Made in Sicily

BORN IN BROOKLYN

NICOLE SCARCELLA

Made in Sicily - Born in Brooklyn

Nicole Scarcella

authorHOUSE®

AuthorHouse™
1663 Liberty Drive
Bloomington, IN 47403
www.authorhouse.com
Phone: 1-800-839-8640

First published by AuthorHouse 08/30/2011

ISBN: 978-1-4634-1287-6 (ebk)
ISBN: 978-1-4634-1288-3 (hc)
ISBN: 978-1-4634-1289-0 (sc)

Library of Congress Control Number: 2011908954

Printed in the United States of America

Any people depicted in stock imagery provided by Thinkstock are models,
and such images are being used for illustrative purposes only.
Certain stock imagery © Thinkstock.

This book is printed on acid-free paper.

DEDICATIONS

To my beloved parents,
Leonarda Genna and Giuseppe Scarcella
In a world fused with imperfection, you were the exception!

To my children,
Teri, Denise, Tony, and Jodi

*From a garden in paradise, God picked the
finest blossoms and sent them to me!*

To my grandchildren,
Ryan, Kristyn, Anthony, Nicholas, Kourtney, Haley, and Taylor
Children of my children, you are loved more than my own children!

To my siblings,
Rose, Joe and Tony
*We share one name and the blessings of our loving parents.
We've shared sorrows, and joys, and a legend of loyalty
and trust. We know each other as no one else can!*

SPECIAL THANKS

To Tony Evans,
The spark that lit the fire.

To my niece Lisa Parker,
For the endearing details about your brother John Scarcella.

To my cousin Ann Marie Fontana,
For the fascinating story about your father Filippo Scarcella.

To my cousin Gae Ganci,
For clarifying the era before I was born.

To my siblings,
For walking alongside me through the layers
and dynamics of our family history.

To my granddaughter Kristyn, my daughter Teri, and my son-in-law Brian, for your enthusiasm, suggestions, edits and guidance towards bringing my words and sentiments to life. To Brian . . . a very special and heartfelt *thank you* for your patience during the final stages!

To Sheilani Romero,
For patiently reviewing the manuscript barely out of a draft format, for your guidance during my exhaustive rewrites, for your tolerance during the baffling computer glitches, for the lovely book cover design, for formatting the pictures, but mostly for your warmth and sensitivity towards my sentiments on the farther side of my words.

To my family, friends and readers, thank you for sharing my journey.

Note to all readers: all errors are my own.

To the many friends, family, caretakers and nameless strangers that crossed my path during a challenging time of my life, I offer my heartfelt appreciation. Please know that I have never forgotten the assistance each of you provided during those years.

To Kelly and Geri,
My heartfelt sentiments of gratitude are being sent posthumously and will wing their way to paradise where the friendship, love, and care you generously provided to Frankie, Teri and I during the difficult years of his illness have been rewarded.

To Betty and Bob,
We are tied forever by a link to the past, the memories imbedded in our hearts, and our friendship, one that continues to this day. Thank you for the support and prayers provided during a truly demanding time of my life, and know that your gifts of love and friendship have never been forgotten.

To Karen and Gary,
The fog of time has never erased the memory of the kindness and support you freely made available to Frankie when the cross became too difficult to bear. My expression of gratitude, though long overdue, is offered sincerely, and with love.

To Dorothy, Arna, Jo and Rebecca,
my biggest cheerleaders . . . finally!

TABLE OF CONTENTS

TO THOSE WHO WANDER THROUGH THESE PAGES . . .

I've written this book as only an American woman born in Brooklyn can write, minus the panache of someone with an English literature degree, embracing instead the flair of my East Coast and Sicilian upbringing. As you wander through these pages, please take into account my less-than-adequate writing skills, as well as the fleeting memory of someone in their seventh decade of life.

I have written this book to honor my beloved parents, for my siblings who have walked many of the same paths, and for my beautiful children and grandchildren to acquaint them with my life and heart.

I have wandered back in time to past generations, to my childhood and adolescent years when life was far simpler and less demanding. Drawn from memory are recollections of a positively enchanting childhood, an unsettling adolescence, two marriages, as well as the peace and tranquility of having lived long enough to enjoy retirement in Southern California.

I've exercised some poetic license in my writing. Although timelines and names may not be on target, they are as accurate as my mind has allowed.

PREFACE

Roman poet, Publius Ovidius Naso, also known as Ovid, once wrote, "Everything comes gradually, at an appointed hour." It did for my parents. Through the years I've often wondered where life would have taken them, what paths they would have chosen had they met when they were young, in the sleepy fishing village Castellammare del Golfo, Sicily. Most likely I would not have been born, and you would not be poised to thumb through this book. Fate had other plans. They met as young adults when they returned to this county, their country *L'America*, leaving behind the footprints of their youth in Sicily, an island dear to them and never far from their thoughts.

Strange as it may seem, the genesis of this book was not inspired by my core connection to Sicily. The inspiration came from an unrelated source. It began while I was at work on a quiet October afternoon in 1998, when a coworker stopped by my office to thank me for an e-mail I had forwarded to his manager.

I'd been asked to be a part of a project improvement work group, to design a database and record the information discussed by the group. At a discussion meeting I met Tony, a technical writer and engineer, someone familiar with the terms and acronyms used on engineering projects, verbiage completely out of my field of expertise. When Tony offered his help in making sense of the unfamiliar verbiage, I was extremely grateful. At the conclusion of the project, I was able to present an intelligent report to the task manager. Being sincerely appreciative for Tony's assistance, I forwarded an e-mail to his manager and made him aware how valuable Tony had been to the project, and to me as well. I also forwarded a copy of my e-mail to Tony.

A few days later Tony stopped by my office. He was smiling as he made his way towards my desk, and I could tell something was on his mind.

"Hey, just stopped by to say *thanks* for sending that e-mail to my manager. I really appreciate what you wrote. That was really nice of you."

"Well you deserved it, Tony. Have you forgotten how much help you were?"

"Actually you had the more difficult part. My part was easy," he continued.

"Are you kidding? I don't think so! If it hadn't been for your help, my entries into that database would have sounded like gibberish. C'mon, I had no idea what they were talking about. You clearly understood the jargon!"

"Well maybe, but what the heck, we got through it and now it's history. By the way, I'm curious, are you French, Spanish . . . what?"

"No, I'm American. Why do you ask?" I teased.

"No reason, just being nosy," he chuckled. "So what *is* your heritage?"

"I'll satisfy your curiosity. I'm Italian. No, actually I'm Sicilian. That's what my mother always told me, that I'm Sicilian—made in Sicily actually. Can you believe it?"

"Honeymoon baby?"

"Something like that. Actually, my parents were both born in the United States but were raised in Sicily. My grandparents were olive oil Sicilians."

Tony smiled. "Hmmm, Sicilian! And where were you born?"

"Well not in Sicily!" I teased back. "I'm a second-generation American . . . born in Brooklyn!"

"No kidding? Brooklyn, wow! Bet you have tons of stories . . . ya know, growing up in Brooklyn . . . Sicilian parents. What was it like?"

"Colorful! Noisy! Loud! All of the above! Lotza music, food, rowdy friends and doting parents. The best!"

"Hmmm, sounds like fun. Do you have any siblings?"

"Yeah I do. I have a sister and two brothers. Say, am I being interviewed?"

Tony smiled warmly. Sounding somewhat apologetic, he added, "Heck no, I'm just curious."

"What's your background?" I asked.

"My background? German. You know cold, severe. I have one sister. Not much fun!"

"Well, growing up was not boring on my end. It was circus-like at times. My father sang all the time, made homemade wine, and my mother cooked and sewed and screamed a lot!"

Although my explanations did sound as though growing up had been fun—and at times it was—in reality, by the time I was seventeen I had eloped and left behind all the "vivid excitement" in my life. As I continued to elaborate on my colorful childhood in Brooklyn, Tony seemed intrigued, somewhat envious.

"You should write a book about your life. From what I'm hearing, I bet you have great memories to share."

"Write . . . me? You must be kidding! First of all, I can't write. I can hardly speak correctly. I still speak Brooklyn-ese! Have you been listening to me?"

"No, I'm not kidding! Hmmm . . . Brooklyn-ese? Hardly! Not that it matters! Think about it, you could write about growing up in a big Italian family. Bet you had rowdy friends! You could include them," he teased. "An accent would add color. Authors don't always use proper English syntax. They sometimes use dialect to make a point. I'm a writer and I have used dialects to spice up the dialogue."

"So you're a writer? Of course you are, I should have guessed. You write technical documents, so you are a writer, and probably a good one!"

"I wrote a screenplay, a few magazine articles and a short story. Nothing exciting, nothing published. A book from someone with your background would be great. I'll help you if you're interested!"

"Tony, I can't write. I don't have a creative cell in my body. Climbing a mountain sounds easier. Honestly, my life was not that interesting. Even if it was, where would I start?"

"Nicole, you can write. I know you can. Your e-mail to my manager had a writer's flair. I'll help you!"

A few days later, Tony stopped by my office with a copy of his screenplay. I'd read many books, but never screenplays. I spent the entire weekend weaving through his work, fascinated with his vivid imagination, the portrayal of characters, as well as the manner in which screenplays are formatted.

When I arrived at work the following day, I left Tony a voicemail and asked him to stop by my office. Later that day he stopped by and I shared that I'd read his play and found it fascinating. We chatted about writing in general. From our conversation I surmised he was a library of information about writing techniques.

Tony began forwarding writers' web sites, brought me books on writing styles along with a stack of writing magazines. The idea was captivating, but it seemed like an overwhelming task.

Although writing was not yet on my "to do" list, he suggested I enroll in a writing class. He told me the class offered at work provided basic writing techniques and would be a great start. When our company posted its yearly technical writing class, I signed up.

Between his gentle prodding and a mild but budding curiosity, Tony had achieved his objective. I not only signed up for the writing class at work, I followed up and enrolled in a writer's workshop offered locally. It was during the offsite workshop when a wave of excitement fell over me. The instructor was an agent and a writer, and I was fascinated by her insight. Being around other writers was stimulating. She provided a myriad of suggestions and ideas about writing in general, noting that a life story or an idea that may not seem important, can in fact be.

"If you place your thoughts and ideas on paper, someone will read it!" she added enthusiastically.

By the time I'd decided to begin writing, where to begin and how to draw on memories remained nebulous. Tapping into the past seemed impossible until I came across a book written by Thomas Wolf, *You Can't Go Home Again*. The title intrigued me. I began to mull over his words as well as my past. Suddenly it came to me: using my mind's eye I could go home again—to the past, to my childhood and the years that followed. All I had to do was close my eyes and reach back.

Tony convinced me that life's experiences take root and remain imbedded deep within our minds. Armed with a cache of information, daily mentoring, four writing classes, a pocket guide to correct my less-than-adequate English skills, a rush of confidence fell over me. After all, God gave us a memory so we might have roses in the December of our lives!

Where to begin and end my story remained a challenge. It was not as simple as clicking the heels of little red shoes. But my goal was firm. Suddenly, like phantasms or ghostly dreams, memories began to flash about in my mind. It was as though setting a goal opened Pandora's Box, and from her urns she gifted me, not with evil, but with the ability to recollect. I began to drift back to when I was very young, to the time my parents showered us with love—untiring love, forgiving love, a love that embraced us like warm rain during a springtime storm. As the essence of their love began cascading into my mind, the memories I'd long forgotten returned and writing commenced.

As moments, events, phrases, songs and prayers I'd heard as a child flashed to mind, I also recalled that my parents were never at a loss for words, especially my mother. Most of her expressions were warm and loving. Some were mysterious. When I was young, she often told me I was not American, a puzzling revelation for a young child to comprehend.

"*Tu non sei Americana, sei Siciliana. Ti ho fatto in la Sicilia* . . . you're not American, you're Sicilian. I made you in Sicily," she'd share wistfully in a soft and dreamy voice, as though she was reaching back to a special moment in her life.

"But Mommy, you told me I was born in Brooklyn, in St. Catherine's Hospital!"

"*Si, e vero, pero ti ho fatto in la Sicilia* . . . yes it's true, but I made you in Sicily!"

When I was old enough I learned I was conceived during a belated honeymoon in Sicily. When I began to write, her words took on an air of enchantment—almost spiritual, romantic—and they inspired the title of this book.

Our home in Brooklyn is where my story begins . . .

MY GARDEN OF MEMORIES

Some of the most endearing memories that often cross my mind are those of my childhood years and my family gathered around our dining room table in Brooklyn for *pranzo*, the most hallowed meal of the day, the hallmark of every tightly knit Italian family. It was the time of day when the trials and tribulations of daily lives were played out like an operetta, and in our family, *pranzo* began shortly after my father arrived home from work.

As I close my eyes and reach back, the scene in the dining room unfolds with my father seated at the head of the table, my mother next to him. I sat next to my father, to his right. Seated next to me was my sister Rose (called Sarah as a child), a rosy-cheeked cherub with a halo of springy, black curls that screamed out in all directions. My mother and my brother Joe (nicknamed Joey), the first male sibling, sat across from my sister and me. Joe, quiet by nature, with fair skin and blond curls, was a stark contrast to the rest of the family. His coloring encouraged a myriad of jokes aimed at my mother and the possible liaison with an Irish milkman or a German baker! Completing the family circle was my youngest sibling, Anthony, a.k.a. Nino or Tony. I was twelve when he came into our world and he took his place at that table next to my mother and sat in a high chair that had been handed down in stages. Tony grew up embracing their Sicilian heritage more than any of the other children.

Mommy was the heart of our family, soft and warm, yet hardy and robust—all wrapped in a tidy package of womanhood! Mommy nourished us with food and love equally. There are no words that can best describe her true essence! She was unique, she was love—she was

1

Mommy, someone who cared little if food spilled or if we washed up before dinner. She would rather hug and kiss her children than bark out orders about cleanliness. My mother was an earthy woman, most comfortable preparing farmer's meals. And in her kitchen, the aromas of garlic, onions, and basil danced about harmoniously, reaching every nook and cranny of our home to tease the fussiest of appetites.

My father was king of his castle, a strong man who worked long hours as a dockworker, was happiest when surrounded by his beloved family. *Pranzo* was the highlight of his day, the time when a hard day's work was put to rest. The scene every night was always a repeat performance of the previous night . . . the table brimming with flavorful foods and the blending of happy voices waiting to eat. And while he poured his homemade wine into his favorite glass, he'd smile through weary, red-brimmed eyes. When we were young, he'd encourage us to drink wine and would pour equal parts of water and wine in our glasses.

"Drink the wine! It makes your blood rich. It's good for you." But we never did.

When I was older, I learned that milk was the preferred beverage served with dinner in other homes. My mother told us milk was meant for baby cows, poisonous to humans, and I believed her!

My mother's entry into the dining room was always dynamic. Wearing a colorful apron and her skin glistening from the olive oil she used liberally while cooking, we'd watch as she placed a mouth-watering platter of pasta directly in front of my father. And as her voice rang out, "*Mangia, mangia* . . . eat, eat," the table would come alive.

After dinner, the scene at our table turned tranquil. While Rose and I tidied up the kitchen, my father would remain seated at the table reading his favorite Italian newspaper, *Il Progresso Italo-Americano*. My mother would return with her battered old coffee maker and soon the flavorful aroma of espresso would fill the air. When the coffee was ready, she'd slowly pour the rich liquid into tiny china cups. As the pleasing taste filled their senses, the fatigue of the day would vanish, and my father would begin to sing, flooding the air with the ageless melodies of his favorite Neapolitan songs. On some nights, holding the youngest on his lap, he would spin Sicilian fairy tales or tell us about his life as a young fisherman.

When news via a letter or the newspaper filled them with nostalgia, they would share bittersweet memories of their beloved Sicily. We learned about the close family bonds and the abject poverty they endured during their young lives. We learned that my paternal grandfather fished each day to feed the family. In vivid detail he would describe the beautiful bay in Castellammare, as well as the majestic castle that guarded the entrance to their quaint village. We learned about our maternal grandparents' farm with olive and walnut groves, and the goats and chickens that lived among them, often sharing their home as well! So picturesque were their descriptions that when I was young I envisioned having lived on that beautiful island as well. Their recollections became my memories, and like flowers in an English garden, leaf-by-leaf, they've unfolded to blossom into my story.

Those were the gloriously happy days in my life!

THE SANDS OF TIME

Long before the birth of my parents in the early 1900s, as Sicily wrestled with famine, a bleak economy, struggles for political power, and the criminal machinations of the Mafia, Sicilians turned their focus on the new world across the Atlantic, and the quest for a better life commenced. Leaving behind families, as well as "*la miseria* . . . misery," they set in motion the making of their own private American dream.

In time my grandparents joined the adventurous Sicilians, those who traveled to the new world on steamships filled with hundreds of men, women, and children. The trip across the Atlantic took approximately two weeks. And when the voyage was over, their eyes would first take in the sight of the beautiful bay and the large woman with spikes on her head holding a lamp that lit the night and welcomed weary travelers to this beloved land of America.

For my paternal grandfather, the new world was not all he hoped it would be. He suffered from arthritis, and the harsh winters in New York aggravated his affliction. After my father was born, they returned to the milder climate of Sicily, to the old fishing village of Castellammare. My father was approximately twelve months old when they ventured back to their island.

As it had been for prior generations, the sea was my paternal grandfather's world and the only means of feeding his family. He returned to mending nets during the day and setting out to sea at dusk to fish through the night. This was the life of a Sicilian fisherman. Unfortunately, the once-plentiful seas flourishing with blue fin tuna and sardines had been fished dry. The bounty was now scarce.

For my maternal grandparents, the new world was not the utopia they'd dreamt about either. The inclement weather combined with the lack of work and less-than-satisfactory living conditions forced them to rethink their situation in the new world. My mother was not yet twelve months old when they returned to their farm in Castellammare and the impoverished existence they'd left behind. Life on a farm, though less devastating than that of a fisherman, was nonetheless bleak.

As the children matured, the struggle to survive in Sicily remained constant. Poverty remained out of control. The stories about the gold-lined streets in America continued to evolve. With little to eat and a lack of medicinal and everyday necessities, the dream of finding work in the new world shifted to the children.

Although my father was born in New York City, he was raised in Sicily and joined the Italian Navy in his teens. After his discharge he returned to his family. As the oldest son, he was responsible for the care of the large family, but the circumstances for island fishermen turned desperate, and only one option was available: travel to America, find work and support the family from afar.

After my maternal grandfather passed away, maintaining a farm became a struggle for my grandmother. The needs of a large family were vast, and a renewed interest in the new world began to blossom. My grandmother made a difficult-but-necessary decision—send my mother and her son (Giuseppe) Joe to America.

Filled with hopes and dreams to improve the lives of their families in Sicily, my parents set sail (separately) across the Atlantic, and in approximately two weeks they arrived at Ellis Island.

My mother was barely fifteen at the time and deeply devoted to her grandmother. Being forced into leaving her grandmother triggered an avalanche of bitterness in her young heart towards her mother, a deeply rooted resentment that remained for the rest of her life.

After his tour of duty with the Italian Navy, my father, now in his early twenties, also arrived in the new world. Each settled in the homes of Sicilian families already living in New York, where strong bonds between immigrants provided shelter and opportunistic links for work.

In the beginning, my father had a business arrangement with his uncle in the famous New York Fish Market, but the relationship soon fell apart. With no education and few work skills other than those tied to the sea, my father found work on the docks making repairs on large ships moored on various anchorages from New York to Baltimore. It was dangerous work, and only men with a strong back and a rooted motivation could endure the unforgiving North Atlantic winters. Being young and ruggedly strong, he worked hard, earned a generous salary, and remained firmly committed to providing financial support for his family in Sicily.

My mother settled in the home of her mother's sister Nina and cousins Anna and Sophie. There she was taught to sew and was soon hired as a seamstress in the garment district. During this era, factories provided a less-than-adequate working environment. Women (some very young) worked ten-hour days, six days a week in buildings that were either too hot or too cold depending on the season. Regulations pertaining to safety and to worker's compensation were non-existent. Discomfort was commonplace. Yet it mattered little to my mother. This was her only opportunity to support herself and her family in Sicily as well.

Many years would pass before my parents would meet. Each settled separately into new lives, remaining dedicated to their promises of financial help to those left behind in Sicily.

This was an era characterized by speakeasies and gangsters, a time when the business of bootlegging was booming and undeniably profitable and when even average citizens broke the law. Much of the bootleg alcohol was manufactured in clandestine home stills and largely by the hands of criminals and gangsters. People who once were law-abiding citizens became criminals. Sadly, most of the men involved in the Mafia were young immigrants, as was my mother's brother Joe. He considered legal work nefarious and readily fell under the spell of life as a Mafioso. Less than a year after they arrived in New York, his life was cut short. There are, however, two versions as to how he met his final demise. One testimony chronicles his death as having come from gunshot wounds after a muddled Mafioso deal. Another account describes his last moments otherwise, that he was asphyxiated during the manufacture of bootleg alcohol in an unventilated basement. His death was reported as carbon monoxide poisoning. His ties to the Mafia were undisputable, and for my mother, it was a tragic ending to someone so young.

IL PRIMO AMORE . . . FIRST LOVE

The world for Sicilian females in America had not evolved with changing times. Their lives remained shackled to century-old traditions. Females were closely guarded from the world outside the home. The Sicilian female in the new world would never be exposed to the modern nuances of life the American female enjoyed. In the eyes of fathers, brothers, and caregivers, the old traditions remained the safest way to keep the female in her virgin state for the right man. For the most part, marriages were arranged. When two people were considered a good match, those in charge made all the necessary arrangements.

For my mother, her aunt was in charge. Ten years would go by before the right man for her niece would come to her attention.

It began one day after rumors about a potential husband for my mother began to circulate throughout the tight network of Sicilians and eventually reached my mother's attention. She was told that his name was Giuseppe (Pepino) Scarcella and that he was quite handsome and had been raised in Castellammare, where his family still maintained a home on the marina.

They described him as a dynamic man with marriage in mind and mentioned that he and his uncle owned a successful fish market business in New York City—intriguing information that fed my mother's curiosity. After a conversation between my mother and her aunt, the seed was planted and the dance began.

My father was told about a woman named Leonarda (Nardina) Genna from Castellammare. And likewise he was intrigued. Being so far away from his family in Sicily, anyone from his beloved town held a special fascination, and he let his interest in meeting her be known.

My mother's life suddenly took an exciting and dramatic turn. Except for the men in the family or those whom she worked with, she'd never been in the presence of other men. The possibility of meeting someone with marriage in mind held her mind captive. As the arrangements moved forward, the dinner date was set, and the anticipation in my mother's heart intensified with each breath.

My mother on her engagement day

On the morning of the introduction dinner, the moment my mother opened her eyes, her stomach began churning. The day dragged on endlessly, and she could barely contain her excitement. Later that evening, when a knock at the front door signaled his arrival, she had to remind herself to breathe.

The scene that evening mirrored that of the pre-marriage scene in *The Godfather*. After the introductions were made, they gathered in the dining room and were seated around a large table. My mother sat at one end and my father (to be) at the other—close enough to steal quick glances at one other, yet too far to be able to engage in conversation.

The sight of the handsome man on the far end of the table must have set my mother's heart beating wildly. The rumors she'd heard from her cousins did not justify how handsome Pepino actually was.

I have always imagined my father was intrigued as well by the svelte woman, sitting barely a breath away, looking lovely and beautiful in a stunning dress she'd sewn especially for this occasion. I will assume there was an immediate attraction as well.

After dinner, Pepino and Nardina let it be known they would like to meet again, and after receiving her aunt's approval, several more dinners were planned. In time they expressed their desire to marry and plans for a wedding were set in motion.

I've always assumed they did not fall head-over-heels in love on the first night they met, but I am certain the moment their eyes met, a warm glow entered their hearts. They did not feel the draw of emotion that begins instantly—with a spark that kindles and erupts into a flame and fills you with unspeakable desire to meet again and to remain together always. Their love would build slowly, with each passing day, like fermenting wine, intensifying with time.

Following the customary rules of wedding protocol, an engagement party was planned. At this party the wedding date was announced and engagement rings were exchanged.

During the time leading up to the nuptials, Pepino and Nardina would continue to see each other; however, they were never left alone. Pepino would visit her, but the setting was always in the well-chaperoned parlor in her aunt's home. There would be no private moments for just the two of them, no chance encounters, no opportunity for a heart-stopping kiss.

The days and weeks that followed were deliriously happy. Having decided to sew her wedding dress, together with her aunt and cousins they shopped for fabric and made decisions regarding flowers, music, food, and the reception. Once the dress was completed and all preparations were in place, she anxiously waited for her wedding day.

CE LA LUNA MEZZO MARE

APRIL 8, 1934

My mother and father on their wedding day

In the dressing room of Our Lady of Mount Carmel Catholic Church, while my mother fretted impatiently, the pews began to fill with relatives and friends who'd come to witness this fairy tale wedding. For my mother, the realization that her wedding day had arrived was more than she could bear. She wondered if those around her could hear her pounding heart.

At the foot of the altar, my father fidgeted nervously, knowing his bride-to-be would soon make her appearance. When the wedding march announced her arrival, his eyes locked on the positively stunning woman walking towards him in a princess-like wedding dress, with an elongated train trailing behind her and a bouquet of Calla lilies in her arms. Likewise, her eyes were focused directly ahead, at the handsome man with a miniature Calla lily boutonnière in the lapel of his black tuxedo jacket.

The ceremony was brief: a quick blessing, an exchange of rings and vows, and promises of fidelity and love—a love that would blossom in their hearts with each passing day. My cousin once told me my parents looked like movie stars walking hand in hand down the aisle and waving to friends and family.

They gathered in her aunt's house to celebrate; however, the honeymoon would be postponed for another time. And when the dawn of their special day came to an end, my parents made their way to a tiny apartment they'd call home for many years.

They settled into married life, worked hard, and remained firmly united in their commitments to their families in Sicily. Each month money and packages filled with an assortment of clothing made their way across the seas to Sicily.

Soon after they were wed, the business relationship between my father and his uncle ended, necessitating a challenging change in my father's life. With no education or skills, his only option was to accept work on the docks repairing ships the size of the Queen Mary.

Pepino adjusted to the bitter cold winters until one unforgiving winter day when an accident nearly took his life. From the tenth deck of the ship where he was working, he lost his grip, hit his head on the side of the ship, and fell into unconsciousness, into the icy waters below. He floated lifelessly but awakened quickly, and when he stretched out his arms, he realized he was under the ship. My father was a powerful swimmer with strong arms and lungs. His strength enabled him to find his way into the air and the arms of a rescue crew, and he was taken to the hospital with multiple injuries.

Although their world had been turned upside down, they never abandoned hope, and the road to recovery would be bumpy. After days and weeks of praying, he began to recover. Many weeks would pass before he was well enough to return home, and many months would go by before he regained his robust strength—time used to ponder the unforgiving dangers surrounding his work. With no other options to fall back upon and armed with a clearer understanding of his job, when he was well enough to work, he returned to the docks.

HONEYMOON IN SICILY

Married life fit my parents like a glove. They were well suited for one another and extremely happy. While continuing to support their families in Sicily, they frugally saved for their own future, one that included a family of their own. However, by their third anniversary, their hopes of having a family had turned into an unreachable dream. When a belated honeymoon was suggested, the idea immediately captured their attention. Reuniting with family, coupled with the possibility of coming home pregnant, sparked an irresistible desire to travel home.

Amidst the hectic and exciting dynamics of ships leaving the New York harbors for Europe, they embarked on the long overdue honeymoon to Sicily. Only this time they traveled stylishly with meals prepared by on-board chefs and slept in private quarters at day's end. During the day they relaxed on beautiful decks and shared their thoughts about Sicily, the families waiting for their return, and the hope of returning home with child.

During the last night at sea, while waiting for night to fall away, they chatted away the hours, and at dawn they watched as the ship made its way into a port in Palermo. It felt like an eternity before the ship anchored. Soon they were walking down the gangplank, drawn towards the roar of voices shouting their names and the arms of loved ones they no longer recognized.

Many years had passed since they were last home. The lives of their loved ones had greatly changed, the look of radiance and good health was riveting, and the transformation warmed their hearts. The aid they'd provided so diligently from across the sea had been put to good use. Life had improved beyond their wildest imaginations.

And when it was time to make their way to Castellammare, they relaxed and enjoyed the sights in the back seat of a car rather than on a hard bench in the back of a donkey cart. Soon they would be aware of many other remarkable changes their families were enjoying.

Many had gathered at the edge of town, waiting and watching for the first sighting of an approaching car, eager to warmly embrace Pepino and Nardina and to share with them the remarkable benefits their generosity had made in their lives.

The passing of time had fashioned many remarkable changes. Brothers had grown into manhood, sisters were now mothers, siblings and cousins had moved north and to other parts of Europe, and sadly, many elders had passed away.

Having been raised on the marina, the sea was a haven for my father, and the turquoise waters of the bay were never far from his thoughts. As a young boy, he would swim to the old castle on the far end of peninsula to explore its hidden mysteries. Now that he was home, he wasted no time and made his way to the waterfront where he and his father had mended nets during the day and fished through the night.

Standing on the shore, he gazed out towards the horizon and listened to the melody of the waves as they crashed against the rocks. He'd never forgotten the beauty of the sea that now sparkled under a bright sun. The tranquility of being surrounded in quiet stillness when he swam in the warm waters of the emerald giant had never been far from his thoughts. Once again the sound of sea called to him, and he dove into the surf and swam until he'd spent the last drop of energy.

For my mother, the most endearing moments were those shared with her grandmother. She had missed her and frequently dreamt about her. Yet their time together was bittersweet; her grandmother had become fragile with age. My mother wanted to remain with her in Sicily or take her to live in America. Since neither option was possible, they shared as much time together as possible, reminiscing about the days and months and years leading up to my mother's voyage to the new world. Leaving her grandmother would now be a far greater torment than when she first left for the new world. It was painfully obvious she'd never see her grandmother again.

Although my father had missed the sea, his thoughts were mostly of his siblings, his parents, but mostly of his beloved mother. Her softness, kindness, and the sweet sound of her voice calling his name was always with him, but now, as the time to depart for their return trip home drew close, he wondered if he'd ever see her again.

The gloriously happy hours and days of their belated honeymoon in Castellammare flew by faster than birds in flight on a windy day. They had shared many happy hours with friends and family and acquainted everyone with life in America. But soon they were packing for the return trip home, and the honeymoon would be relegated to a treasured memory.

After their tear-filled departure, a hidden joy would soon brighten their lives. Two had traveled to Sicily and three were returning home to America!

Sicilian honeymoon . . . the homecoming

FIRST BORN

January 13, 1938 was the day I embarked on the most difficult journey of my life. The time had arrived to leave the contented environment of my mother's womb and meet my parents, those responsible for the muffled growls and rumblings, the clatter and clamor that kept me from a sound sleep, and the enchanting sounds that somehow encouraged a tranquil slumber.

Nine months had elapsed; my living quarters had become cramped. With not a moment left to ponder, I thrust forward and set in motion the first welcoming signs of labor. This was the day my parents' lives would change forever, as would the customs of an unsuspecting hospital.

My mother's pregnancy had been normal and completely uneventful. As anticipated, in the ninth month, they were awakened by the unmistakable but welcoming signal that the birth of their first child was imminent. Her bags had long since been packed, and soon my father was nervously helping my mother into the waiting cab for the short drive through the sleepy streets of Brooklyn. At St. Catherine's Hospital, the doctor waited for their arrival. By the time they entered the front door, my mother was deep in the throws of labor and was immediately wheeled into a labor room. Unbeknownst to my parents and the hospital staff, a cloud of controversy was lurking close by.

Sophisticated technology for obstetrical care in those days was non-existent. Prior to the onset of labor, doctors had few tools to determine if a normal delivery was possible. In time the doctor became aware that my mother's labor was not progressing normally, and a vaginal delivery was not possible.

The deeply concerned doctor led my father into his office where he shared his apprehension; my mother's life was in danger and more than likely the baby would not make it safely through the birth canal. My father was also made aware that Catholic hospitals did not, under any circumstances, perform birthing surgeries, and St. Catherine's would abide by that strict religious policy.

Although his world had taken a terrifying turn, he knew he wanted no part of their religious rationale. This was America, not Sicily, not the Vatican. He insisted a surgeon be called in to perform a caesarian section, but the hospital staff could not oblige. All attempts to console him and quell the situation had no effect. His anger began to escalate, as did his goal not to abandon my mother or his baby. And although his English speaking skills were lacking and he felt like a foreigner in his own country, they understood his frustration. Yet their hands were tied. He began to rant about the absurdity of religious laws in a hospital environment, and when his rage turned to fury, the staff had no choice but to summon security and the police.

The clock was ticking and he felt helpless; something had to change quickly. When two police officers arrived on the scene, they found themselves in the midst of a chaotic situation. The staff explained the situation, adding how in the past the hospital had never been taken to task regarding a birthing situation.

As fate would have it, the police officers were Italian and spoke both languages fluently. They reassured my father they would do all they could to bring this situation to a positive conclusion. While the officers struggled to convince my father that help was on the way, the issue was reported, and a judge was summoned, someone who took compassion on the situation and set the wheels of justice in motion.

The issue was resolved and a surgeon performed St. Catherine's first C-section. And when it was over, my father was led to my mother's bedside, followed by a trip to the hospital nursery for a glimpse of his tiny daughter wrapped in a pink blanket and sleeping peacefully in a tiny bassinet.

My mother often spoke of that day, how my father, with the help of two Brooklyn police officers and a compassionate judge, reversed the archaic doctrine of the Catholic Church, consequently saving the life of his firstborn, possibly my mother as well, and sealing the fate for all future, difficult births.

Firstborn

BE IT EVER SO HUMBLE

After two weeks in the hospital, the time had arrived to say goodbye to the hospital nursery. With my father by her side, my mother waved goodbye to the staff, and with her baby bundled in layers of warm blankets, they headed to the waiting cab, through the streets of Brooklyn to the large red brick apartment on 68th Street, my home for the next four years.

While I peacefully slumbered in my mother's arms, the cab pulled up to the curb in front of our apartment where neighbors had braved the blustery January day, anxiously waiting to welcome us home. After many warm greetings, my father led the way up the long flight of stairs to the front door. Once inside our cozy apartment, my mother placed me in the brightly decorated pink bassinet.

I would not be aware of these first precious moments—my first trip outdoors, my pretty bassinet, and my surroundings—not for a while longer.

Memories of this apartment have clouded with time, yet faint recollections remain, especially those of our neighbors, La Signora Pina and her teenage daughter Rosanna. I may not remember their faces, but I clearly recall the friendship they shared with our family and how I dearly loved hearing La Signora Pina's voice speaking in a delicate sounding Tuscan dialect. La Signora's articulation was my first introduction to the singsong sound of the Italian language, a sharp contrast to the harsher-sounding Sicilian dialect spoken by my parents.

Many details of our cozy apartment are now fuzzy, yet some remain—the elongated room by the front door that united the dining room and kitchen and the small table where I drew pictures, where my father read his newspaper, where we ate our meals. The kitchen included the usual suspects: an icebox, a stove, a sink, and a window overlooking the courtyard below. I vaguely remember my bedroom that doubled as a living room as well and the closet where each morning I'd pick from a long row of pretty dresses my mother had sewn for me.

Snuggled tightly between the kitchen and the dining room was a washbasin. In that basin, using a washboard and a bar of hard soap, my mother would wash our clothes. When she was done, she would hang the wash on a clothesline that extended from the wall outside the kitchen window to a tall tree at the far end of the property.

The washbasin remains a distinct memory. Each morning my mother would close the tin lid of the basin, set me on top, and comb my hair and tie my shoes. Like most children, if danger is lurking, they will find it. Unbeknownst to my mother, a miniscule sharp edge lay hidden on the underside of the basin lid, an area where only a tiny finger might find the waiting danger. And when I lifted my bloody finger and reached towards my mother's face, her deafening scream was heard through the kitchen wall, into the apartment of La Signora Pina, who immediately raced over to see what was wrong. As a nurse she knew exactly what to do. While attempting to calm a hysterical mother, she bandaged my finger, and we made our way to a neighborhood doctor.

I'm not aware if medications to dull pain were available for young children in those days, but I recall how the pain from the four stitches I received hurt more than the cut.

I was only three years old when that accident occurred. The tiny scar remains to this day and keeps the memory of that apartment and that washbasin fresh in my mind.

AUNTIE ANNA

It didn't take long for me to recognize my mother's intense love for family and friends and how much she treasured the warm vibes of these relationships. Within this group of kinships was her cousin Anna. My mother and her cousin were inseparable, closer than most sisters.

Anna was married to Philip. Their home was the middle level of her mother's house on 69th Street, a few short steps from our apartment. Anna and Philip were never blessed with children of their own. Because of their close friendship with my parents, it was not surprising that my mother shared her firstborn with her cousin and best friend.

Auntie Anna was my second mother. She loved me as though she'd given birth to me. During those early years, Auntie Anna and her husband Philip were a vital part of my life. We spent endless hours together playing games, taking long walks and sharing meals. During quiet times she would spin Sicilian fairy tales, and at bedtime I would cuddle between her and Uncle Philip. I loved her as much as any child could love someone other than her own mother.

When Auntie Anna heard about my finger accident, she decided a new doll was justified. My mother agreed, and plans were made to take me shopping.

After seeing a picture of my father in his Navy uniform, I had begged my mother to make me a sailor suit—a little girl sailor suit. It was no surprise when the sailor dress she made for me became my favorite outfit. On the morning of our doll-shopping excursion, I bypassed all the pretty dresses smartly lined up in my closet and chose my favorite outfit—the pleated white skirt and a navy blue top with a large, square white collar.

Carefully guarding my bandaged finger, I sat nestled between my mother and Auntie Anna for the train ride downtown. We traveled to Canal Street, home to many unique stores, an area perpetually bustling with shoppers looking for bargains, those who cared little for the dynamic and eye-appealing ambiance of large department stores. This was a lackluster area in New York City, where buildings soared high, almost touching the sky, and warm rays of sunshine never had an opportunity to snake through the streets and storefronts and brighten each day.

Most of the stores were unattractive, dusty, and every inch of space was crammed with items I had little interest in. Many toys of that era were homemade, and there were precious few dolls for sale, but Auntie Anna had a goal. We walked past several stores before entering an establishment where several rag dolls and stuffed animals were neatly displayed on a shelf.

I spotted the doll I wanted immediately, and I began yanking on Auntie Anna's dress, pointing to a doll with a black cloth face and long, dangly arms and legs on the top shelf. It was dressed in a sailor suit, one closely resembling my outfit except for the pleated skirt. My mother and Auntie Anna looked surprised.

My choice seemed odd. The other dolls on display had long hair that matched mine and wore pretty dresses. It was obvious my choice had all to do with the doll's attire and not the color of its face and hands.

"*Sei sicura che vuoi questa pupa* . . . are you sure you want *this* doll?" they asked. "Look at this one! Her hair is like yours! I'll make you a dress just like the one she's wearing," suggested my mother.

Their prodding did not sway me from my choice, and my attention never wandered from the black-faced doll wearing a Navy outfit. Like most three-year-old little girls, my doll and I played house during the day, and she snuggled in bed with me at night. Just as Auntie Anna had hoped, my new doll distracted me from the discomfort of my stitched finger.

IN THIS CORNER

In most Sicilian families of past generations, a misunderstanding or a misspoken word often led to revenge and retaliation. These disturbing episodes often led to lasting feuds that took years to resolve. Many disagreements were taken to the grave. For some, forgiveness or reconciliation occurred only after a major event in the family—an untimely death or the blessed birth of a baby.

An argument between my mother and her aunt (Auntie Anna's mother) resulted in a long-standing feud. Understandably, everyone took sides. Auntie Anna stood by her mother, and the close friendship the cousins had enjoyed ended. I was strictly forbidden to see Auntie Anna, a decision that left me devastated. This classic Sicilian feud lasted untold years. I never knew what provoked the disagreement, but I remember the day it occurred vividly—the disturbing moment when Auntie Anna's mother slapped my mother across her face and the upheaval that followed.

I was only four years old at the time and dearly missed Auntie Anna. Not being able to visit her was crushing. The argument had been with Anna's mother and not between the cousins, yet my mother barely ever spoke her name again. When I was older, I'd sometimes see Auntie Anna waiting on the corner. And when she saw me, she'd wave, and I'd run towards her. Auntie Anna would hug me, smother me with kisses, and caution me not to tell my mother I'd seen her. Before leaving she'd tuck a quarter in my hand and tell me to save it. But I had to tell my mother! How else could I explain the quarters?

"Mommy, I saw Auntie Anna on the corner, and she gave me a quarter!"

On those special days, my mother would look at me sadly and tell me to put the money in my piggy bank. She never forbade me from running to Auntie Anna when I saw her. At times, and stubbornly, I'd ask if we could visit Auntie Anna, but the answer was always the same—NO! All that remained were the quick encounters on the corner.

We never again had any contact with Auntie Anna, not when we learned that she'd adopted a child, nor when her husband Philip passed away. But the storm of time often clears the senses. I was married when they renewed their relationship. By this time, both were widows. Although the friendship was rekindled, unfortunately the relationship was never the same.

FLOWERS FROM THE SAME GARDEN

On February 26, 1942, my sister Rose was born. I was only four years old, and my mother had not shared this noteworthy detail—that a baby would soon share our happy home. I don't recall how my father explained my mother's absence during her two-week hospital stay, yet I remember the day she returned home and how my world suddenly and dramatically changed.

I'd missed my mother's warm hugs and sweet kisses. She was never far from my mind, nor were the songs she sang, the prayers we recited before I drifted off to sleep each night. "She'll be home soon" were the only words my father spoke as I waited for the blessed day when my world would return to normal.

On the day my mother was returning home, La Signora Pina and I sat gazing out of her apartment window to the street below. La Signora told me my mother had a big surprise.

"Tua momma ha una supressa . . . your mother has a surprise!" she whispered sweetly.

To a four-year-old time has no reference, and after what seemed like an eternity, I watched a taxicab slowly pull up to the curb. With my eyes focused directly below, I watched with a strained imagination as my mother stepped out of the cab carrying a tiny bundle in her arms. La Signora took my hand, opened the front door of her apartment, and from the landing outside the door, I stood anxiously waiting to feel my mother's arms around me once again. Suddenly the door below opened and my mother appeared. From the landing I could see her warm smile, heard my name echo through the hallway, and watched as she slowly made her way up the stairs. And when she reached the top step, she bent down to kiss me and shared the surprise—a tiny baby swaddled in pink blankets and wearing a pretty bonnet. I stared at the cute, pink face with tiny, black ringlets peeking out of her bonnet. It looked like a doll; a warm, pretty doll.

"This is your sister, give her a kiss!" she said, her voice gushing joyously.

I'd never been around newborn babies. Actually I'd never been around any children, even those my own age. My mother told me her name was Rosaria, named after my mother's mother, and she was quickly nicknamed Sarah.

While my mother was away, someone had decorated my sister's first bed with beautiful ribbons, colorful bows, fluffy blankets and a lace pillow. I wondered why my bed was not as pretty. My mother reassured me I'd slept in that same bassinet when I was born and the adornments were every bit as beautiful.

Many more surprises were waiting for me. Unlike my dolls, this baby squealed and squirmed and let out bloodcurdling cries when she was hungry.

I discovered I was no longer the lone princess. In the blinking of an eye, my mother was no longer mine alone. And with her index finger crossing her lips, she began training the volume of my voice.

"*Nicoletta, shhhh, tua sorella dorme, parlate piu piano o si sveglia . . .* your sister is sleeping, speak softly or you'll wake her!"

My mother spent endless hours in a rocking chair lulling my sister to sleep. And while she slept, she boiled bottles and nipples, prepared formula, washed mountains of diapers and hung them to dry on the clothesline outside the kitchen window. Soon I was folding diapers, and from time to time—under her careful watch—I held my sister.

But the best time of my day took place when the three of us sat cuddled together in a rocking chair. My mother would rock us and sing beautiful Sicilian lullabies, songs she learned from her grandmother— songs I would later sing to my own children and grandchildren.

MAMMA, COS'E LA GUERRA . . . WHAT IS WAR?

In September 1939 chaos erupted in Europe, shattering the uneasy balance of peace in the world. Although I was young and sheltered from the world outside our home, I learned a new word, one that spoke of fear and death. It didn't take long to hear the word repeated on the radio, on street corners, in churches, and in stores—*guerra*—war.

I would later learn the war began without warning when Germany invaded Poland and signaled the beginning of World War II. In June 1940, with Mussolini at the helm, Italy declared war on Britain and France. On the morning of December 7, 1941, Japan attacked Pearl Harbor, a dark day that marked America's involvement in the war. After the surprise attack on Pearl Harbor, air raid drills, scrap drives, and food rationings became part of our lives.

The dawn of May 1943 marked the beginning of darker and far more daunting days for American Sicilians. The United States invaded Sicily, and American soldiers of Italian descent were sent into battle against their cousins, in the land where roots were deep and loyalties were tested.

Cousins fighting cousins triggered anger and heated conversations at dinner tables. Auntie Anna's nephew, Salvatore Randazzo, was one such soldier. Sal was born in the United States, drafted into the army, and like many other American Sicilian men, he was sent to Sicily to fight against his cousins.

After the war, the American soldiers who'd been sent to Sicily spoke of having faced little resistance on the island and instead were warmly welcomed. The soldiers shared heartwarming details of the Sicilians who rejoiced en masse, welcoming American soldiers in jeeps and trucks as they drove along the narrow old streets. Our soldiers also spoke of an old Anglican church where a memorial mass was celebrated for fallen Americans and attended by General Patton and other officers.

For a child living in that era, air raid drills were terrifying. My parents did their best to ease my fears. When the sirens sounded, everyone scrambled for safety, and my world switched gears. Often the sirens sounded at night, signaling "lights out" in homes, buildings, and streets, and the eeriness of being plunged into total darkness was terrifying.

During nighttime air raid drills, my mother would turn off the lights and drape a black cloth over one small light fixture in the kitchen. In this quasi darkness we would wait for the "all clear" to sound and for light to return to our world.

When sirens sounded during school hours, we hid under our desks. Years later, I learned that during one drill, Japanese war planes were only ten minutes away from reaching their target.

On August 6, 1945, an American aircraft dropped an atomic bomb on Hiroshima, and Japan surrendered. This single act resulted in the end of World War II. I was seven years old, yet I remember with absolute clarity the day the world stopped to rejoice.

It was mid-afternoon when the bells from Our Lady of Guadalupe began to chime. As the sound echoed through the neighborhood, people ran out of their homes wondering what had occurred to trigger the joyful pealing. News reports were not immediately disseminated during that era. It would take a while for radio stations to announce the news they'd longed for, news that the war had ended. People gathered on stoops, in doorways, in stores, and some made their way to church to speculate. And when shouts of *"Japan surrendered, the war's over, our soldiers are coming home"* were heard, the news exploded like a wildfire, and madness erupted.

The hours that followed were wildly joyous. The air was electrified, filled with a plethora of festive sounds. The clamor resounded throughout each neighborhood. Cars began racing up and down the streets, and the sound of screeching brakes added to the jubilation. It was the Fourth of July and New Year's Eve all wrapped into one September afternoon, and we were captivated by the pandemonium.

As the euphoria continued, pandemonium began to build, and chaos erupted. It was inevitable something might occur to mar the ecstasy.

While we were sitting on the front steps of our house, a police car slowly pulled up to the curb in front of the house next door. Two somber-looking officers slowly made their way to our neighbor's front door, respectfully removed their hats, knocked on the front door, and were soon led inside. A few moments later a chilling scream pierced the air, a sound that spoke of tragedy. My mother quickly ran to our neighbor's door and returned to tell us that their young son Pete, the youngest of seven children, home on leave from the Navy, had been killed in a motorcycle accident less than a mile from home. Only moments earlier the family had been celebrating the happy news, but now this day held another meaning, one of sadness that nothing could erase.

Although the war had ended, far more disturbing news eventually made its way to our home. A few weeks after the war ended, my father rushed to answer an anxious knocking at the front door. A man in a Western Union uniform handed him a telegram, one with a black border encircling the envelope. The border indicated disturbing news, and he called to my mother. Noting an odd tone in his voice, she rushed to his side.

They sat side by side on the living room couch and slowly opened the envelope. Upon reading the words in the telegram, a wail erupted from deep within him. The telegram stated his youngest brother Camillo had been killed a few days after the war ended. Numbed by the news, my father began crying and calling out his brother's name—*Camillo, Camillo.* His agonized sobs reverberated throughout our house, shattering the joyfulness of the war's ending. My mother joined him in his grief, and they remained huddled together on the living room couch, crying long into the night.

Frightened and stunned by their grief, I sat on the floor close to them. Later I went to my bedroom and fell across my bed. I wept for the young soldier uncle whom I'd never met, who had been killed by the evils of war, but I mostly cried for the gut-wrenching pain that pummeled into my parents' hearts. Throughout the years, the memory of that day has never left my mind.

From that day forward, and for the year that followed, an all-consuming stillness fell over our household. My mother began wearing black mourning garments, the radio was silenced, the window shades and beautiful velvet drapes in our dining room were drawn closed, and the sound of my father's voice in joyful song was hushed.

While still in the grips of pain over Camillo's death, another telegram arrived noting the death of my mother's brother Mario. He had also been killed at the end of the war. His death compounded the sadness at a time that should have otherwise been devoted to elation over the end of war.

1945: Camillo Scarcella's funeral

Castellammare Del Golfo, Sicily

OUR HOUSE ON 72ND STREET

The birth of my sister Rose created an urgent need for a large home, and the search for one began immediately. Houses at that time were in short supply. Within my parents' tightly-knit circle of friends, news of their need spread quickly—a large house with many bedrooms, a backyard for children to play, and a basement with a wine cellar for my father.

It was pure luck when they learned of a house for sale in Bensonhurst, an area of Brooklyn not far from the apartment. The owners were considering a move, and the house was not yet on the market. My father was told the house was located in a much-desired neighborhood of quaint old homes, nearby schools, churches, and shopping.

Wasting no time, he walked to the corner of 72nd Street and 14th Avenue. In the center of this block of five homes, one stood out—a large white house with an enclosed red brick porch and an arched hedge above a black wrought iron entry gate. He could not look away, hoped this was the house, and crosschecked the address on the front door against the note in his pocket. Noting they were one and the same, he rushed home to share the news with my mother.

He already knew what my mother's reaction would be and was anxious for her to see the house through her own eyes. Houses in the neighborhood of Bensonhurst would sell quickly, and an appointment was promptly made to speak to the owners.

The following Saturday morning, with my sister in a baby carriage, we walked the few short blocks from 68th Street to 72nd Street and 14th Avenue. My mother spotted the house immediately—the one he'd described so eloquently—the white house with a row of well-trimmed hedges marking the front border, tall pines standing guard by the front windows in front of the enclosed, red brick porch.

The house in no way resembled the other traditional homes in this well-established neighborhood. It stood out proudly, outrageously flaunting its own brand of beauty—very white, very bright. From where they stood across the street, she imagined the house calling to her, to a large family with many children to move in and fill the air with the happy sounds of laughter, for music to resonate through the house, and for fragrant aromas emanating from the kitchen to waft from room to room.

It was love at first sight. The house was "over the moon" beautiful, far more upscale than the other custom homes on that block. If the truth were known, my parents were ready to buy the house—inside sight unseen.

One can only imagine their excitement as they crossed the street, opened the black wrought iron entrance gate, and walked under the horseshoe shaped hedge. Bright blue hydrangeas graced each side of the path leading to red brick steps and the front door where they nervously knocked.

The owners warmly welcomed my parents inside. After a tour, my parents decided the house felt like home—their home. The sale was toasted with espresso coffee and a check for $4000, money they'd sacrificed and saved through the years. After the legalities of home buying were completed, my parents became proud owners of a beautiful home on a lovely, tree-lined street in Brooklyn. All that was left was packing and moving.

The interior of our new home was bright and spacious with many windows, and to the side of the living room was a cozy nook where a wall-to-wall mural had been painted on all three walls. Of the four levels, only two were occupied. Directly under the pitched roof, nearly ready for occupants was a partially finished attic. Since renters lived on the second floor, we would live on the first level with easy access to the basement and backyard.

Although the kitchen was tiny, it had all the features my mother needed to comfortably cook and feed her family. Except for the kitchen and one tiny bathroom, the rooms were spacious and bright, especially the dining room where the family would spend most of their waking hours.

In time, the enclosed front porch would become a lovely bedroom for my sister and me. My mother purchased stylish white bedroom furniture, sewed pretty green and white bedspreads for the two beds arranged uniquely end-to-end, and she decorated the wide span of windows with curtains to match the bed coverings. She created a room with a lovely feminine ambiance for her daughters to enjoy for many years.

I loved this room, especially when I became a teenager. It was isolated from the rest of the house, hidden from view by the trees. In the winter, when snow was falling, I'd open the blinds and peer out of the window at the stunning sight of snow-laden trees—a winter wonderland of picture-postcard worthiness!

The basement had a coal burning stove and a room used to store a season's worth of fuel. Towards the back, directly under the master bedroom, was a large room that in time was remodeled (sparingly) and used as a den.

The most charming area of the basement was the "man cave" my father's wine cellar—an area that had been carved deep into a wall, with dirt shelves that held odd-sized bottles. A heavy aroma of wine emanating from empty wine barrels completed the ambiance. The wine cellar became my father's hearty haven.

The backyard was everything my father desired. By springtime the rambling rose bushes lining the back border of the yard burst out in living color. By the end of the first summer, the backyard became an Italian garden, an oasis in the city. The yard, though small, had ample room to plant trees and to grow a variety of vegetables—tomatoes, onions, zucchini squash, and everyone's favorites, sweet basil and tasty mint. The following spring, my father planted fruit trees—nespoli and fig. Most had origins from Sicily.

Above a rickety old wooden table was a pergola with grape plants in each corner. By midsummer of that first year, vines covered the trellis, and large clusters of red grapes hung lazily above the table teasing birds as well as my parents. It was at this table where, weather permitting, they'd sit and enjoy their after-dinner espresso.

In the back and to the side of the house was a small garage, enough to comfortably house a medium-sized car. Since we had no plans to purchase a car, the garage was leased to someone lucky enough to own an automobile.

The dining room was center stage, the main gathering place, and the room I remember nostalgically. My mother purchased a beautiful dining room set with a table large enough to seat twelve guests comfortably. Many of my memories were created around that table. Be them sad or happy moments, at this table the dynamics of the family were played out daily—where discipline was imposed, homework was completed, decisions were made, and of course, where the family gathered at dinnertime to enjoy *pranzo*.

At this table my father wrote letters to his siblings, my mother stuffed packages to be sent to our never-forgotten families in Sicily, and my father sang and told us about life in Sicily.

In the dining room was a freestanding radio, very stylish for that era. During the early years, before television entered our lives, after dinner we'd gather around the radio and listen to music or to a variety of funny or scary evening soap operas. Programs such as *The Inner Sanctum, Amos and Andy*, and *Burns and Allen* were very popular.

During my teen years, every Saturday morning at exactly ten o'clock, I'd tune in to the *Hit Parade* and sing away the weekend chores. Music always made the chores less boring.

The kitchen, my mother's culinary kingdom, was always bursting with a kaleidoscope of enticing aromas. The room was tiny, with barely enough room for a table. Luckily, one fit perfectly over a black and white tiled area. At that table my mother served breakfast, lunch, midday coffee breaks and after-school snacks. A corner pantry was used to store staples, and a modern electric refrigerator replaced the icebox we'd used in the apartment. The stove, not much larger than most camp stoves, was perpetually in use with coffee percolating on the back burner or the beginning stages of an evening meal simmering. A window above the sink looked directly into our neighbor's side yard, where, depending on the weather, neighborhood children gathered after school to play.

Once the furniture was in place, my mother stocked the pantry—the shelves in the basement—with her favorite supplies and hung the velvet drapes she'd sewn over the large dining room windows. Soon our neighbors began welcoming us into the neighborhood and the house on 72nd Street became a happy Sicilian home and would remain so for many years.

Cloaked with the charm of the old country, weekend visits from relatives and friends were commonplace. During these festive gatherings, our home became an Italian fun house, filled with the happy sounds of laughter from the women as they cooked, gossiped, and complained about their husbands, from the children as they ran about aimlessly, and the men as they sang, drank homemade wine, and played cards into the early morning hours.

During the early morning hours on those festive weekends, the men would often turn their attention away from playing cards and focus on their growling stomachs. Soon the aroma of *pasta cu l'agia e l'olio* . . . pasta with garlic and oil would fill the air and quell their noisy bellies.

My parents filled our home with love, laughter, music and an ambiance of old Sicily, where their ancient traditions reigned for many years. But we lived in America, and as the children came of age, customs fell by the wayside and new traditions quietly assimilated into their lives, much to my father's chagrin.

Our home on 72nd Street

On June 5, 1943, my mother came home with another surprise—a new baby. This time the bundle was blue . . . a baby brother named Joseph, named after my father and grandfather (Giuseppe) and nicknamed *Joey* and later *Joe*. He was an adorable baby, cuddly and cute, with a lovable smile he generously shared with anyone looking his way.

My parents were overjoyed; the birth of a son was a grand event. They savored the euphoria of having a male child. One would think a king had been born to claim his throne. It would be some time before my sister and I understood the importance a male child held in a Sicilian household. To my parents—my mother in particular—a son was king and daughters were princesses.

The five of us

In spite of our place in line, Rose and I never lacked for love and attention. My father adored his little girls, and my mother never failed to share her loving heart with her daughters. We never felt slighted; both parents were equally generous with their feelings in a million ways.

THANKSGIVING DAY SURPRISE

With the onset of fall that first year in our new home, Thanksgiving Day soon began to inch closer. Although our Thanksgiving table had not evolved to the level of the American genre of celebration, the meaning was the same: to be thankful to God for good health and for our new home. In lieu of turkey, my mother served roasted rabbit or duck or whole chickens, plus the standard mosaic of Italian foods.

Thanksgiving Day in our new home may not have included the usual suspects—turkey, gravy, mashed potatoes, and pumpkin pie—but we feasted on a surprise of a different nature. It began early Thanksgiving morning after my father poured his coffee and headed down the hallway for a cursory check of all exterior doors. When he reached the front of the house, he opened the door and something immediately caught his eye. My mother and I were seated at the kitchen table when we heard his voice ring out.

"*Nardina, veni ca* . . . come here!" he shouted.

The frenzied tone of his voice suggested something out of the ordinary had occurred. My mother and I rushed and found him standing by the open door holding a beautifully decorated basket.

"*Che ha successo* . . . what happened?" my mother asked while glancing at the large basket in his arms.

"*Tallia che cosa ho trovato davanti la porta* . . . look what I found outside the door!"

The basket was brimming with an assortment of Italian cookies, chocolates, hard candies, and fancy Italian breads, as well as a small wooden turkey we later placed in the center of our table (in lieu of a roasted bird!). We were both delighted and bewildered. Without a card or a note, the giver remained unknown.

On Thanksgiving morning of the following year, the moment we woke up, we rushed to the front door hoping to find another surprise. We were not disappointed. Waiting by the door was another beautiful basket chock-full of delicious goodies much like those of the previous year.

For many years, we looked forward to Thanksgiving Day, not for a roasted turkey on our dinner table, but for the baskets, a charming compliment to our Thanksgiving Day celebration. Yet the thoughtful person, the giver, remained a locked-room mystery. The basket was a topic of conversation when visitors stopped by. For a while everyone imagined it was Auntie Anna, yet no one knew for sure. She was the likely candidate.

Five years after the first Thanksgiving surprise, an early morning dash to the front door left us disappointed. No basket was waiting to be enjoyed, and the caring giver remained a mystery.

After we'd settled into the white house, when La Signora Pina and her daughter Rosanna stopped by to see us, the house would suddenly come alive with the sounds of lively chatter and laughter. Rosanna kept me occupied by playing games and checking my latest schoolwork and my wardrobe of pretty dresses, and my mother and La Signora indulged in lively conversation and drank espresso coffee at the kitchen table.

A few days after our painfully disappointing Thanksgiving, Rosanna stopped by the house. This time, she came alone.

"Where's your mother?" inquired my mother.

Rosanna took hold of my mother's hand and softy whispered, "Signora Nardina, I wasn't sure anyone would stop by to tell you. My mother passed away last week. She had a heart attack during the night and passed away in the hospital."

The news stunned my mother. She immediately embraced Rosanna and wept in her arms.

"Signora, my mother loved and missed all of you so much. When you moved away, she took it hard. She never stopped thinking about you. I'm not sure if you ever figured out who left the baskets every Thanksgiving. It was my mother."

The news of her passing hurt deeply. While Rosanna shared how much La Signora enjoyed shopping for the basket and the goodies she knew the family would enjoy, my mother cried.

"It gave her so much joy to deliver the basket in the early morning, before anyone was awake!" Rosanna sadly added.

My mother shared her feelings for La Signora as well and told Rosanna how much their friendship had meant through the years; how special the Thanksgiving Day baskets had become in the Scarcella household.

Rosanna visited for a while longer. As though La Signora was there with them, they cried and sipped espresso and reminisced about the years when both families shared the top floor of the apartment house on 68th Street. Before she left, Rosanna took my hand, looked at my scarred finger and said, "Promise me that every time you look at your finger you will remember my mother."

Never be sad for what is over;
just be glad that it was once yours.

BUT I DON'T WANNA GO TO SCHOOL

When I was a little girl, I thought everyone was Italian. And why would I feel differently? After all, the Italian language with a Sicilian dialect was the only verbal communication used at home.

Although my father took great strides in promoting his heritage, he was born in New York City and proudly called himself an American. He was tremendously mindful of the opportunities the land of his birth had provided. Yet he was also mindful of his roots and had his opinions.

"If you're Sicilian, that's better than being Italian, but we're Americans, and that's even better! There is no country like America. You should be proud of that!" he'd say in a determined voice.

I was never sure what being an American meant. As far as I was concerned, we were Sicilian, more Sicilian than Italian. Until my first day in school, I had never heard another language spoken in my presence.

The English language was nonexistent in my world. By the time I was four years old, my parents were painfully aware that in order to attend school, something had to be done about my language skills.

One of the neighbors suggested speaking to someone at the local Catholic school. Taking their advice, my parents contacted a priest at St. Rosalie's Parochial School, and a workable solution was available with one requirement—a Catholic baptismal certificate was needed.

Although my parents were married in a Catholic church, they did not practice the religion. As far back as I can remember, we attended a "speaking in tongues" church in our neighborhood every Saturday night. This religious practice occurred during the years when Auntie Anna and the entire family were close. After the feud, our attendance in church became a distant memory. Faced with the urgent need of a baptismal certificate, the wheels were set in motion, and godparents were quickly chosen.

I was four years old when I was baptized in St. Patrick's Cathedral in New York City and was immediately enrolled in St. Rosalie's Catholic School, an event that initiated the beginning of a new chapter in our lives.

My life changed the morning my mother and I made our way to St. Rosalie's Catholic School. She'd spent months preparing me for school, yet her attempts had failed miserably, her words falling on tiny deaf ears. Each time she uttered the word *scuola* . . . school, the more convinced I was that something sinister was about to enter my safe world. I was frightened. Not wanting to add any further anxieties, she avoided telling me I would be left alone, with strangers.

With tears streaming down my face, she led the way, reassuring me that school would be fun. I wanted to be home with her. The only moments away from her had been when Auntie Anna or La Signora Pina had been a part of our lives.

I'm sure it pained her to leave me in a strange environment where I would not understand what was being said, yet she had no choice; there was no other way—attending school was my destiny. And when it was time to leave me with the nun, I cried openly, passionately, and with the strength of a vice grip I clung to her leg. The nun attempted to pull me away from her, but I held on, begging her not to leave me. Eventually she left and probably cried all the way home.

My parents may have given some thought to the difficulties I would experience in a classroom full of strangers that spoke an unfamiliar language, yet they would never be aware of the classroom bullies that took advantage of me, made fun of me, shoved and punched me until I cried. Thankfully most of the girls were more assertive than I was. They always came to my rescue and would shoo away the bullies. These incidents were never reported to the nuns or to my parents.

To say I was in shock is to understate my feelings during those first few months, before I stopped crying every morning on the way to school, before I began understanding what was being spoken.

For the longest time I mostly listened and absorbed. In time the nun was able to devote more time to her youngest student with a unique need, and I began to understand conversations and to form little sentences.

Every night I'd proudly share what I'd learned in school with my parents and they would repeat the words back to me. I became their tutor, and soon our conversations were sprinkled with the sound of English words. By the end of my first year in school, the ambiance at home began to change, but never completely.

Having little exposure to English, it was far more difficult for my mother to learn the language. Most neighborhood vendors and neighbors spoke Italian; few spoke both languages. My father had more exposure. Some English was spoken at work, although he mostly learned work-related words. In time he was able to communicate with English-speakers, more so than my mother. Both learned enough English to understand and be understood.

A semester was a long and endless span of time for a four-year-old. Thankfully, by June I'd fully acclimated to my new life in school. Much to everyone's amazement, especially the nuns and my parents, my test scores surpassed expectations, and I graduated to second grade.

Being able to speak English, I was transferred to Our Lady of Guadalupe, a parish closer to home. In this new school I quickly made friends and invited them home to meet my parents. Although my friends were also Italian, their parents were acclimated to the American lifestyle. English was spoken in their homes, a sharp contrast to the communication in my home. My parents insisted I speak English, but responded in Italian. When my friends visited and listened to our dual mode of communicating, they found it amusing and would giggle!

BRUKOLINO—1940

Life in the 1940s was far simpler than in today's modern world. In our Brooklyn neighborhood, hardly anyone owned a car or a television set, the home telephone had not yet made an appearance, and home entertainment was derived via the radio. Child molesters were unheard of, and children played in front yards and were allowed to ride bikes freely around the neighborhood. Families ate together when Daddy came home from work, meals were homemade, especially in Italian homes, and families rarely ate in restaurants—at least not mine. Men wore classy Fedora hats but respectfully took them off before entering a building, Mercurochrome was the miracle drug of the time, and children were told that storks delivered babies.

During this era, the horse-drawn delivery cart was representative of daily life in Brooklyn. The sound of vendors' carts clip-clopping down the streets in the early dawn, delivering milk, ice, vegetables, even junk, was commonplace. Iceboxes were used to store cold foods, and the iceman carrying blocks of ice in steel grips was an everyday sight.

Although indoor plumbing was available in the city, "backhouses" were still used in country homes. Hair dryers were not available for home use, and the family wash was hung on outdoor clotheslines. Only a limited amount of canned products were sold in food stores, and "take out" was not in our vocabulary.

A few blocks from our house was a rather unique business: a chicken house. When chicken was on the evening menu, fresh hens were purchased at this establishment. However, the chickens in that store didn't come in neat, clear cellophane packages; they were alive, clucking away, probably pleading for mercy. Needless to say, it was not my favorite place in the neighborhood, and their squawking could be heard long before you set foot in the front door. Once inside, feathers could be found everywhere—on the floor, floating in the air, and on counters. Adding to the offense was the overpowering odor of burnt chicken skin. Whenever my mother sent me on this mission, knowing two birds were about to get their necks wrung was absolutely disturbing.

Soup for dinner always called for a trip to the corner vegetable stand as well. "Here's five cents," she'd say while tucking a shiny coin in my hand. "I need soup greens." My mother never failed to remind me to come home with two carrots, two onions, two sticks of celery, and fresh parsley. And to be careful, not to lose the money!

Supermarkets had not made the local scene during this time, at least not in our neighborhood. The shopping environment consisted of specialty stores: the fish market, the butcher shop, vegetable and fruit stands, bakeries and delicatessens. There were no quaint clothing boutiques in our neighborhood; we traveled downtown to large department stores for clothes shopping.

In the early hours of the morning, the aroma of bread would snake through the neighborhood. No Italian would dare eat Wonder Bread. There were many bakeries in each neighborhood, and every Italian family patronized their favorite establishment. The local baker was held in high esteem, and shoppers were loyal. Hands down, Romano's Bakery on 13th Avenue was our favorite bread store.

Fish markets had their own unique environment, offering a variety of specialty and exotic fish to choose from—including snails—and contained the unmistakable aroma of the sea. My father did most of the fish shopping; he was the expert in that field and took great pleasure in making the selection for Friday night dinners. He knew the fishmongers personally. For my father a trip to the fish market was a visit with friends. Having been raised in Sicily where no part of the fish was wasted, fish soup was among his favorite meals, as was a tasty feast of snails. However, seeing fish eyes floating in your dinner plate or snails floating in some indistinguishable sauce made us all cringe.

No foods were labeled "bad" to eat—food was good, even crème puffs and cannoli—mouthwatering treats that were passionately enjoyed. Ice-cold lemonade, tasty egg creams, frosty milk shakes, and iced espresso coffee were among the popular non-alcoholic drinks during that time. Coke and 7UP were the most popular brands of soda. Our Sunday dinners included cream soda, a refreshing treat we looked forward to with gusto.

And who can forget the tasty "Charlotte Russe", pronounced "Charley Roosh" in Brooklyn, purchased at the corner candy store to be eaten while walking along the avenue. The tasty treat was contained inside a white cardboard tube with a scalloped edge and was a slightly dry but yummy sponge cake. The best part was the whipped cream on the very top. As you ate, you pushed the cardboard disk up from the bottom. Delish!

While most Italians enjoyed the poetic Neapolitan songs and operas, big band music was all the rage during the '30s and the '40s. The wildly popular genre swept the nation and was listened to on radios and played in jam sessions, and couples would swing to the music in clubs and ballrooms such as the Roseland in New York City.

Bold, bright colors were used in kitchens, and bright yellow was my mother's color choice. Crocheted doilies were used on couch armrests, and plastic see-though covers were placed on living room couches. Venetian blinds and lace curtains framed many windows, and shiny linoleum floors, chrome kitchen sets, and built-in storage cabinets were in vogue. Curtains, drapes, slipcovers, and bedspreads echoed matching colors and fabrics throughout the house.

Organdy was a popular fabric for kitchen windows and dresses as well. Thanks to my mother, my closet was filled with many pretty organdy dresses; each one made me feel special and very pretty. I loved swirling 'round and 'round and watching my full skirts swell up like a puffy parachute!

My sister was blessed with long, pretty curls. I had soft waves. To equal the playing field between sisters, my mother would often twirl my hair around long strands of cloth before bedtime. In the morning I'd enjoy lovely, long banana curls. The long twirls always made me feel like a princess. I learned early in life that a little discomfort was to be tolerated; the end result was all that mattered!

Two sisters

During the grueling heat of summer, children cooled off by running through water gushing freely from open fire hydrants and drank water burping out of a backyard hose. Babies slept on their tummies and wore cloth diapers. No one wore helmets when riding bikes or scooters, and we stayed out all day, returning home before dinner or at the sound of our mother's voice echoing loudly down the streets.

Children's toys were simple and uncomplicated during this era. Boys took great pleasure in playing marbles in the dirt, and girls enjoyed playing jacks on stoops. Candy Land and Silly Putty made their debut, and the world of Tonka trucks fueled little boys' dreams.

Many toys were homemade. Little girls played with rag dolls with button eyes, and boys played with war toys often concocted from garage scraps.

Children made colorful parachutes from their fathers' old handkerchiefs and enjoyed the construction process as well as the finished product. The fun began by decorating one side of a handkerchief or an old cotton swatch of cloth with colorful crayons, tying four strings of equal length to each corner, and securing the ends together with a rock. Standing on a high place, they would hold the center of the handkerchief, let it drop, and watch as it filled with air and floated gracefully to the ground.

When it wasn't raining, summer evenings were magical. Catching fireflies (lightening bugs) in glass jars happily entertained us for an entire evening.

My first bike

Sis feeding the birds

INDIAN MARY AND MIKE

Every neighborhood in Brooklyn had its own uniqueness, an oddity that made it an original. Ours did as well!

Located in the middle of 100-year-old stately homes was an eccentric home/business enterprise with a peculiarity all its own. Barely a stone's throw from our house, the quaint old structure sat back from the street and was divided into two sections: a candy store in the front, a barber shop in the back. Living quarters were somewhere in the back of the property, away from any curious view. Although sweet shops in those days were plentiful, this candy store was distinctive and unrivaled.

The store was lovingly referred to as "Indian Mary's Candy Store," and every adult and child throughout the area had at one time or another stepped into Mary's world. A long path led you from the sidewalk to the stairs, and soon you were standing on a dilapidated wooden porch with an old rocking chair to rest as needed. On the left side of the porch was an old Indian statue standing guard by the front door. On the right was a standard barbershop pole with whirling red, white, and blue stripes.

The owners were known as Indian Mary and Mr. Mike. Mary's title was not only due to the Indian statue on the porch; it was mostly her long, black hair worn in braids, framing the high cheekbones of her weathered face. Some of the neighborhood children often referred to her as "Crazy Mary," but she was not. There was never a doubt in anyone's mind . . . Mary *looked* like an Indian so she must be!

The candy and ice cream areas of the store were Indian Mary's domain. No matter what time of the day, children were always clamoring about, ogling her tempting wares. Along the walls, an assortment of items, including large bottles of soda, were on display as well. On the right, a large glass-enclosed counter was filled with a large variety of candy, and on the left was an ice-cream freezer jam-packed with summertime deliciousness. In the back of the building was the barbershop, Mr. Mike's domain. These were the days before high-tech salons, a time when men frequented barbershops for a good haircut and lively conversation, all at a fair price.

The walls were decorated with old pictures and other peculiar objects. One of the images displayed always captured my attention. It was a picture of dogs sitting around a table, smoking cigars, and playing cards. It always made me stop and stare for a few moments.

Wall décor in Indian Mary's Candy Store:
7 dogs playing poker, artist: CM Coolidge

It mattered little when you visited the store, the sights and sounds were always the same: Mary, wearing long and colorful dresses standing behind the candy or the ice cream counter, the happy voices of delighted children scampering about in their decision-making moments, and male banter echoing from the back of the store where Mike trimmed hair and the men shared jokes and told tall tales.

No one had ever seen where Mary and Mike ate, slept, or bathed. Based on the appearance of the barbershop and candy store, everyone surmised their living quarters probably matched the exact ambiance of the store—dusty and rustic!

Summer days in Brooklyn were long and hot and muggy. After dinner my mother would give me three nickels to buy ice cream for Rose, Joe, and myself. While I ran to the store for the treats, my two siblings would patiently wait on the front stoop of our house. Soon the three of us were feasting on the cool, smooth taste of chocolate-coated ice cream bars, a refreshing treat at the end of a smoldering day.

It was during those early years when I took my first journey through the "garden of good and evil" tiptoeing ever so lightly on the evil side. The heat of the day had spilled into early evening. My siblings and I were still sitting on the front stoop when my father came upon the scene. Having just finished eating the ice cream I'd purchased with the money my mother had given to me, my father failed to notice our chocolate-lined lips.

"Here's some money, go get some ice cream. It's still hot out!"

He had no idea my mother had already treated us, and I had no problem keeping that fact to myself. However, while enjoying our second treat of the evening, my mother suddenly appeared.

"Are you still eating ice cream?" she asked.

My father looked puzzled. He told her he'd just given me money for ice cream.

"Joe, they already had ice cream. You gave your daughter money for the second treat."

My father was not pleased with me, and he let his annoyance be known vocally. This was the first time he had ever raised his voice towards me. My mother made her disapproval known as well, but after seeing me in tears, she began laughing.

"Ah c'mon Joe, it's hot out, leave her alone!"

I was only eight years old at the time, very young and not clever enough to deliberately pull the wool over his eyes. That incident may have set my father up on his heels and subconsciously planted the seed to keep a watchful eye on his eldest child. And he did.

STOP THE CLOCK

Two months before I turned ten, a new chapter in my life began to unfold. I didn't have an older sister to fill me in on the intimate details of a woman's changing body. Matters regarding the body, male or female, including menstruation and childbirth, were strictly taboo in my family. Even the word "pregnant" was never used in conversation. One can only imagine how shocked and frightened I was by the strange pink surprise that greeted me early one morning.

I had no idea what the early morning surprise meant and was too scared to ask. I assumed I was ill and would soon die. By the time I was dressed and ready to go to school, the situation worsened and I turned to my mother.

Due to my age, my mother was upset and marched me over to the doctor's office. After she tearfully explained the situation, he smiled and reassured her that nine years of age was young to begin menstruating but not unheard of. And as though I was invisible, I was left in the dark, confused and frightened.

When we arrived home, she smiled and reassured me I was not sick, I was not going to die. She told me that the event happens to all girls when they become women. "*Ora tu sei una femina* . . . now you are a woman," daunting words for a nine-year-old to digest. I was still playing with dolls, not prepared to be *a woman*! I had no idea what "being a woman" meant. Having no choice in the matter and trusting that I was not dying, I swallowed hard and went along with the program.

She kept me home from school that day and spent the morning preparing me for the monthly ritual. Later we went shopping, and I was rewarded with new shoes. My mother was happy, seemingly proud that her daughter had reached this milestone, and she shared the news with all the neighbors. On that morning, my world changed, and nothing made any logical sense.

The next day I shared this troubling experience with my girlfriend MaryAnn.

"Oh, you got your period?"

"My what?"

"Your period, the curse—didn't your mother tell you about it?" MaryAnn continued.

"I have no idea what you're talking about. Do the nuns know about this?" I asked in complete innocence.

"It's normal," she responding reassuringly.

"Normal?"

"Yes silly, it's normal. It has to do with babies—how they are made—with the egg and stuff!"

"What are you talking about?"

"BBB!" she laughed. "The birds, the bees, and babies."

Although my mother never shared the reason for menstruation, she had no problem sharing old wives' tales, urban legends, and folklore beliefs surrounding the monthly ritual.

"Don't ever wash your hair during that time of the month or you'll get real sick. And don't touch plants or flowers either. If you do, they will die."

Many superstitions, some unrelated to menstruation, were widely believed and accepted as truth in the Italian culture.

Malocchio ... the evil eye, is a curse placed on someone due to jealousy or envy by another party. The *malocchio* supposedly manifests itself in a misfortune to fall upon the cursed person, usually in the form of some physical ailment. Many Italian women in my Brooklyn neighborhood had that "evil" look in their eyes!

One other superstition followed me into adulthood, namely the ubiquitous power of a St. Joseph statuette. It is believed the statuette planted upside down in the front lawn of a house for sale will inspire a buyer.

THE NIFTY FIFTIES

On the cusp between the '40s and the '50s, my youngest sibling Anthony, a.k.a. Tony, was born. It was November 17, 1949, and this time around I was aware my mother was pregnant and I was actually given permission to select his middle name. For months I pondered over this honor. I decided on *Mario*, the name of a classmate who always made me blush when I caught sight of him looking my way. Mario was also the name of my mother's deceased brother, and the name met with her approval.

Tony topped the scales at 9 pounds, 13 ounces, a healthy handful for a newborn. Tony had olive skin and a full head of black hair—distinctly Sicilian. This was her fourth C-section, but things did not progress smoothly. After surgery, she developed a mild infection, was placed on Penicillin and sent home. But the infection worsened. The medication caused a severe case of hives, and she was bedridden for two weeks. I was kept home from school to help with my new baby brother. My contribution to his care was limited to feeding, changing diapers, and running errands to the local markets. Formula preparation was still a tedious chore that included boiling bottles and nipples and mixing various elements of dry ingredients including Dextri-Maltose. Relatives stepped up to the plate and stopped by every day to prepare the formula, wash clothes, and manage the larger shopping needs. My father did the cooking in the evening, a task he thoroughly enjoyed.

Stick 'em up cowboy—whatta cutie

The '50s was a time I recall with great fondness and nostalgia. It was a generation that did not feign affection, belittle friendships, or look upon love as a fleeting moment in time.

By 1953, the three-year Korean conflict was over, thereby warming the Cold War and bringing the illusion of peace and security to the world. Although issues with Communism continued to bubble on back burners in Washington, teenagers for the most part had little interest in politics, and those in my circle of friends were not politically minded.

From Coney Island to Times Square, Queens to the Bronx, teens were wrapped up in the genre of the times. They wore the trendiest fashions and listened to the most popular music, parents were respected, God was revered, and one's sweetheart held great importance.

No one would dare argue that the '50s was an era when timeless songs filled the air! From Frank Sinatra to Elvis Presley, from rhythm and blues to doo-wop, music rocked! Teens dropped endless coins into jukeboxes and danced to "It's a Dream" or "Earth Angel." During those glorious radio days, a famous disc jockey, Alan Freed, was at the helm and was dubbed "king of rock and roll."

Due to the large Puerto Rican and Cuban population in New York City, teens included Latin music in their repertoire of listening enjoyment. The "lindy hop", an offshoot of the 1930s-40s swing era dances, was now the hottest dance craze. And a new invention called the portable transistor radio made its appearance.

At the movies, the world of Technicolor™ made its appearance, and we were introduced to movie stars like Rock Hudson, Liz Taylor, Esther Williams, Debbie Reynolds, and my favorite heartthrob Tony Curtis in living color.

Men's hairstyles were eclectic in the 1950s, often inspired by movie stars like James Dean, Troy Donahue, and Elvis Presley. The "DA" (duck's ass or ducktail), the "flattop", and the "pompadour" were the styles mostly worn by younger men.

When one thinks of the 1950s male youth, the white t-shirt or rolled-up long-sleeve shirt (revealing biceps), leather jacket, jeans or pegged (tight rolled) pants were wildly popular but also considered very much the look of the "bad boy". A guy wearing jeans, a black leather jacket, and a slicked-back ducktail was the best tool to attract the girls. Some lucky gals wore their boyfriends' high school jackets and were envied by the ladies "left on the sidelines"!

Teenage females wore full skirts with motifs; the most popular was the poodle with a leash and full petticoats—great when dancing. Capri pants, dungarees, sweater sets, cinched belts, and pleated skirts were in also style. Topping the popular footwear list were penny loafers, moccasins, and white tennis shoes.

None of my friends dabbled in drugs, but most smoked. We met in ice cream parlors to listen to the latest hits on the jukebox and enjoy sweet treats. Our favorite meeting place was The Milk Bar on New Utrecht Avenue where we'd indulge in eating fries or drinking tasty milk shakes, sodas, as well as egg creams, a tasty drink made with chocolate syrup and soda water.

Elvis and Little Richard topped the rock-and-roll and rhythm-and-blues charts. Yet teenagers enjoyed another genre as well: pop music. Songs sung by Ol' Blue Eyes (Frank Sinatra), Perry Como, Eddie Fisher, Tony Bennett and Frankie Laine were among the top headliners. My father loved Perry Como!

Each Italian home was a clone of another with the same foods, the same conversations, and the same greetings. My friends called my mother

"*Mom*" and my father "*Mr. Scarcella.*" I returned the same respect in their homes. Divorce in the '50s was a rarity; no one within my circle of friends came from a broken home.

After school and on weekends, we rode our bikes and played stickball, street hockey, kick-the-can and hide-and-go-seek. *Ringolevio*, a hide-and-capture game, also deserves an honorable mention. There were few indoor games during that time, although playing cards, checkers, and Monopoly™ were popular. Young girls played "jacks" on stoops, and boys played "marbles" in the dirt. Everyone read comic books . . . Superman and Batman and Archie ruled.

During summertime, young children and teens were always outdoors, and no one worried if they wandered away from home. At some point during the day or early evening, a mother's booming voice could be heard shouting out the name of her child to come home. A familiar whistle designed for a particular child also signaled importance. Italian mothers never needed a megaphone; their voices (or whistling) would echo far and never failed to reach their targets.

Trains, buses, trolleys, and bicycles were the favored mode of transportation. Your bike was your escape. We pedaled for hours on end. During the summer, my friends and I would take daylong bike rides through other Brooklyn neighborhoods, with no repercussions for the long hours away from home.

Betty Crocker's famous cookbook made its appearance in bookstores. Men whistled at pretty girls passing by, and gals regarded their wolf calls a compliment. With the passing of spring, every teenager's biggest goal was getting a tan, the darker the better. Warnings about the dangers of UV rays were as yet unknown, and "catching rays" was considered "healthy."

Child molesters or sexual predators were unheard of, although we were warned to stay away from strangers. Except for the Lindbergh baby kidnapping, reports about children disappearing were rare.

Every man, woman and child in the early '50s feared polio. Until Dr. Jonas Salk's miracle discovery in 1955, this disease was considered an epidemic. It brought terror into the hearts of parents and fear to children old enough to understand. The only preventive tool known was hand washing, and reminders were posted everywhere.

Two of my friends succumbed to this killer. The first death occurred when I was in fourth grade. It wasn't unusual to be sick and stay home from school, but it was unusual when someone was gone for long periods of time. Joan Cappolla had been absent for one month when our nun tearfully announced she had polio. Knowing the consequences, we began to cry. Even tough little boys could not hold back their tears. We wrote little notes to her expressing how much we missed her. One morning, our nun walked into the classroom and told us Jesus had taken Joan to heaven. For many students, it was the first time they had come face to face with death. The disturbing news shook our world, and the entire class began to sob uncontrollably.

On the day of the funeral, our fourth grade class sat in the front pew of the church and sobbed throughout the entire mass, as did our grief-stricken nun. Soon the entire congregation joined in our grief, and the anguished sobs overrode the priest's prayers. On that sad morning, the Monsignor was forced to cancel classes, and we were all sent home.

In 11th grade, the death of another friend, Marilyn, was equally devastating. She lived in our neighborhood, and every morning we would walk to school together. The disease began innocently after what seemed like a harmless head cold. In less than two weeks, Marilyn had passed away from polio. Much like Joan, losing Marilyn was devastating and never forgotten.

However, the happy times helped mitigate the grief, especially when "the boys of summer" began training, initiating another magnificent season of major league baseball. My father was not into sports. He showed absolutely no interest, a viewpoint that I found disturbing.

"Daddy, I know you know who Joe DiMaggio is," I'd remark with a hint of sarcasm in my voice.

"Of course I do. DiMaggio, he's Italian right? And he plays ball!" he'd answer teasingly.

By no stretch of the imagination was my father a jokester; however, he did his fair share of taunting me about the Dodgers and would make weak attempts at teasing. When his compulsion to annoy me peaked, he would say, "Ya know I heard the bums stink!"

With three local teams to root for, New Yorkers enjoyed the games with gusto. From the sweet smell of success after a win to the long ride home after a loss, long-suffering fans remained fiercely faithful and spewed their abhorrence for the opposing team on street corners, in subways, over the radio, in homes, and along school corridors. Dodger fans hated the Yankees, Yankee fans hated the Dodgers, and no one liked the Giants!

Famous athletes often visited schools and spoke to students during assemblies. On the day Jackie Robinson was scheduled to visit New Utrecht High, students, the school faculty, and many parents and fans waited in the large assembly hall to hear him speak. It was a day I remember fondly, yet I was disappointed since my parents were not among the crowd of spectators.

It was as though the whole world followed baseball—except my parents. Whenever teams were in town, fans flocked to Yankee Stadium and Ebbets Field. I was envious of my friends who bragged about going with their parents to ballgames.

In all fairness, my father's greatest pleasure was drawn from his family, his garden, and his music. He also enjoyed going to Italian films and writing poetry. When I was very young, he took me to an opera. Later on, expanding his horizons, he took me to see *The Wizard of Oz*.

When television came into our lives, Cousin Nick would stop by to watch the baseball game on our newly acquired novelty, the television set. My father would turn on the set and would leave Nick to watch the game alone. Nick accepted my father's odd behavior. He didn't mind. As with all devoted fans, watching the game was all that mattered.

The 1955 World Series matched the Dodgers against their archenemy, the Yankees. The Yankees were considered a shoe-in. When the Dodgers turned the tables and won, Brooklyn exploded. This was their first World Series championship! The long-cherished dream became a reality and literally blew the lid off Brooklyn.

In the '50s smoking was in vogue and ads promoting cigarettes were everywhere. If you smoked, you were considered cool. Most adult males smoked—my father did not. I thought smoking looked cool; especially when someone blew large puffs of smoke and formed smoke rings in the air—like the famous Marlboro Man billboard in Times Square. The image of this rugged cowboy was considered to be one of the most brilliant advertisement campaigns of all time.

A visit to Coney Island topped everyone's entertainment list. After a twenty-minute train ride through Perfume Bay—a polluted patch of landfill—Brooklyn's wonderland was a breath away. Coney Island was more than a beach; it was home to Steeplechase Park, the world famous

Cyclone, the Parachute Jump, Nathan's Hot Dogs, and the Wonder Wheel.

Today, the Cyclone remains a landmark in Coney Island. The ride opened in June 1927 as the world's largest and fastest ride. Although it continues to be copied by other amusement parks, it clearly remains *the* most famous rollercoaster ride. Many years would pass before I mustered up enough bravado to ride its wooden cars.

In July 1988, the Cyclone received National Historic Landmark status and is now listed in the New York State Register of Historic Places. Furthermore, a quote by Charles Lindbergh in *Time* magazine compared the Cyclone to his first solo flight across the Atlantic! Imagine that!

During this time, children of Sicilian descent held fast to a myriad of century-old traditions. Among these old customs were greeting protocols, how children greeted adults. Calling someone older than oneself by his or her first name was considered rude, *maleducato* . . . impolite. If a child disrespected this rule, he or she would immediately feel the sting of a slap across the face.

An older person very close to the family (but not related) was greeted as an *aunt* or an *uncle*, and adult acquaintances were greeted as *Mr. or Mrs. "so and so"*.

Years later, I would realize how deeply engrained these rules were in my life. When I later arrived in California, imagine my surprise when I heard my brother Joe's fifteen-year-old girlfriend Pat greet my mother by her first name. My friends had always greeted my mother as "Mom" or "Mrs. Scarcella." I found it odd that my mother was not offended.

"Hey Joe, since when do your friends call Mom by her first name? And what do you call your girlfriend's mother?" I asked sarcastically.

"Mom doesn't care?" he replied.

"You're kidding! So Mom's changed?" I queried. "And I can call her friends by their first names?"

"No, I don't think so," he snapped back.

"Oh I get it, Californians are rude and Mom doesn't care—WOW!"

"No, it's different here and it's not rude. Besides, I told you, Mom doesn't care!"

When I asked my mother why she didn't mind Pat's seemingly irreverent greeting, her reply was brief and to the point. "Oh I don't care. He's gonna forget all about her—you'll see!"

The matter was laid to rest until a few days later when an expected visitor stopped by and introduced herself as Doris, Pat's mother, and asked if she could speak to me.

The visit came as a surprise, but I invited her inside. And while my mother made coffee, Doris and I began chatting. She explained how things were in California—how the use of first names for those you love and care about is proper. She asked me not to take offense.

"In California, formal greetings are used for people you work with and for casual acquaintances," she explained.

Doris was so sweet. I listened respectfully and thanked her for explaining *her* traditions. I also took the opportunity to clarify mine and made it clear that Italians feel differently; they believe it is rude and highly disrespectful for young people to be on a first-name basis with their elders. She smiled and told me she understood and insisted that I call her Doris.

Other than clarifying her point of view, and mine as well, I wasn't sure what good came from her spontaneous visit. As far as I was concerned, she was wrong—dead wrong—at least in my mother's house. And I was positive Pat would continue to greet my mother by her first name.

I was mistaken. From that day forward Pat greeted my mother as "Mrs. Scarcella" switching to "Mom" after she and Joe married.

As I met people and acclimated to the new Californian lifestyle, Doris' greeting made good sense, and I incorporated it into my own life . . . outside of my mother's house, of course.

ONE RINGY DINGY

During this era, everyone used public telephones, and many were conveniently located in various business establishments as well as on street corners. The public phone booth, encircled by glass doors, became your private communication domain.

When home telephones became available, the desire to have one in our home exploded quickly. However, the wait list was lengthy, and the monthly rates were costly—too costly for most families.

I was thirteen when the odd-shaped device with a round numbered dial and a long cord made its appearance in our home and was placed on the shelf in our living room. Although I can't recall the phone number, I do remember our "Cloverdale" prefix, the method used by the phone company prior to the use of numbered prefixes—a bit of nostalgic trivia I've never forgotten.

The "party line" was also a source of entertainment for curious teenagers. They enjoyed listening to other conversations, especially when they recognized the voices on the other end.

In the beginning, use of the phone was limited to my parents—mostly my mother. In time my father's work assignments were received via the telephone, thereby eliminating long waits on the docks each morning. As with all technology, prices eventually came down and home rates were more affordable. By the time my friends had telephones in their homes, I was allowed to use the phone freely.

After a few years, everyone had a phone and it was no longer considered a novelty or a frivolous expenditure. In due time private lines also became available, yet most families continued to use party lines. As the benefits of owning a home telephone mounted, especially for emergencies, it was no longer considered a toy for the rich.

BATTA BING

When I was young, discussions about the Mafia or (*La Cosa Nostra*) were held in hushed tones behind closed doors. By the time I entered my teenage years, names such as Lucky Luciano and Joe Bonanno—members of the Mafia—were openly discussed. Heated debates about the Mafia were overheard when family or friends visited our home, yet I never had a clear vision about the origins of this ominous organization. When I entered high school, my friends enlightened me, and it was obvious that my parents' views differed from those offered by my friends.

"Mom, my friends told me the Mafia started in Sicily!" I was always chided for that comment, yet I suspected my mother's views were questionable.

"There is no Mafia in Sicily. Sicily had Giuliano, a good man, like Robin Hood. The Mafia began in America."

My parents spoke kindly of Salvatore Giuliano, the famous Sicilian bandit, and labeled him an Italian Robin Hood, someone who took from the rich and gave to the poor. Sicilians regarded him as a hero and a patriot. I was told how during his lifetime, women adored him, children prayed for him, fathers looked up to him, mothers protected him, and in the mountains above his home village of Montelepre in Sicily, young men became soldiers in his army.

Many years would pass before the ambiguous history of the Mafia became clear. It occurred after I read a book written by Gay Talese, *Honor Thy Father*. The author discusses the origins of the Mafia and its beginnings in Castellammare del Golfo, Sicily, the town where my parents had spent their childhood years. The author tagged the quaint fishing village as the birthplace of many American Mafia figures, including Salvatore Maranzano, Stefano Magaddino, and Joseph Bonanno. However, he noted that the underground crime world, and the transgressions by the American Mafia, did not begin until they arrived in America. In many ways, my parents' beliefs held merit.

When I was older, discussions about the Mafia were always prefaced with assurances that our family had no affiliation with this organization, other than my mother's brother Joe and his decision to join the Mob when he arrived in New York.

As a teenager, I was suspicious of one person we respectfully called *Uncle Nick*, a non-blood relative. He was but one of the "uncles" in our midst, yet his actual connection to our family was hazy. Nick and his family (wife Josie and two daughters) lived in an apartment close to our home. Josie, Nick, and my parents enjoyed a close friendship; the two families often visited.

One day, and for reasons never made known, Nick announced that his family had been evicted from their apartment. During that time apartments were scarce, and since our home was spacious, my parents felt compelled to offer them accommodations—in our house—an arrangement that lasted two years.

Our house, though large, did not have guest rooms; the mid-level was rented out, and the attic did not have a bathroom. Nonetheless, my father felt an obligation to offer his assistance. Soon Nick and Josie were settled comfortably in our home.

The logistics of the room assignment between the two families made no logical sense, and the reasons behind this odd rationing were never shared.

Our beloved dining room, kitchen, bathroom, and the two back bedrooms—the best rooms of our house—became Nick and Josie's new apartment.

Our family had a less desirable arrangement. Our cozy living room was turned into sleeping quarters for my parents and brothers. My sister and I remained undisturbed, sleeping in the refurbished front porch bedroom.

Our daytime living accommodations were relegated to the basement where we shared space with the furnace, a coal burner, my father's beloved wine cellar, and a large room where coal was stored for the winter. The basement lacked the warm and cozy ambiance of the rooms above. There were neither warm floor coverings nor carpets over the cement floors, nor beautiful velvet drapes for privacy.

After a modest facelift, we ate our meals in the large back room of the basement where odd pieces of furniture (an old couch and a large dining table) created a modest resemblance of a dining room. Aside from the tiny window above the kitchen area, narrow windows across the top back and sidewalls of the basement dining room brightened the darkness of our eating environment. The sink where water drained from the washing machine was now used to wash dishes, and a stove and a refrigerator were purchased to complete the mock kitchen. Fortunately, my father had recently installed a new bathroom with a shower across from the kitchen area.

This bizarre arrangement made sense to my parents but not to me, a teenager deep in the throws of puberty with many restrictions on her comings and goings and no say in the matter. With little patience to spare, my protests echoed loudly each time I headed down the wooden steps to our dark quarters in the basement.

Nick and Josie were gregarious by nature and fun to be around. On weekends we all shared the upstairs dining room and our home abounded with sounds of laughter and music.

Nick and Josie's married daughter lived in Brooklyn with her family. Their youngest daughter did not live at home. After a serious altercation with a teacher in junior high, she finished high school in a Catholic boarding academy and came home once a month for a weekend and on holidays. We were the same age, and when she was home, weekends were fun. My father never protested when I asked to go out with her. It was as though he viewed her sentence to boarding school as an award. I never questioned why he did not consider her to be a dangerously out-of-control teenager. Strangely enough, neither did her parents.

Towards the second year of our odd living arrangement, I was told the telephone was off limits. No explanations were given. My siblings and I were ordered to come straight home after school. The tone was clear and ominous. Like good little Sicilian children, we obeyed. Conversations between the adults were now hushed or held behind closed doors, and the jubilant sounds of laughter suddenly disappeared.

"Mom, what happened? What's going on?" I'd ask.

She would "shush" me into silence and remind me not to use the phone under any circumstances. She eventually revealed that the problem was tied to Nick and swore me to secrecy.

One afternoon, my father, seemingly nervous and anxious, ushered the four of us into the porch bedroom and instructed us not to leave the room under any circumstances until he returned.

Sprawled on the beds with nothing to do, we stared out of the front windows until a large, black car pulled up to the curb. Four well-dressed men in stylish suits stepped out of the car and walked up the path to the front door. The shiny, expensive looking car and the well-dressed men seemed oddly out of place in our neighborhood. When the doorbell rang, we heard our father's footsteps as he made his way to the front of the house. We heard the door open, and our father's greeting as he invited the men inside.

The french doors of my bedroom had sheer curtains that allowed one to look past the living room and directly into the dining room. The scene around our dining room table looked peculiar—my father and Nick dressed in casual attire seated across the four well-dressed men in dark suits. My father kept pouring Vermouth into their glasses, but there were no smiles, and the conversation appeared to be agitated, heated, or so it appeared. Suddenly, the seemingly tense discussion ended, the men stood up, and my father and Nick led them towards the front door.

A few days after that strange meeting, Nick disappeared. Josie was visibly upset and my parents seemed preoccupied, on edge. Yet my mother refused to share any details.

Approximately one month later, Nick reappeared. Although phone use continued to be off limits, for the most part, the ambiance in our home was back to its jolly ole self. However, a nagging curiosity kept me wondering about the mysterious men, the odd meeting in our home, and Nick's unexplained disappearance. More than anything, I wanted to know where Nick had been, but my mother maintained her silence.

A few weeks later, Nick and Josie made a much-welcomed announcement: an apartment had become available, and they were moving. It had been two long years. As much as I'd enjoyed the festive mood at home, I hated the basement arrangement and wanted my house back.

After Nick and Josie moved away, we moved as well, back to our cozy little kitchen, the bright dining room with velvet drapes on the windows and our comfy living room. Once again the house was ours, along with a new phone number.

Once things settled down, my mother began revealing small bits of information. The police suspected a connection between Nick and a Mafia-involved murder in Chicago, and Nick had been arrested. But Nick was cleared of any connection and released. My mother refused to reveal the identity of the mysterious men in dark suits.

WHERE'S THE REMOTE?

I recently read that in 1952 only forty percent of all Americans owned a television set and most television viewing was concentrated within a 40-mile radius of New York City. In other words, most Americans were not watching television during that era. We were among the lucky few. Once television made its appearance, it topped the list of unique home entertainment venues, outranking the uniqueness of the home telephone.

We were introduced to television after an invitation to visit the home of our (real) cousins Mary and Marty. When we arrived, everyone was gathered in the living room and all eyes were glued to a rather odd piece of furniture they referred to as a "television set". I'd never seen anything like it, nor had any reference to "television" been made at school.

Marty was anxious to explain what television was all about. After pushing the "on" button, a strange blue light lit up the round, odd-looking screen. After a few minutes, a hazy picture began to appear. He kept fussing with the long pieces of metal on top of the set he referred to as "rabbit ears" until images of people in a living room setting appeared on the screen. It reminded me of a movie theatre screen on a far smaller scale and not nearly as clear. In order to continue watching what was being broadcast, every few minutes Marty would jump up and wiggle the rabbit ears until the images returned with clarity.

On the way home that evening, my parents were inundated with our demands: "Daddy please, please, please, can we get a television set too?" A week later a similar piece of furniture was in our living room as well.

At that time only two channels were available, but it didn't matter; we were glued to watching whatever was being broadcast and we loved it.

It took a while to get the hang of turning on, tuning in, and fiddling with the rabbit ears until the picture cleared, but from that day forward, life in our home changed dramatically. *"Howdy Doody"* joined us during *pranzo*, followed by fifteen minutes of news. After dinner we gathered around the television set and waited for the bumper music to announce the start of another program. Before long, new shows and programs were on the air and we were allowed to stay up later during the week. On weekends we watched television until the screen went blank at midnight.

Sadly my father lost his top billing as chief storyteller and crooner for our after-dinner entertainment. He'd been replaced by the weird looking wooden box with the unusual screen that lit up on demand. Clearly the novelty had taken over and revamped our lives.

Today's audience would deem some of the programs we watched as boring. Bar none, my mother's favorite drama was "I Remember Mama". Broadcast live, the program revolved around the lives of a loving Norwegian family living in San Francisco around 1910.

Nothing distracted my mother from watching the dynamic interactions between Mama (Martha), Papa (Lars) and their four children: Nels, Catherine, Christina and Dagmar Hanson.

The behavior archetype of the Norwegian family was endearing, especially the calm logic used by the parents to quell issues and problems that entered their lives; methods far removed from the fiery ambiance in our home yet filled with same love of family.

It didn't take long for many new programs to hit the airwaves. Parental guidance was not needed back then, programs were not sexually oriented, there were no morality issues, and the stars never made political comments. Programs were pure and simple entertainment. Much like today's "American Idol", "The Original Amateur Hour" topped the list of most watched television shows. On Tuesday nights we watched "The Milton Berle Show", and on Sunday nights we looked forward to "The Toast of the Town", hosted by Ed Sullivan. The madcap adventures of "I Love Lucy" and "My Little Margie" kept everyone glued to their sets. Westerns ranked high: "The Lone Ranger", as well as the king of the cowboys: "Roy Rogers". And who can ever forget "It's a bird, it's a plane, no it's . . . !" Yes, "The Adventures of Superman" also took its place in the long list of successful and unforgettable television programs. Soaps soon made their debut: "Guiding Light" and "The Edge of Night".

"American Bandstand" was making great strides in Philadelphia when 1956 until a clean-cut 26-year-old named Dick Clark took command as the new host. With Dick at the helm, the show became a hit and was soon broadcast widely. Dick and his new program quickly stole the hearts of every teenager who loved to dance and were now glued to their television sets after school and emulated the newest dance steps in front of mirrors.

Dick Clark—host on American Bandstand

By 1955 the television set had made its way into almost every American household. Television became the main media for home entertainment and new words such as "channels" and "rabbit ears" became part of everyone's vocabulary.

FATHER KNOWS BEST

My father was a daddy in the truest sense of the word. He was soft as butter on warm toast and hard as nails when appropriate. He loved his family, loved being a father, and wore his heart on his sleeve.

He was a proud American, politically minded, and a resolute Republican. However, having been raised in Sicily, our lives mimicked the world he left behind. His ideals and beliefs about raising a family were definitely Sicilian-oriented—not American.

My father was a small man, 5 feet 6 inches tall. Although he cast a small shadow, he left a large wake in his path. He was a father to his children, a friend to many, and loved by all. Although he came from a generation of men who didn't openly vocalize their love, he was different and expressed his feelings openly towards his children. When we were young, *"ti voglio bene* . . . I love you" or *"tesoro mio* . . . my treasure" were words he often verbalized, words that continue to resonate in my heart to this day.

Barely educated beyond third grade, my father's learning was derived from real life experiences. He was a self-taught marine biologist with a clear understanding of the sea through hands-on experiences, knowledge passed down through generations of fishermen.

My father was a poet and loved sharing his poems with his siblings via letters. He was also an eloquent storyteller, spinning tales almost every night to a captive audience . . . his children! Until television came into our lives, it didn't take much prodding for him to oblige us with the legendary tales that had been told to him by his mother.

Hands down, the most requested story was *La Crapuzza e La Crapazza*, a fanciful child's fairytale about two wildly rambunctious goats and their daily misadventures.

"Daddy, please, please tell us the story about *La Crapuzza e La Crapazza!*" we'd plead.

"Oh c'mon, you've heard it a million times! You know the story, why do ya wanna hear it again?" he'd tease back.

"We just do!"

"But you know how it ends!"

"No, Daddy, it's different, it's always different."

We'd beg, he'd tease, and he'd snake through the bone-chilling fable, pioneering new twists and turns, adding fresh sound effects, as well as another spectacular ending. Being surrounded by his children was my father's greatest joy and seeing the wonderment in our dark eyes was his only gratification.

When he passed away, we honored his never-forgotten storytelling. The following words were engraved on his headstone: In honor of the stories he told to his children, especially *"La Crapuzza e La Crapazza"*.

My father was handsome! My girlfriends would swoon over him and tell me I was so lucky. There was a short span of time when I developed a rather unsettling crush on him. I secretly carried his picture in my wallet until I experienced a crush on someone my own age.

Be it an opera or a Neapolitan folk song, Frank Sinatra or Carlo Buti, music scored his life and stirred his heart.

"Music is like breathing," he'd say. "It feeds the soul . . . it's the fuel that makes you dance through life."

With the introduction of the 8-track player and recorder, communication between himself and his siblings in Sicily changed dramatically. Hearing a voice behind poems and songs opened a new and exciting world. Suddenly Sicily seemed closer.

My father's warm tenor voice added a melodic timbre to the poetic Neapolitan songs, and it led to a short singing engagement on a local New York City radio station. He considered himself fortunate when asked to sing live on the air. However he was shy and found it difficult to schmooze with radio types. The programs were aired live, and the hours he was needed at the station made it impossible for him to keep up with his regular work. Sadly his radio music career ended and became a fond memory.

In the 68ᵗʰ Street apartment we called home before the white house, he taught me to sing old Neapolitan songs. When he was home, I'd sit on his lap and we'd sing by the kitchen window where neighbors in the courtyard below listened and applauded. It was then when his love of music found a place in my heart as well.

Until I turned fourteen, our home always glowed with the happy ambiance of love and laughter and hugs and kisses. When I entered high school, my demands became a clear threat to my father's authority, and the peaceful tranquility we'd once enjoyed began to unravel. He was unprepared to deal with an American teenager. As far as he was concerned, the old Sicilian ways were best: keep daughters at home, safely away from all marauding males. This was his mantra, his goal for my immediate future, and I began to distance myself from him.

During my high school freshman year, my father tightened his grip on my comings and goings and the activities I wanted to attend, those my friends enjoyed and I could not. His beliefs and opinions touched all levels of the American lifestyle. When I asked if I could wear lipstick, he said no. When I asked if I could go to the movies or roller-skating with friends, the answer was always the same, an emphatic no. Needless to say, dating was out of the question. As far as he was concerned, all entertainment outside our home was forbidden, unless my sister tagged along. He'd often make negative comments about my attire, but due to my mother's influence on this topic, he always lost the clothes battle.

He made his viewpoint and values clear, and I protested—vehemently. Conflicts at home became an everyday event, and no amount of pleading, crying or reasoning softened his views. My mother felt sorry for me, but her efforts to change his mind always failed.

Some nights, after he went to sleep, she would come into my bedroom and give me permission to go out, and I'd give her a solemn promise to be home by a certain time. Eventually, I'd sneak out after *she* went to bed.

Although my father was strong willed and held firm to his goals, there were many happy times during my adolescent years. When I turned sixteen they decided to honor my milestone birthday with a sweet sixteen party, something very popular back then. I assumed the party would be for my friends with a small mixture of our family and their friends. I was excited until I learned the party was for their friends and our relatives. However, they compromised and I was given permission to invite a few friends. Clearly, the party was an extension of the merry weekends with the usual suspects of their close friendships. As the plans progressed, I relaxed and secretly hoped my sixteenth birthday might signal a turning point in his *no dating* rule.

The birthday celebration would not mirror the "typical" sweet sixteen parties brimming with birthday banners, balloons, hot dogs, hamburgers and rock-and-roll. The ambiance was clearly an Italian celebration with homemade Sicilian pizzas, yummy Italian cookies and pastries from Romano's Bakery, and of course Neapolitan love songs.

I invited three couples and one male friend, Elliott, a Jewish guy who lived in our Italian neighborhood and close friend with one of the couples. Elliott was a dreamboat but someone I was not interested in romantically. Had I been, he would never have passed my father's smell test. Elliott was not Italian; he was German and Jewish and would have been a difficult sell!

The evening's music agenda for my friends was rock and roll in the basement den; for the adults, the standard fare, Neapolitan songs sung around our dining room table on the main floor.

After that night, my father began to lighten up—somewhat—not entirely. He allowed me to go out with groups of friends, but only if they picked me up and brought me home. He continued to oppose dating—passionately, and I was made aware that the timeless art of choosing a mate for the daughter was solely the father's duty and responsibly.

"I will find the right man for you, a man who will jump over the moon and bring you a star!"

DON'T ASK THE WINEMAKER
IF HE HAS GOOD WINE

My father lived in a world of perpetual motion. He never rested, never napped. He just kept moving. Although he was a fisherman, he was also a man of many talents. He loved preparing tasty fish dishes, made all the repairs around the house, and his gardening skills were admired by neighbors, friends and family alike.

He also earned the title of master winemaker and *his* wine was his beverage of choice. He never drank in excess and savored only one glass with evening meals. Since cow's milk was considered indigestible, the children were served small amounts of wine mixed with water with meals. However, we never indulged; strong tasting wine was not palatable to young taste buds.

For Italians who enjoyed the winemaking process, the celebration was a grand event! In advance of the much-anticipated winemaking day were weeks of planning. The basement became the most important room in our house. The winemaking paraphernalia was cleaned and readied before the grapes arrived. Wine barrels and bottles were marked for the following year's harvest, and the fermentation vats were filled with water and guarded carefully as they swelled.

On the day the grapes were due to be delivered, my father and Uncle Nick would stand by the curb and patiently wait for a truck to arrive with the precious cargo of California grapes. After what seemed like an eternity, the truck would pull into our driveway, and crates of grapes were carefully unloaded and stacked.

The ritual began the following morning when the crushing was launched and the basement became a festival filled with voices lifted in song, hardy laughter, and even arguments at times. Their faces, hands, clothes, walls, and floor soon replicated the deep burgundy color of grapes. Once the crushing was completed, the vats were filled with wine and the winemaking process was relegated to memory.

From that day forward, my father spent vast amounts of time in the wine cellar. He had a profound reverence for the grapes fermenting in those old barrels. He also loved the solitude of his wine cellar—sitting on an empty crate—drinking in the cool, musty air and the aroma of fermenting grapes.

It would be many months before the wine could be tasted and enjoyed. Now was the time to be patient and to take pleasure in what remained of the previous year's harvest.

GARDEN OF WEEDIN'

Primavera . . . springtime, a time of rejuvenation . . . when flowers, trees, and gardens, as well as my father came alive. It was a glorious season; when memories of the harsh winter months were cast aside, when warm breezes, gentle rains, and the colors and fragrances of spring were welcomed like a warm embrace after a long, painful absence.

My father—a seaworthy Sicilian fisherman, sailor, and winemaker—was also a capable and dedicated farmer! He took fastidious care of the soil in his garden—insurance for a sumptuous and tasty bounty come summer. By April he moved outdoors and devoted most of his time to his garden. His techniques were odd by today's standards, but his garden thrived and that's all that mattered!

He attributed his successful harvest to the rich soil in our tiny Brooklyn backyard, a product of his dedication. His technique of nourishing the earth was derived from my mother's knowledge about farming and common sense. His garden was nothing more than a large compost pile where every scrap of biodegradable leftovers (fish bones, meat bones, chicken bones, banana skins and eggshells) were buried. If something once lived, life would continue after a garden burial! It was no wonder our cats loved the outdoors, preferring to scamp around our backyard instead of the warm, cozy beds my mother provided indoors.

Our backyard mimicked those in Sicily. An old wooden table outside the back door was nestled under a trellis. In the spring, vines from his grape plants would spread over the lattice. By summer, when large wreaths of tasty red grapes dangled above the table, they sat and enjoyed their after-dinner espresso and the trials and tribulations of the day were discussed and then discarded.

My father was proud of his garden. Under his watchful eye, fig and nespoli fruit trees never failed to give birth to a sumptuous yield each summer. His burgeoning garden was a profusion of tomatoes, zucchinis of various varieties, beans, onions, mint, and rosemary. But it was the basil that made him proudest. Year after year the leaves grew to prizewinning proportions. The intoxicating aroma and delectable taste of this herb never failed to tempt the pickiest appetites. Since fresh basil was not available after summer, freshly chopped basil disappeared from our dinner table by September. Once the basil went to seed, the long seed stems were cut and hung upside down to dry in the basement and waited to be rejuvenated the following spring.

In preparation for the freeze of winter, after the harvest, he would wrap and bind the bare trunks and branches of his trees securely with old sheets. In appreciation for his due diligence, the trees would blossom again the following spring and bear delicious fruit to be enjoyed throughout the summer.

My father respected the earth and looked upon gardening as a labor of love, a devotion that deepened when they moved west to their new home in California. When I arrived, I was not surprised to find a profusion of basil with leaves as large as elephant ears in the back yard. Seedlings from his peach, fig and loquat trees had traveled with him as well, and were now thriving under the warm California sun and a generous growing season. Although the setting was different from our Brooklyn backyard, the ambiance remained my father's wonderful garden!

MOMMY

My mother was an original. I called her "Mommy" well into my teens! She was someone any child could comfortably attach a hook into if they could, an earth angel with an unwavering love for motherhood. My mother was blessed with a natural ability to nurture, a task she performed effortlessly. She was inexhaustible, and no demand was too great. Everyone who knew her would easily attest to her true essence and calling to motherhood.

She loved to cuddle with her children, sing old Sicilian lullabies, and share fairy tales from her childhood. When I became a mother, I sang the same sweet lullabies to my children. And when I heard my children singing the exact songs to my grandchildren, I marveled at the legend she'd left.

My mother was blessed with incredible good health and boundless energy. Although her days were busy, she never asked for help with chores, except to set the table for pranzo and wash dishes after dinner. When we left for school in the morning, she managed all the chores. Even after I began working, she continued the routine of making my bed and washing my clothes.

Mothering meant caring for her family, and she did it all with a smile on her face and a song on her lips. She shopped and cooked and ironed and mended and sewed and did it all as only a mother with boundless love in her heart for family can do!

My mother celebrated her role as a mother, a dynamic attribute that became unmistakably clear when one of us became ill and she became "Dr. Mommy." Her fervent devotion held no boundaries.

"You don't look too good," she'd say. "Come over here, whatza matter? Lemme see if you have a fever. Do you have a stomachache?"

Taking immediate action, she would press her cheek against ours and check our foreheads for unusual warmth. If she suspected we had a fever, she'd take our temperature—not orally since that option was not yet available. Half an aspirin followed by an alcohol rub was next in her line of defense. If there were no signs of a tummy ache, a cool enema was sure to bring down any fever! From sore throats to tummy aches, bay leaf tea and chicken soup were the meds of choice on her "get well" list. And when nighttime rolled around, she sat in a rocking chair by our beds until morning. Our comfort became her priority; no task was too demanding, no request was ever denied.

Before we drifted off to sleep at night, she'd kneel by our bed, and folding our hands into hers, she'd ask us to pray and ask Jesus to watch over our family. The prayers, those she'd once recited with her grandmother as a child, always began with "The Lord's Prayer" in Italian; *Padre nostro che sei nei cieli, sia santificato il tuo nom . . .*

My mother was hooked on Italian soap operas, and Italian radio stations broadcasted several soaps throughout the day. Once the bewitching hour rolled around, she'd wait for the bumper music to begin and settle into the comfort zone of the radio stories. While her babies slept and I was in school, she sewed and listened as the never-ending dramas unfolded. This was her "getaway" time of day; when the house was quiet and she could drift along with the tragic productions.

My siblings and I were not blessed with robust appetites, yet we loved most of what she prepared. Our favorites included, homemade pasta, chicken soup, breaded veal cutlets, and her famous lemon chicken. Not all meals met with our approval, especially a dinner of *fava* beans, *bacala* (cod fillets), *lenticchie* (lentils), or *babaluchi* (snails)—my father's favorite. And no amount of enticement could make me eat breaded calf's liver.

When you're raised in an ethnic environment, you are mostly familiar with the foods of that nation. In high school, I was introduced to the American foods served in our school cafeteria and was envious of those who feasted on what appeared to be a gastronomical banquet.

One day I caught a break and ate lunch in school. This was the day I was introduced to *mashed potatoes* and immediately fell in love with the creamy texture. We seldom enjoyed potatoes for dinner, and when we did, they were home fries. When I got home from school that day, my mother asked about lunch, and I shared what I'd eaten. I told her about the mouth-watering potatoes and gave her the simple recipe described by a friend. Seeing my excitement, she agreed to surprise me some night. One evening I was surprised. She told me she'd prepared mashed potatoes for dinner . . . Italian style, a dish that had some resemblance to the American fare but tasted nothing like the potatoes I'd eaten at school. I leaned that she'd boiled the potatoes with the skin on, smashed them, and added olive oil, garlic, salt, pepper and parmesan cheese.

"Mom, you're supposed to peel the potatoes before cooking. You're supposed to add butter and milk, not olive oil. Don't you remember what I told you? It's so easy, why didn't you follow the recipe?"

"No, no milk!" she responded. "Olive oil is better and the potato skin is good for you! Now stop complaining and eat!"

She may have been the first cook to serve *garlic smashed potatoes* long before it became a popular food. From time to time, she would make her "smashed" version—a touch of Italy in everything she prepared.

Having worked as a seamstress when she arrived in this country, she continued to work when I was little (when Auntie Anna was in the fold) but gave up her career after the feud with her aunt. After the birth of my brother Joe, an acquaintance introduced her to the owner of a dress factory close to our house. With his help, she purchased a professional sewing machine and set up a workplace at home. He delivered packages of cut fabric right to the front door and picked up the completed bundles based on a schedule. She loved contributing to the family income, and being able to do so from home made it worthwhile. She worked only while I was in school and while my younger siblings were asleep.

In the beginning of her "home" career, she set up shop in the enclosed porch (before it was renovated into a bedroom). Later, the basement became her workplace with only the Italian radio soaps to keep her company. With little time for cleaning, sewing dust and microscopic fabric cuttings from her work could be found nestled in every corner of every room in our house and remained there until she had time to clean up.

When her workday was complete, she'd go upstairs and listen for the clanking sound of the front gate announcing my arrival home from school. To welcome me home, a cold glass of milk and a generous portion of homemade Italian cookies on the kitchen table was a welcomed sight. This was the only time she served milk. By the time my siblings were old enough to attend school, we were introduced to Ding Dongs and other American cookies.

When I was old enough, my mother decided the time had arrived for me to understand the connection between work, money and a saving's account. She began by teaching me the dangers of her power sewing machine. When she was confident I would not sew my finger to the cloth, she taught me how to sew a straight line on old fabric pieces. Soon I was paid one cent for every collar or cuff with a straight row of stitches. After I'd earned my first dollar, she took me to the bank and opened an account, something I was proud of and continued to contribute to through high school.

When I was young, she sewed most of my clothes. I loved all the cute, little dresses with puffed sleeves, flared skirts, and stiff crinoline slips. As I got older, the clothes became mostly utilitarian. By the time I was in high school, I envied the trendy outfits my friends wore. I looked like an immigrant. My mother had no clue about American teen styles, but when she noticed what my friends wore and how cute they looked, she understood my frustration with her collection. It was during this time when our shopping excursions to Fulton Street began. She was generous, and my closet was always brimming with trendy new clothes.

These were among the happiest years of her life; years I remember with great fondness, love, and admiration for an amazing mother!

IF SHE WAS SITTIN', SHE WAS KNITTIN'

Hands down, homemaking was my mother's forte. Among her skills was a love for knitting. Her nimble fingers could transform a ball of yarn into a thing of beauty in record time; one day a ball of yarn, the next day a beautiful new sweater or a warm blanket to cuddle up with in the winter. It was one of the many crafts she learned from her grandmother.

Before I was born, she knitted a beautiful rose-colored angora coat with a matching brimmed hat. I wore the sweater until it no longer fit, and later it was passed down to my sister. Although my sister and I were too young to enjoy the beautiful rose-colored sweater as much as she did, I am grateful a picture of her lovely creation remains.

Modeling my mother's springtime collection in sweater wear

To keep us warm during the winter, she knitted vests that were worn under our clothes. I assumed everyone wore such a garment. When my friends noticed the vest, they viewed it as strange and not very pretty. I ran home from school in tears and refused to wear the vest. Although she worried I'd get frostbitten without her vest, she no longer insisted I wear it.

As the queen of thrift, nothing went to waste. When we outgrew an item she'd knitted, it was passed down to the youngest, or salvaged to live a new life in another knitted creation. It was not strange to come home from school and find her unraveling a sweater to be reincarnated soon into a new garment.

During my sophomore year she knitted a beautiful a white jacket. Weather permitting I wore it often. Everyone envied my jacket; even the guys offered compliments. Fond memories of that jacket often come to mind; how happy and pretty it always made me feel.

During the dark days after my father's death, to ease her loneliness, knitting became a welcomed distraction. Although she no longer knitted pretty sweaters, she spent countless hours weaving beautiful blankets. Even though she was much older, her fingers still had the dexterity of her youth.

One of her precious blankets remains with me to this day. Whenever life gets me down or I'm worried and upset, I reach for her blanket and wrap myself in the warmth of her precious creation. During these moments she returns to me, and I can feel her love comforting me until my world is again safe.

MOMMY'S HOMEMADE PASTA

My mother was an earthy cook. Most of the foods she prepared were healthy farm-type meals; not fancy, not sophisticated, just healthy. Many of her meals left a lasting memory.

Hands down, my siblings will agree the meal we enjoyed best was her homemade pasta. It was my mother's specialty, one that never failed to turn *pranzo* into a gourmet *festa*.

On the days she decided to make pasta, preparations began well in advance. It was a labor of love, an all day event. Somehow she always managed to complete the process before we came home from school. To be greeted by the yeasty aroma from long strands of pasta strung out to dry around the house was a delightful treat. Chocolate would not have been as enticing.

Barely five feet in stature, she stood tall in our tiny kitchen and always made the process look easy, a task of love that made her smile widely and made her family happy.

On her pasta-making days, the process began after she tucked her hair under a kerchief and wrapped her favorite apron around her waist. After gathering all the needed ingredients on the kitchen table, her hands would flutter over a floured board, mixing and stirring and kneading the doughy ingredients until it reached a perfect consistency. With her face dotted with flour, she'd shape small portions of dough into tiny balls, then work the balls onto long, thin reeds. Sliding the pasta off the reed was tricky, but she had this feat mastered. The pasta was then hung to dry on lines strewn throughout the house or on clean sheets on beds.

When we arrived home from school, the sight of pasta hanging everywhere aroused our appetites. Eating raw dough was also treat. If she caught us sneaking a strand, she would shout, "Stop it, don't eat raw pasta or you'll get a stomachache!" But that never stopped us.

Complaints to the chef on homemade pasta nights were non-existent, and her only reward was watching her family indulge until stuffed.

Making homemade pasta was a task I was never capable of mastering. My fingers lacked her gifted agility. My only indulgence in homemade pasta is derived via the memories she created—strands of pasta drying throughout the house—platters of tasty red pasta in the middle of our dining room table; a vivid memory of her love for family during those gloriously, happy times of my life at home in Brooklyn.

BON APPETIT

My parents were adamantly opposed to eating out. In their eyes restaurants were nothing more than havens of pestilence and disease-laden illnesses, as well as a waste of hard earned money.

"If you eat in restaurants you'll get sick, your hair will fall out and then you'll die!"

My friends would often comment on restaurants they'd gone to with their families. Having no idea what the eating out experience was all about, I felt left out of these worldly pleasures. Although I loved my mother's pizza—it was the best—I wondered about pizza by the slice at the local bakery!

The passing of time brought about inevitable changes including my mother's views on restaurants. During one of our Saturday shopping excursions, she told me we were going to eat lunch in a Chinese restaurant before going home. I wondered when she'd developed this sudden desire for Chinese food and why she was no longer preoccupied about eating in disease-infested restaurants. Although I was curious, I never questioned her decision.

She seemed to know the way, and after a short walk we entered a Chinese restaurant. Her familiarity with the restaurant's location was surprising. Once we were seated she wasted no time, and sounding quiet familiar with a particular dish, she promptly ordered chow mein. From that day forward eating chow mein became part of our shopping experience. I'm not sure what I loved best about our shopping days—the new clothes or the Chinese food. Probably both.

She also loved the tasty knishes served out of pushcarts on Fulton Street. We never went home without enjoying this tasty treat as well. It became a shopping day dessert.

Many years had gone by since I'd last heard my parents rant about the dangers of eating in restaurants. On their thirtieth wedding anniversary, my siblings and I decided to take them out for dinner and foolishly assumed they'd enjoy an adventure on their milestone day. We decided it was best to stick with Italian food, and a well-known restaurant in the area seemed to be the right choice. For those living in the area, a trip to Vince's Spaghetti House was a treat. Although the sauce was not on par with my mother's outrageously tasty pasta, it was flavorsome. For those who'd never tasted homemade sauce, it was judged as the best.

We told my mother of our plans. Although she didn't decline or make a fuss, she warned us my father would probably not enjoy eating out. Ignoring her comment, and trusting that once we were at the restaurant he would relax and enjoy the adventure, we went ahead with our plans and left it up to her to tell him what was in store for their anniversary.

When their special day arrived, we picked them up at home for the short drive to the restaurant. In the backseat of the car, my mother sounded happy, or so it seemed, yet my father was silent, never said a word and never shared his thoughts. Caught up in the excitement of the day, we ignored the impassive look on his face—a obvious signal he was not exactly thrilled about the adventure.

At the restaurant we were immediately seated at a large table. We began chatting and looking over the menu. My father's nervous demeanor was obvious to everyone, including the restaurant staff. When the waitress came to take our order, my father immediately made it known he was hungry and wanted to know when we were going to eat. When the server returned with our salads, he looked puzzled and began to mumble. In most European homes, salad is eaten after the main course. This was backwards. He grumbled about the bread, told us it wasn't crispy. But the worst occurred when the pasta came to the table.

"What is this stuff? This is not sauce and the pasta is overdone," he mumbled under his breath loud enough to be heard.

By this time, my mother wasn't any happier. She always sided with him, at least in his presence, and true to form she chimed in with her own displeasure. "This is such a waste of good money. And no leftovers—what a shame!"

Anniversaries are often personal, yet at times children do intervene. Our motive was to join them and celebrate with a special treat. However, this was their anniversary, and in retrospect, we should have honored their ways.

It has been said that in order to maintain good mental heath, you should make it a habit to learn one new thing each day. For my siblings and I, what we learned on that day is the following: You can take Sicilians out of Sicily, but you can't take Sicily out of Sicilians!

NEW UTRECHT HIGH

After graduation from elementary school, I quickly recognized my parents goals were far different than mine. There was nothing I desired more intensely than going to New Utrecht High, a co-ed school close to home, the school most of the neighborhood teenagers attended. They insisted I enroll in Bay Ridge High School, an all girls school miles from home. This decision had nothing to do with education and had all to do with my interaction with males.

I'd been dreaming about dressing in cool clothes, meeting up with friends—feeling normal—at least during the day. Located in the heart of what was known as "guido land," New Utrecht had the reputation of being the coolest school in Brooklyn. Armed with an unwavering resolve to keep me away from the male population, my father insisted I attend Bay Ridge High School. Making matters worse, attending Bay Ridge High entailed traveling each day on crowded buses.

But I was determined and I set my sights on accomplishing this goal. I began telling them Bay Ridge was swarming with a "girls gone wild" crowd. Yet my daily litany of complaints about this school didn't faze them in the least. They remained unconcerned, telling me not to worry, adding it was up to the teachers to take care of any problems.

I was persistent. When the first plan failed, I spent endless hours scheming various scenarios. While I pondered and planned, an event took place at school that paved the way towards achieving my goal. All I had to do was sit back and let the game play out. Unfortunately, the incident happened to my closest friends: MaryAnn, Edie, and Ann. Fortunately I was not involved.

Teen smoking was very popular back then and understandably frowned upon by parents and teachers, especially during school hours. MaryAnn, Edie, and Ann had taken up the habit; I had not. The fourth floor bathroom was *the* place where students met and smoked after lunch. Since the teacher's lounge was on the first floor, the fourth floor bathroom was seldom checked during school hours. I did not smoke, and never had any desire to venture into that smoky bathroom.

Our day began normally, by the bus stop on 75th Street. After arriving on campus we each went our separate ways. Shortly after lunch, the fire alarm sounded and students and faculty were evacuated. From across the street we watched large plumes of smoke billowing out of the fourth floor bathroom window and firemen aiming water hoses at the angry flames. A rumor soon began to circulate about three students who'd been taken off campus. But their identities were unknown.

When MaryAnn, Edie and Ann didn't show up at the bus stop for the ride home that afternoon, I was certain I knew the identity of the three students.

When I got home I immediately called each of them and was promptly told they could not come to the phone. The following morning I rushed to the bus stop hoping they were waiting for me. And they were—none-too-happy but willing to share the events of the previous day and one careless moment . . .

By the time MaryAnn, Edie, and Ann joined the smoking crowd in the fourth floor bathroom, the barely breathable air was thick with smoke. Most of the students were already preparing to leave. However, they'd arrived later than usual and lingered a while longer. A trail of smoke followed the students as they made their way down the hall directly into the path of an oncoming teacher.

"Fire, I smell fire!" screamed the teacher as she ran towards the firebox and pulled the alarm. Sensing the smoke was coming from the bathroom she threw open the door but didn't find the raging fire she suspected. She walked into a room reeking of smoke and three startled students standing by the sink holding lit cigarettes.

"Put out those cigarettes, get your things, and come with me!" she shouted.

In that terrifying moment of panic, they snuffed out their cigarettes and carelessly tossed the butts into the trash bin. One cigarette had not been completely extinguished. On the way to the principal's office, the butt burst into flames, and the trash bin erupted into an inferno. By the time the fire department arrived, the room was engulfed in flames, and the threat of fire reaching the lower levels attributed to the chaos that followed.

MaryAnn, Edie, and Ann paid a dear price, ended up with a four-year probation, and were placed on restriction at home as well.

As for me, the outcome was far different. After telling my parents what happened—carefully omitting the names of the culprits—I repeated my "I told you so" comment and ultimately got my wish. Two days later, I was transferred to New Utrecht, and the rest was history.

My first day of school at New Utrecht High marked the beginning of many happy days. It felt wonderful to be walking in sunshine, and not on a crowed bus, in step with a caravan of neighborhood friends and students going my way.

New Utrecht was an institution-type structure consisting of five levels and a basement where the lockers were located as well as an Olympic-sized pool. I fell in love with this large, red building the moment I entered its massive domain. There were no elevators, and searching for classrooms, bathrooms, the lunchroom, and the gymnasium entailed running up and down long flights of stairs, and running blindly from point-to-point. Yet I loved every inch of the building and looked upon the mass pandemonium that took place between classes as exhilarating.

New Utrecht High School

Although confusing in comparison to the simplistic orderliness in elementary school and Bay Ridge High, my first day at New Utrecht was wildly entertaining. The school was all I'd imagined it would be, and my four years at New Utrecht, minus the first few weeks at Bay Ridge High, were among the happiest years of my life.

In my wonderful new world, bright with promise, were many new faces and many new discoveries to unearth. It was inevitable that one person would stand out. Her name was Michaela. She was Sicilian, no surprise; most students were Italian, many were of the Jewish faith. Michaela and I had much in common and we'd been assigned to many of the same classes. We immediately became close friends—two peas in a pod.

As the routine of high school settled in, Michaela and I noticed that students often ditched school and bragged about how incredibly easy it was to get away with it. Since most homes did not have telephones, truancies were reported by mail. We quickly learned the schools had only one tracking mechanism—truant officers. Although their dark suits made them easy to spot, those who braved the streets during school hours feared them.

Giving no thought to consequences, we decided that ditching might be fun. The idea promoted an all-consuming fascination—for one day. We decided to chance it on a Friday when teachers were busy with their end-of-week curriculum. After registering in homeroom, we walked past the auditorium towards the unlocked exit doors where students and teachers came and went at odd times. Leaving the school grounds could not have been any easier. After opening the massive front doors, we bolted down the long flight of stairs to the soda shop across the street (the soda shop seen on the "*Welcome Back Kotter*" television show). Our goal was to get to the train station one block away. We were cautious, tried not to call attention to ourselves, and we began to walk slowly, pacing ourselves carefully.

We rode the trains knowing full well truant officers were mostly posted on transit systems. After a few suspicious sightings and a quick lesson in the art of dodging, we found ourselves in Times Square. With little spending money, after a few hours of aimless walking we decided to go home, to Michaela's home above the bakery shop her parents owned, where food was plentiful.

Since things had gone so well on Friday, we decided to ditch again the following Monday morning. This time we ended up in Coney Island and continued to scrutinize every man that crossed our paths as a potential truant officer. After a few could-be sightings, we headed back to Michaela's apartment.

Feeling confident, on the following week, we no longer signed into homeroom. We met by the train station each morning to decide on the day's agenda. There were places we could easily walk to and not be seen. Dyker Park on 86th Street was one such area, a short jaunt from school and void of people during weekdays.

Soon we began to wonder how our parents would react if they found out what we'd been up to. My father would have chained me to my bed forever. In retrospect, considering how I'd schemed and clamored and connived my way into New Utrecht High, I am not sure why I thought ditching would be fun.

On the third week of our school-day vacation, we decided to stay in Michaela's apartment. Not only was it safer, we could listen to music and eat to our heart's content. Her refrigerator was always packed with leftovers and delectable pastries from their bakery.

By this time, we were aware that our absences had probably been duly noted, and absentee letters was surely on their way. We began planning a way to get back in school. All we needed was a written excuse. For me, this would be a cakewalk. In the past, whenever I was absent from school, with my mother's permission, I wrote the excuse notes and signed her name. Michaela's situation was considerably different. Her parents spoke English fluently and were not easily manipulated.

On the day the truancy letter arrived at my house, I was quick to snatch it out of the mail slot, write an excuse on the back of the letter stating my absence was due to an illness, and carefully forging my mother's name on the note. The excuse was not questioned and no issue was made of my absence. However, having missed so much schoolwork, I failed that semester.

Michaela got lucky as well. After retrieving the truancy letter from her mailbox, she returned to school the next day sans a written excuse. She was prepared for the consequences and promised not to implicate me. When they questioned her, she told them she'd been ill but did not want to worry her parents as they had a family business to operate. For reasons unknown, they accepted her flimsy excuse, and her parents never found out. Michaela failed the semester as well.

Oddly enough, the school officials, including the homeroom teacher, never made a connection between the two of us.

To make up for lost credits, Michaela and I attended summer school. My parents were never aware that summer school was only three hours a day for six weeks, and by noon we were headed to Coney Island to meet friends and enjoy hours in the warm summer sunshine.

In the fall I entered tenth grade with an entirely different outlook on school. I buckled down and studied. The notion of "ditching" made me cringe. I dug into my schoolwork and kept busy with the new curriculum.

As time moved forward, I began noticing things other students enjoyed. Conversations were always about weekend dances, Friday night basketball games, ice-skating in Rockefeller Center or seeing the latest movies—things forbidden by my father. All my friends were dating. Needless to say, dating was out of the question; any mention of this subject always made him angry.

Everyone was having fun. Everyone also felt sorry for me. I felt left out of the world students lived in. As my envy for their lives mounted, resentment towards my father began building, rapidly, with each passing day.

When excitement at school for an upcoming event reached fever pitch, I'd get caught up in their enthusiasm, especially when Friday night games were scheduled against a rival school. All my friends were making plans to attend, and I was envious. Time and time again, my father refused to let me go, and I was embarrassed to tell those who asked that I was "not allowed to go out."

On one particular night, I was determined to get my way. But the more I begged, the angrier he became. When I realized I was not going to win, I accused him of being unfair and heartless. I told him he didn't love me. My scolding angered him further, and he stood up and shouted; "Look at me, you are not going out at night, not tonight, not any night. Do you understand? Don't ask again." Turning to my mother he continued, "This is all because of that school. If she doesn't stop asking, I'm gonna pull her out of school, and she can stay home with you."

Normally he'd just say no, glare at me and mumble about young people in America. Not that night. I'd pushed him to the edge.

After the dishes were done and the kitchen was tidied up, I ran to my room, fell across my bed and cried. My mother tried consoling me, but when I told her how much I hated him, she shook her head, and walked out of the room.

I learned early on that Italian wives never challenged their husbands in matters of discipline. It was tradition. During these confrontations my mother always rallied on his side. But when we were alone, she'd admit he was too strict and would offer to talk to him. If she did, it never helped. That night marked the beginning of a deep-seated resentment towards him, one that lasted until the day he walked me down the aisle.

During those early teen years, I felt as though there were two worlds: my life at home with a domineering and overly protective father, and the rest of the world where my friends resided—a world I was not a part of.

THAT'S AMORE

All my friends were in love. MaryAnn, Edie, and Ann had boyfriends and were going steady. Although I was on a short leash, inevitably someone caught my eye. It happened in 11ᵗʰ grade when I met Eddie. He was in my homeroom, and whenever I looked his way I'd catch him staring at me. In time we began chatting. I'd find him waiting for me before my next class, and he met me during lunch hour.

One day Eddie opened his wallet and pulled out a picture of me standing by the soda shop across from school. On the picture were tiny cut-out words from a newspaper that read: POST NO BILLS. When I asked him how he got my picture, he told me one of my friends had taken the picture and had given it to him. From then on Eddie was constantly on my mind. I'd go to bed thinking of him, and the moment I awakened he was there waiting for me. I'd race around all morning and practically run all the way to school.

When Eddie asked me out on a movie date, telling him I was not allowed to date made me feel like a child. I knew he was disappointed. I certainly was. He said he understood, and our relationship remained a school-day romance.

Soon after I met Eddie, talk around school began circulating about a Friday night party close to home. Everyone was invited, including Eddie. I brooded for days knowing my father would never give me permission to go. Going with Eddie to this party meant the world to me, and I would have sold my soul to be able to go.

Mindful of my father's feelings, on the night of the party I decided to ask him for permission. I carefully planned my approach and also promised myself not to raise my voice. Once things settled down at the dinner table, geared for battle, I pleaded my case.

"Daddy there's a party just down the street. It's really close by, on 70ᵗʰ Street. Can I please go?"

"*Ancora* . . . again? I said NO. You're unbelievable! It's the same old story. What's the matter with you? How many times have I told you not to ask if you can go out at night?" he shouted angrily. "How many?"

"A lotta times, Daddy. But you never explain why I can't go out. Everyone feels sorry for me. Just tell me *why* I can't go to this party."

"Because it's dangerous!"

"What's dangerous?"

"Boys are dangerous!"

"Boys? Boys are dangerous? Well maybe in Sicily they are. Maybe *you* were dangerous when *you* were young. This is America and boys are not that way! You're wrong—you just don't love me. You say you do, but you don't!"

No one spoke—stunned at what I'd just accused him of—waiting for the backlash—wondering what was about to happen. Normally he would have raged for a while, and then left the table to tend to his chores. That night was different. From the look in his eyes, I knew I'd better back off and not say another word. For a few moments, he just sat and glared at me, but then he pushed himself away from the table, stood up, and walked toward the kitchen. Suddenly, he stopped, turned around, and said, "You better be home by ten!"

I'm not sure what angel was standing by me that night, but I didn't care; I had permission to go to the party, and that's all that mattered. Of course he didn't know about Eddie, but my mother did.

I had a wonderful time that night. Eddie and I danced every dance. During one of the slow dances, he slipped a friendship ring on my finger, and my heart began to swell. On that night, I could not have been any happier.

I continued to see Eddie at school, but I hardly saw him during the summer. In the fall we were no longer in the same homeroom. My first romance had fizzled, yet I was not disappointed; it had run its course. Not being able to pick me up to go a movie or a school function like other couples had doused the flame for both of us.

GREGORY THE CHICKEN

Long before Eddie and I stopped seeing one another, he told me about his pet—a lame and lonely chicken named Gregory. With no other chickens for companionship, the chicken spent her days wobbling around in his backyard. Why the chicken was given a male name was never clear, neither was the reason she was lame.

In time Eddie and his brothers had grown tired of their pet and were told to find her another home. After hearing about the chicken, I shared this sad predicament with my mother.

"*Portarla ca* . . . bring it here!" she said. "I'll take care of the chicken!"

I could hardly wait to tell Eddie the good news, and he wasted no time arranging a personal delivery. My mother was excited and immediately made plans to welcome Gregory. After the preparations were in place, Eddie made a personal delivery, and Gregory had no problem adjusting to her new home. Soon she was wobbling and pecking around our backyard as though it was her birthright.

My mother had grown up on a farm and had been around farm animals. She had a plan—a goal—and went to work to fatten up Gregory's puny bones. Under my mother's loving care, it didn't take long for the bird to gain weight. Gregory quickly became our pet, imbedded in the family, well-fed and living life in a loving atmosphere.

From across the seas and coast to coast, Italian homes on Sunday were always busy with food preparations. Some mothers went to church—mine did not. For my mother, Sunday church services were held in her kitchen preparing dinner for her family.

When I arrived home from church on this particular Sunday, I went outside to check on Gregory, but she was nowhere to be found.

"Mom, have you seen Gregory? I can't find her!" I stammered.

My mother shined on Sundays. Noontime dinners meant getting an early start on preparations. Unless she had a headache or someone died, she was always upbeat and chatty. Yet, on that Sunday, she seemed pensive. I kissed her and asked her again about the chicken. But she continued to cook and did not respond.

"Here, taste this," she insisted and handed me the piece of bread she'd dunked into the sauce.

"You okay?" I asked again. She said she was fine and continued to cook. But suddenly she turned towards me and said, "I have to tell you something. The chicken died during the night. I dunno what happened. Maybe she was sick."

I felt as though there was more to the story; something didn't feel right. I ran to my room and sat on my bed to sort things out more clearly. Although I was heartbroken about Gregory, my mother's unusual demeanor puzzled me.

From time to time there had been pets in our household. My mother loved cats, and they were very much a part of our family—even Queenie, the little mixed breed dog, was lovingly cared for. When our animals ran away or died, not having our furry friends scrambling around the house was always sad. Yet I'd never felt as bad about our cats, or for Queenie, as I did that day for that lame little chicken.

The mood around our Sunday dinner table was subdued that day. Once we were all seated around the table, she entered the dining room with the first course, a Sunday standard, a huge platter of pasta. When we were done, she returned with the second course, her delicious lemon and garlic roasted chicken. In light of Gregory's passing, I could hardly believe she'd prepared chicken. Seeing chicken parts on a platter was upsetting.

It didn't take long to make the connection. Pointing to the platter of chicken in the center of the table, I stood up and asked, "By any chance, is this Gregory?" Neither my father nor my mother responded. I wasn't sure if my siblings caught on—they were younger—but I knew what had happened.

Later, while tidying up in the kitchen, I could no longer hold back my feelings. "Why did you let Daddy kill the chicken? Why? And how could you cook it?" I questioned. "And how could you both sit there and eat that bird, our pet? I can't believe it!"

"Because chickens are meant to lay eggs or be eaten, that's why!" she shouted back.

"That's so mean. Gregory was crippled. She was a pet and you cooked our pet!"

"No—chickens are not pets! Dogs and cats and birds are pets, chickens we eat!"

For the longest time, whenever my mother served chicken, I thought about poor Gregory. It took forever to come to terms with what they'd done. That Sunday was living proof they were still living in Sicily and nothing could alter their principles and values.

SO MANY RELATIVES . . .
SO LITTLE TIME

There are many surprises that cross our paths on our journey through life, and it's fair to say some surpass others! One such surprise occurred to me after I arrived home from school one day. After opening the front gate, I heard a jumble of cheery voices echoing from inside my house. I rushed up the back stairs, opened the door, and I was immediately greeted by what appeared to be an army of strange and unfamiliar faces.

A petite and pretty woman greeted me by the door, introduced herself as Zia Barbarina (Aunt Barbara) and began smothering my face with noisy kisses. Smiling from ear to ear, my mother explained that Barbarina was her sister from Sicily. She'd arrived earlier that day with her family: Lorenzo, her husband, and five young children: Tony, Nino, Rosalie, Sadie, and Maria.

Until that moment their names had only been words I'd heard in conversations. I'm not sure if their visit was a surprise for my mother, but it was for me. My mother and her sister had not seen each other in many years, not since my parents had returned to Sicily for their belated honeymoon.

Front: Maria and Uncle Lorenzo (Lawrence)
Back: Nino, Aunt Barbara, Tony, Rosalie and Sadie

My mother was thrilled. It was as though she'd won the lottery. For many days and into the following week, laughter filled the air and our home seemed smaller, cozier, and sweeter!

It was a wonderful reunion. The sound of children speaking a foreign language held a special fascination. For Italians, first cousins are more like sisters and brothers. And when my mother's sister Nina arrived from Detroit, she ignited further excitement. The three sisters were inseparable, and for two weeks people visited our home every day. Swallowed up in a flood of new family energy, our home was a perpetual whirlwind of fun, food, and festivities.

But two weeks flew by quickly. Once Zia Nina went home, things began to settle down. My mother had hoped her sister Barbara would remain in New York. My father was positive he could find Zio Lorenzo work on the docks, but they had other plans. Per immigration laws, Zio Lorenzo's sister has secured a job for him in California. Having just rekindled their relationship, the news shattered the happy ambiance in our home. And when the time came for Aunt Barbara and her family to leave Brooklyn, my mother was devastated. Three thousand miles was a world away from Brooklyn, and their departure left a deep emptiness in my mother's heart.

After my aunt settled in California, she began calling and writing and sowing a "move to California" seed in my mother's mind. Flowery letters described California as beautiful, similar to Sicily. She spoke of the mountains, the trees, the flowers, and the wild vegetables growing on hillsides.

"*E como la sicilia*—just like Sicily," she'd share. Aunt Barbara told my mother California was where she should be as well.

In the beginning, moving to California seemed impractical, a day dream with little chance of happening. With little education and less than adequate English language skills, life outside Brooklyn would be difficult for my parents. However, my aunt was persistent and her metaphorical descriptions of California were explosive. She wrote about the Italians already settled in the area, as well as the Italian mayor who'd been a tremendous help to them—someone willing to find work for my father as well. With the possibility of a job, my aunt convinced my parents to consider moving.

The following winter, my father came down with a cold that developed into pneumonia, and he was unable to work for many weeks. The illness took a debilitating blow on my father's strapping good health. He was painfully aware it was only a matter of time before he would no longer be able to work on the docks. And the accident that occurred aboard ship when he was younger could easily happen again, only now he was older and not nearly as agile.

After my father recovered from pneumonia, the idea of moving to California took on a life of its own. It was no longer a pipe dream or a far-fetched idea. As I listened to their discussions, including the problems and challenges they might encounter along the way, the reality of this move sounded like a frightening nightmare. As for me, the thought of leaving Brooklyn, my friends, and school seemed unfathomable. The idea of never again seeing the friends I'd known most of my life began to weigh heavily on my mind. Whenever California was discussed, my apprehension intensified.

There were other daunting pieces to the life-in-California puzzle. For my parents, work was of utmost importance, as was transportation, now available on every corner in Brooklyn and non-existing in California, not at the level we were accustomed to. After hearing a discussion about purchasing a car, I shuddered. I could not fathom my father learning to drive. How would he be able to pass a driver's test? I was certain the task of driving would fall on me. The only knowledge I had about a car was the useless and mundane information regarding engines and spark plugs I'd learned in Driver's Ed class.

Aunt Barbara's mesmerizing descriptions of California had cast a spell on my parents. I wondered if they had given any serious thought to what they were about to surrender. My mother loved the city, the trains, buses, trolleys, the neighborhood and our neighbors, her beloved house. And my father had a job he could rely on, although it was taking a heavy toll on his health.

Actually, I didn't care if they moved; I wanted to stay in Brooklyn. One afternoon, after mustering up what my father described as absurd bravado, I asked if I could stay in Brooklyn and live with a relative or—God forbid—a friend. My father thought my question was a joke. In the fifties, a young woman living on her own, even with relatives, was unacceptable, unrealistic, I knew I was trapped in their goal to move to California.

"Ma tu sei pazza? No, mai, . . . are you crazy? never. You're moving with us!"

THE TASSEL'S WORTH THE HASSLE

Although I was aware the move would not happen quickly, the thought alone cast a shadow on my future. As plans began to firm up, thoughts about living in California became a distractive force. I began to fret about my future and I thought about it every waking moment of every day.

In the fall I returned to school as a senior. Setting aside my anxieties, I joined the Madrigal Society. Singing always brightened my days, and the high school choral was an excellent venue to stretch my vocals.

Since I had not made known any desire to study nursing or to become a doctor, attending college was not in my future. However, a program offered to seniors caught my attention: an internship with a major organization, one that entailed alternating work and school weeks. Applicants were tested scholastically and placed with major corporations. Students were coached on how to dress and behave, and were instructed about safety while traveling via the subway.

When I was accepted and assigned to work in a large legal firm to be trained as a paralegal, I was thrilled and could not wait to tell my parents. On the day I received my assignment, I rushed home as though I'd spouted wings, completely unprepared for my father's reaction.

It was Friday afternoon and I knew my father was already home from work. I ran as fast as I could, flung open the front gate, ran up the stairs and opened the back door. Both my parents were at the kitchen table enjoying their afternoon espresso. My heart was racing wilding. I was excited to share the news about my very first job and yet, I had barely uttered my last word when my father's reaction fractured all traces of excitement.

"No, oh no, you're not working for a lawyer. NO, you can stay home and help your mother!" he shouted.

I was stunned. I ran to my room and tossed myself across the bed. Closing my eyes, I wondered about my life. He'd already forbidden me from taking part in many high school and teenage experiences, and now he was about to deny my rite of passage from high school into the work force, the world of an American adult.

After checking into homeroom the following Monday, I asked for a pass to see my counselor, and after listening to the details of my father's reaction, the counselor labeled him closed-minded.

"This is absurd. I've never had anyone react this way. I'll speak to him. This is a great opportunity for your future, and you're perfectly suited to work in this firm!"

I explained how difficult it would be to reason with him. After learning he spoke little English, she decided not to go to battle. She changed my assignment and scheduled an interview with Goodbody & Company, a large brokerage firm on Wall Street.

Based on his first reaction, I wasn't sure how he'd react to my new assignment. Working on Wall Street might set up another red flag. However, the counselor reassured me she'd speak to him if he objected the second time. Fortunately, when I described where I'd be working, he made no further comments. Yet the missed opportunity to work and train in the legal field fed my resentment towards my father.

Training for work was fun, as was shopping for clothes with my mother. I could barely contain my excitement and imagined the wondrous world I was about to enter. Mingling with classy professionals on Wall Street seemed exciting and mitigated the disappointment over the lost opportunity to train as a paralegal.

On the first workday I raced through my morning routine. My first day's outfit had been decided the night before: a black velvet jumper over a red sweater. I stepped into a pair of black pumps, reached for my purse, and made my way into the kitchen for breakfast. When I was done, I kissed my mother goodbye, tucked her smile in my heart and raced out the door.

I'd often ridden on the trains but never during the early morning rush hour. It would be the first of many new adventures. The train platform at 72nd Street Station was crammed with early morning travelers. Several trains came and went until the one headed downtown pulled up to the platform. There were many people in front of me. Most were taller and more experienced travelers. When the train pulled to a stop, the door opened and I was pushed forward into the train by the mob of anxious people behind me. There were no seats, and I stood all the way, holding onto the center pole, clinging tightly to my purse with the other hand as suggested in the training program at school.

The offices of Goodbody & Company were located on the third floor of an older, historic looking building. The elevator was a model from the past with pulleys and cables and iron bars. It looked like a cage. I was certain I'd seen the same type in old, spooky movies and hesitated before stepping into its strangeness. I hesitantly pushed the third floor button and rode to my destination. Once it stopped I scrambled out and decided to take the stairs from then on.

A few steps from the elevator were the offices of Goodbody & Company. Although I'd been trained for this moment and knew what to expect, I was nervous. I opened the door and entered a large, well-lit room with many windows and many people busy at their desks. I'd never been in a business office environment with various conglomerations of office paraphernalia on desktops and along the walls. The sound of clicking typewriter keys and ringing telephones, though noisy, was exciting.

Towards the back of the large room was a glass door with the name Mike Murray imprinted on the window. I knocked, and a male voice asked me to enter. A young man stood up and offered to shake my hand, a gesture I was unaccustomed to, especially from a man. Shaking his hand felt odd; kissing was the only familiar greeting in my world. He introduced himself as the manager, and from his name and red hair I knew he was Irish; the first non-Italian man in my life. Unlike the Italian men in my world, Mike was soft-spoken and quickly put me at ease. After a quick overview of my tasks, I was assigned a desk with a telephone and an electric typewriter. Mike introduced me to other employees and proceeded to describe my duties: answer and field calls, type customer statistics and changes on small information cards, and file the cards in a metal cabinet framing the entire back wall.

Other seniors from various high schools were also working in that office. All were friendly; all made me feel at home. During that first week, we went to lunch and took our breaks together. When work was slow, we chatted and shared stories about school and friends and neighborhoods. The wheels were in motion for life after graduation and it felt wonderful.

By the end of my first week, I'd adjusted to the ride to and from work, my manager, my peers, my job, and I actually hated going back to school.

When I returned to school the following week, someone with an adorable nickname captured my attention. We met in our home economics class and her name was *Cookie*. Since we were wearing the same hairstyle, everyone thought we were sisters—blond and brunette sisters. Cookie and I immediately bonded.

I learned she was turning seventeen, her mother was planning a birthday party, and I was invited. Unlike my sixteenth birthday party, Cookie's party was geared towards our age group, and I was looking forward to her celebration almost as much as she was.

On the night of the party, I rushed to get dressed, then walked a few short blocks to her house. During the evening, I noticed a guy standing in a corner. He was tall, really good looking, and he definitely had my attention. Cookie told me his name was Nick. Although he kept looking my way, he never smiled and made no attempt to speak to me. I didn't think he was interested in meeting me until the following day, after Cookie told me he'd asked for my number. The news sent me into orbit!

Nick was an Italian, a senior at another high school, and worked in the family butcher business. I was sure—I was positive my father would approve of him. And when he refused to meet Nick, I was reminded of the myopic world of (most) Sicilian fathers of that era who honestly believed the man whose seed would bring forth grandchildren would be the father's choice, not the daughter's, and certainly not that of a pursuing young male on the prowl.

When Nick called and asked if I'd like to go to the movies, I was thrilled. When I asked him to meet me at the local movie theatre and not at home, I was embarrassed. Yet I rose above the awkwardness, and we met and dated for a while. After a few months of sneaking around, I no longer accepted his calls and blamed it on my father. I was seventeen, Nick was eighteen, and my father's rules had had a negative effect on our young relationship. Although he continued to call, I never saw him again.

Back in school, "senioritis" was rampant. Plans for prom and graduation were moving ahead, and the air was a frenzy of excited energy. Due to my work schedule, I felt somewhat detached from most activities. Although school and work were going well, the uncertainties of life beyond graduation distanced me from the happiness my peers were enjoying. I would miss the familiarity of old red building and my friends, especially the Madrigal Society.

Making matters worse, my friends were moving forward in various directions, embarking on new and exciting lives. And when my school counselor told me Goodbody and Company offered me a job with a pay raise (from $1.20 an hour to $1.35), I had mixed emotions. The job would be short term, the trip to California was moving forward, and I could not help but wonder what my future life would be like.

At times I felt as though the world was spinning. I was on board—yet I had no ticket to ride.

TODAY I MET THE MAN
I'M GONNA MARRY

MaryAnn and I had been close friends since second grade. Although we attended different schools, our friendship remained solid. She was going steady with Joe, a senior at the New York School of Printing. Joe had plans to join the Army soon after graduation. Both MaryAnn and Joe kept hoping I'd meet someone special before Joe left for the Army.

One morning MaryAnn called and asked me to meet her and Joe at the Milk Bar. She told me Joe wanted to talk to me about a guy, someone in his graduating class, someone he was anxious for me to meet.

"Joe thinks he's great, real cute. He lives in the Bronx!" MaryAnn shared excitedly.

"The Bronx? Are you kidding? Forget about it. It's too far."

"Too far? I don't think so. Besides, he'd be the one traveling. Not you! Joe said he's gonna join the Marines after graduation, so it really doesn't matter where he lives. Trust me, Joe thinks you guys would make a good match!"

"Really? What's his name?" I asked.

"Frankie. He's Italian, Sicilian actually. That'll make your father happy!"

"Are you freaking kidding? There isn't a guy on earth that would make my father happy, unless *he* picks one!"

Although I had major reservations about meeting someone outside of our neighborhood, MaryAnn's excitement was contagious, and I agreed to meet her and Joe at the Milk Bar.

Once I arrived at the Milk Bar, Joe began bombarding me with accolades about this great guy, insisting that I meet him.

"Trust me, you'll like him. I'm positive you will. Even your pain-in-the-ass father would like him. He's clean cut, clever, has a great sense of humor. And . . . ba da bing, he's Italian!"

When he was done, Joe opened his wallet and pulled out a picture. He held it at arms length, just close enough for me to catch a quick glimpse of a male face. When I reached out to snag the picture, Joe extended his arm upwards, out of my reach.

"Oh no, no picture unless you say you'll meet him."

"Gimme the picture. I can't say yes unless I see his face."

Joe continued to tease until I was able to snag the picture from his grip.

"Okay, is this a joke?" I asked. "He looks like a movie star! Who is this guy?"

"Who is he? I just told you. His name is Frankie. No joke. He's in my class, and I've known him a long time."

"Really? Well, how come you never mentioned him before? Did you tell him about me?"

"Of course I told him about you, and of course he wants to meet you. Say yes and I'll set it up for next weekend—the four of us. I'll even warn him about your dad. On second thought, maybe not—don't wanna scare him away!"

I agreed to meet him the following weekend, and after parting ways, I put the picture in my wallet. On the way home I stopped several times to sneak a quick peek at the face on the picture. There was no denying; he was cute. I could hardly believe he wanted to meet me. When I got home, I was excited to show my mother his picture. She looked at the picture, smiled and asked, "Is he Italian?"

Joe made arrangements to meet him in Coney Island the following Saturday night. Meeting him quickly became an all-consuming fascination, and waiting for the weekend felt like an eternity. On Saturday I spent the entire afternoon poking around my closet for the perfect outfit. The plan was to meet Frankie at 6 o'clock by the roller coaster. At 5:30, Joe and MaryAnn stopped by to pick me up for the short train ride to Coney Island. After what seemed like the longest ride ever, the train pulled up to our stop, and my heart began to pound.

It was a short walk from the train station to the roller coaster. As we got closer I spotted a guy standing by the corner and I knew it had to be him. Joe waved, the guy waved back, and I immediately recognized the smile . . . the same smile I'd been staring at all week!

While Joe nervously made the introductions, I could hardly draw my eyes away from his sunbright smile, his eyes, big and blue as a summer sky, and thick raven black, clean and shiny and smartly styled. He seemed shy, very shy—somewhat uncomfortable at first. He hardly looked my way unless I was speaking to him.

Joe kept the conversation going and talked about school, graduation, and his plans to join the Army. Frankie relaxed and shared his plans to join the Marines right after graduation as well.

By the time we stopped for a soda, Frankie had warmed up and we were all chatting. Joe asked him about his family, and he told us he had five brothers and a sister, describing most of them as pranksters. He shared stories about his life in the Bronx, and when he was done, he asked about my family, if I had any brothers and sisters.

Coney Island in the summertime always had an air of whimsical madness, and the trip was never complete without indulging in a tasty Nathan's hot dog, a ride on the heart-stopping Cyclone, or taking a spin on the merry-go-round. In spite of the usual rowdy ambiance of bright lights and people running amok, I had my own private attraction, and he was already filling the void in my heart.

By the end of the evening, I could tell Frankie had enjoyed the evening as much as I had. Three hours later, while walking towards the train station for the trip home, he reached for my hand and squeezed it tightly. It felt warm, and wonderful, and I knew he wasn't disappointed.

Frankie began calling regularly, and we met every Saturday night. It didn't take long for Sunday afternoons to become part of our agenda as well. We'd meet in Times Square or at the local movie theatre. Other times we'd just walk for hours, talking and laughing and bonding. It became obvious we had much in common, except for our goals. Frankie was set on joining the Marines, and more than likely I was headed for California.

It felt as though I was gliding along on a beautiful rainbow. MaryAnn and Joe were thrilled the setup had worked. My mother kept asking about him, and from the tone of my voice she knew it was time to tell my father. A few days later, a shockwave fell over me when she told me my father wanted to meet Frankie. It was hard to fathom the reason behind this sudden change of heart until I realized it had to do with the Marines.

My father had thought it out carefully: we'd be in California, Frankie would be serving his country, the relationship would come to a grinding halt, and for now, I'd be happy.

The more I saw Frankie, the more I liked him. I'd tucked him deep in my heart and secretly hoped he'd change his mind about the Marines. During one of our dates, I told him about California. Frankie was surprised. In those days, families hardly ever moved.

"You're kidding! Moving across the country—why?"

"A few reasons—mainly because of my father's health." I told Frankie about my aunt, her move to California, and how she'd been busy filling my mother's head with magical, almost fairytale stories about life in the wild, wild west—a utopian desert. I don't want to move. We've been arguing about it, but I don't have a vote in this decision. Looks like I'm going."

We began sharing information about our parents and siblings. It was clear we'd shared few commonalities. Frankie told me his family lived in a small apartment in the Bronx and they struggled financially, especially after his father contracted tuberculosis and lost one lung. My parents were not rich—not by any means—but we lived in a large, beautiful home in one of Brooklyn's most desirable neighborhoods, and every necessity and comfort was lovingly provided.

I decided to ask Frankie to take me to my prom, hoping he would not turn me down. When he said yes, my heart exploded. It was my first formal event other than being a bridesmaid four times. For the first time in the four years of high school, I felt normal, like everyone else. I was seeing someone steady and I was going to the prom. Life could not get any better. He was all I thought about, like a melody that wraps around your mind and replays again and again.

Going to prom was exciting, and I knew what I'd wear: the blue lace strapless dress with matching shoes and purse, the ensemble I'd worn as a bridesmaid.

On prom night, Frankie arrived with a corsage. When he smiled I felt his eyes bore deeply into mine. My insides began to flutter wildly; I was deliriously happy, flying high above the clouds. Surprisingly, my father did not ruin the night by posting a 10 p.m. curfew.

Prom was held at the Waldorf Astoria. It was a mystical evening; I felt like a princess with her blue-eyed prince at her side. Through the years that night has remained in my heart—an endearing reflection of a thrilling evening.

Frankie and me at prom

New York School of Printing graduation day:
Frankie, me, MaryAnn and Joe

Once prom was tucked away to memory, graduation was straight ahead, then boot camp. We spoke on the phone every day, and continued to see each other on weekends. It didn't take long for Frankie and I to become close. I missed him when we weren't together, and he told me he felt the same about me.

I learned that joining the Marines was something he had dreamt about for many years, a desire that reflected warmly in his eyes. He told me he'd miss me—asked if I'd wait for him. Just as he'd planned, the day after graduation, Frankie joined the Marines and was scheduled to leave for Parris Island, South Carolina on August 9th.

Frankie's military physical had been scheduled for earlier that same day. On that day he would share something that in time would return to haunt us. He told me about a small lump, about the size of a tiny pea, on his shoulder blade. The lump had been there for years and had been checked by other doctors in the past. During his enlistment physical, the military doctor joined the ranks of previous doctors he'd seen, and Frankie was again assured the tiny lump was nothing to be concerned about. He passed the physical, was accepted into the Marine Corps, and all thoughts about the tiny lump were set aside and would be dealt with at another time.

The morning of the 9th, fighting back tears was a challenge. I'd taken the day off from work and rushed to make my way to the depot early, before he took his pledge and boarded the train for the ride south. We met, but our time was brief. We shared our feelings, and I promised to write every day. Frankie kept telling me how much he loved me and how much he would miss me. After a quick embrace, Frankie broke away. I watched as the men took their pledge, and I joined the other teary-eyed women waving to their men as they boarded the train. Soon Frankie's face disappeared in the flood of men and metal.

Ninety days seemed like an eternity. In the beginning the days were long and very lonely. Although I'd never met our mailman, I found myself thinking about him every day, hoping he'd delivered a letter from Frankie. He'd warned that writing might be difficult at first. When the first two weeks passed by with no mail, I wondered if I'd hear from him again. But then one night, after I arrived home from work, my mother told me there was a surprise in my room.

My heart exploded when I read the name Frank Attardo on the top left corner of two envelopes. After locking his handwriting into memory,

I tore open the first letter, then the second. The letters were long, and I read them over and over, focusing on special words that spoke of love, of missing me, and how he could not wait to see me again. I missed him so much, and his letters now meant the world to me. Soon he was writing regularly, sometimes twice a day. I wrote every day, sometimes during lunch hour. His letters were poetic, fueling my feelings for him. Whether I was writing or reading his letters, each word made me feel close to him, very close.

I wondered about our future, if I'd ever see him once we moved to California, and shared these haunting doubts in my letters. He would always reassure me that nothing was going to keep us apart, and how we'd find a way to be together. Although his letters included a smattering of information about boot camp, he mostly wrote about his dreams for us.

It had been a long, lonely three months. And when the daily countdown reached the six-week mark and the hardest part of the wait was over, I savored the feeling of anticipation, the downward trek. And when the calendar noted Frankie would be home in seven days, a tidal wave of emotions fell over me and my heart felt lighter.

JUST THE TWO OF US

I could hardly wait to see him again. It had felt like an eternity since I'd last seen him, and I'd carefully marked off each day on my calendar. Finally, on one very special morning, I awakened to the day when I no longer needed to mark an X on the calendar.

Our plan was to meet at Grand Central Station at 9:30 that morning. Pounding rain during the night had kept me awake. By dawn the sky had brightened. I rushed to get ready, drank my mother's eggnog, raced to the 72nd street train station, placed the token in the turnstile, and waited to board a train for the rush hour ride downtown.

When I arrived at Grand Central, I ran as though I'd sprouted wings, past a maze of people, and stood on the edge of the platform with my eyes locked deep into the dark tunnel. I watched the tiny dots in the darkness become the headlights of an approaching train. A few seconds later the train pulled forward and came to a stop. It took forever for the train doors to open and let the parade of Marines climb down the steps.

They all looked alike; clones of one another, in uniform, with haircuts cropped close to the scalp and trim physiques. I searched every set of eyes until I found a pair of bright baby blues drilling into mine. It took but a few more moments and I was in his arms.

Frankie checked his bags in the depot locker, and we headed outside, into the coldness of a November day. We didn't have a car, but it didn't matter; we were together. I could tell from the look in his eyes and how he kept squeezing my hand that he'd missed me as much as I'd missed him.

As though we were the only two people on earth, we walked towards a café. Later we rode the trains from one end of the route and back and chatted about this training. I learned how boot camp was harder than he'd imagined but worth every minute. I could tell from the tone of his voice he was not only proud to be a Marine, he was happy.

He told me he'd received his orders and would be stationed in Camp Lejeune, North Carolina. He told me about a base in Southern California—Camp Pendleton. However, the news was less than positive. He told me requests for transfers from Camp Lejeune to the West Coast were seldom issued.

Later that day we went to the movies, and in the afternoon we parted—me to Brooklyn and Frankie in the opposite direction, towards the Bronx.

We met everyday for lunch, and he rode home with me after work. Working within the confines of a tight budget, and no car, our weekend routine reverted back to the pre-military schedule: going to the movies with MaryAnn and Joe or talking long walks on the bay. Sometimes we sat on benches by the Belt Parkway and watched the wakes from passing boats beat against the rocks below. During this time I learned how easygoing Frankie was. He had a wonderful sense of humor and a calming demeanor. After his 30-day leave was up, he reported to Camp Lejeune and we returned to writing letters. This time the words we exchanged were far more intense.

He was assigned to the motor pool but asked for a transfer to the tool and dye shop. It didn't take long for Frankie to bond with the Marines he worked with, as well his barracks buddies. He learned that many of the Marines traveled north on weekends, and depending on duty assignments, most likely he'd be home twice a month. Imagine my delight when two weeks later he called and told me he was on his way home.

Among his circle of friends was a Marine named Don and his wife Dana. They lived on base, and Frankie had been invited to their home several times. In one of his letters he told me they lived in a trailer park and described their home as tiny, but cozy.

During his trips home, Frankie spoke of life in North Carolina, about the weather, about the South in general—how friendly the people were. He also described the trailer park where Don and Dana lived. During one of our conversations Frankie casually asked if I would ever consider living on base . . . with him . . . in a small trailer.

"You know—I mean if we were married," he said. "Think you could live with me on base, in a place the size of a dollhouse? If your family moves to California, you wouldn't have to go with them. You would be with me—we'd be together."

At first I answered yes, although I thought he was just making casual conversation. The next time the subject came up I realized his question was more than idle talk. What he'd suggested seemed far-fetched, too big to wrap my mind around. In time, be them in letters or in person, our conversations would inevitably turn towards marriage, moving to North Carolina, and living on base. I was more than positive that his idea, if presented to my parents, would trigger a storm of controversy. My parents would never allow me to marry and move to North Carolina, not in a million years! Of this I was sure.

As plans for California moved forward, I fretted and sulked and finally surmised that if I wanted to continue to see Frankie, getting married might be a plausible solution. The idea began to grow and make sense, and the more I thought about it, the more excited I became. Being with him kept me up at night and distracted at work.

Some of my friends advised me to run with it while others said it was too soon, that I should move to California and let nature take its course. I was positive that if I moved with them, I'd never see Frankie again. I'd become trapped in my parents' world, stuck in their environment with no friends, with little opportunity to work, unless housework counts. I'd learn to drive and become their chauffeur.

As the days and weeks went by and the bond between us grew stronger, Frankie continued to suggest we tell them we wanted to get married—let the chips fall where they may. I assured him the time was not right. Their plans to move were solid, I knew they needed my help, and it was best not rattle the cage.

We decided to get engaged and hoped that our engagement might help them to accept that Frankie and I were serious. An engagement meant wedding plans would soon follow. We spoke to Frankie's parents, and they saw no harm in it and helped us pick out rings. Having no idea how my parents would react, we decided not to tell them in advance.

Once the rings were purchased, our engagement happened quickly. The very next time Frankie was home, we exchanged rings in a romantic downtown restaurant. We were thrilled, very happy, and very much in love. The glow in our hearts could have heated up Brooklyn.

I shared the news of our engagement with my mother during breakfast the following morning. I honestly didn't expect her to jump for joy, yet I anticipated a far different reaction. When I held out my hand, she looked at the ring, then at me, and then turned away without speaking a word. My father never inquired about the ring I wore proudly, although I was sure he was aware.

For a while, Frankie and I took life one day at a time, sustained by the knowledge that, come rain or shine, we'd be together.

Front: Joe and Tony
Back: Frankie and three close buddies from Camp Lejeune

MAY I HAVE THIS DANCE FOR THE REST OF MY LIFE?

Once the Christmas season, New Year's Day, and my 18th birthday in January fell away, we began strategizing ideas. I remained (firmly) convinced that asking my parents for permission to marry would not be wise. Frankie turned to his oldest brother Joey and shared details about the move to California as well as our goal to get married. Without offering an opinion or passing judgment, Joey agreed to help and promised to keep our plans quiet.

With his brother's help, our plan began to take shape. Step one: get a license and get married. Step two: apply for housing. We learned the wait list was three to six months, and I would remain at home until housing became available. Step three: leave together for North Carolina. Step four: call my parents after we were safely on base.

As promised, Joey made arrangements with a Justice of the Peace in New Jersey, and we decided to get married on June 29, 1956. Frankie would be home the night before. I told no one, not even MaryAnn. No one would know. Our plans remained a locked secret between the three of us.

After Frankie bought two white gold wedding bands on base, we applied for our marriage license in New Jersey and my focus turned to something special to wear—something sweet, something feminine but not flashy. During lunch hour I went shopping and spotted a pretty two-piece peach outfit on a store window mannequin. It stood out, and I knew this was to be my wedding dress. I already had matching heels but purchased a lace purse to complete a lovely ensemble. I was ready for the big day!

On the morning of June 29, I woke up before daybreak feeling nervous, anxious to get out of the house. I slipped into my new outfit, a dead giveaway to any other parent, but I wasn't worried. I'd already shown the outfit to my mother; she loved it and didn't suspect it was a bit dressy for work. After drinking her morning eggnog, I kissed her goodbye, headed out the door as though I was going to work. For a brief but pensive moment I hesitated, knowing that the next time I came home I would be a married woman.

Since our families lived at two opposite ends of the city, the plan was to meet downtown. As I boarded the train, fleeting thoughts about consequences and obstacles we might encounter crossed my mind, but they were quickly set aside. For now, in a few hours, Frankie and I would be married, and that's all that mattered.

Marching to the command of the maestro—my heart—I arrived at Grand Central Station, bolted up the long flight of stairs, through the swarm of early morning travelers, to the place where he was waiting.

We had not discussed what we'd wear, but it didn't matter. Frankie was a trendy dresser, always knew what went well together. As I walked towards the newsstand where we'd agreed to meet, I spotted him immediately. He looked positively handsome in a long sleeve casual shirt and slacks. My heart could not possibly race any faster without bursting.

He kissed me, and walking hand in hand, we made our way towards the exit, to the place where we had agreed to meet Joey.

Once we were in the car, Joey asked, "You guys sure you wanna do this? You can still back out ya know!"

"We're sure, just drive on!" Frankie answered and squeezed my hand tightly.

"Say, not sure if I told you, but I can't hang around when we get there. I have an appointment, so you'll be on your own. Hope you're not disappointed. This came up at the last minute, and there is nothing I can do about it."

We told him we'd be fine, and Joey returned to driving. Soon he exited the tunnel and began circling through the city streets until we arrived in Englewood, New Jersey, an old city with many old buildings. He drove until he came to the address he'd been searching for and pulled up to the curb.

"This is it, we're here!" he announced and stepped out of the car. Once again he asked if we were absolutely sure we wanted to go through with our plan. We smiled and assured him we were positive. Joey shook Frankie's hand, hugged me, and wished us luck.

We waited for Joey to pull away, waved as he drove off, then turned to open the large doors of the building. Joey's instructions were clear: take the elevator to the fourth floor and look for an office marked "Justice of the Peace."

It was nearly 9 o'clock, and the building was filled with people scurrying about in all directions. As we rode the elevator to the fourth floor, my stomach was churning and my heart was beating wildly. After a quick search we entered an office, a modest and unassuming office for a judicial officer.

A few minutes later an elderly man with steel gray hair entered the room. He was smiling and in a soft low voice introduced himself as a judge. It was obvious he was expecting our arrival. He motioned for us to follow him into his private quarters, another unpretentious domain for a professional man of his stature. He sat behind a massive desk and we sat facing him, nervously watching as he scanned the information on the license, verifying the spelling of our names and dates of birth.

"Hmmm . . . if you don't mind me asking, why are you getting married? You're both so young, especially *you*, young man!" he questioned in a voice that noted a tone of cautious concern.

We walked him through a condensed version of the "move to California." The judge listened attentively, then questioned if marriage was the only answer to the moving dilemma.

"No . . . well right now it is," I answered nervously. "I love him and we want to be together. My parents would never give us permission to get married, and once they move, the chances of seeing each other will be zero. If they weren't moving, we'd wait to get married, but not for long."

Frankie chimed in, told the judge how he felt, how much he was looking forward to having me with him. The judge asked a few more questions—where we would live—would we have enough income to live on. When he was done, he stood up and led us to a smaller room with a podium and several chairs.

Frankie and I stood hand in hand not knowing what to expect. We made our promises, exchanged rings, and happily said, "I do." And when it was over, the judge smiled, wished us luck, and shook our hands. Amidst the formal ambiance of the judge's office, the ceremony was romantic.

"Congratulations!" he said in a quasi fatherly tone." I don't normally take time to talk to the couple after a ceremony, but I'm retiring, and today is my last day. I won't forget you two. Just want you to know even though you're young, I have a good feeling about this marriage. Just be happy and maintain a sense of humor. Marriage isn't always easy; it's a two-way street. Keep that in mind, young man! I hope you'll stay in touch, send a card once in a while. I'll look forward to hearing from you!"

He handed us our marriage certificate, then reached into his desk drawer for a business card and gave it to Frankie. We thanked him again and waved before walking out of his office. He smiled and waved back.

It was midmorning of a workday, and people were rushing past us on our way out of the building, but we hardly noticed. Soon we were standing by the front entrance. For a few moments we stood facing one another, speechless, quietly contemplating what had just occurred.

"Yeah—we did it, we're married," he whispered and pulled me close.

I can still remember those euphoric moments. We were so happy, and not a thought was given to consequences, not during that blissful moment in time. We were married, and soon we'd be living in Camp Lejeune.

With no car, very little money, and no plans for the rest of the day, we went into a nearby coffee shop and slipped into a cozy booth. Frankie kept squeezing my hand. Although the ceremony was still fresh in our minds, the full impact of being married had not yet embraced us. Not being able to share our special night together, we simply wrapped ourselves in the joy of the day.

"I can't wait till we go home, to our home. It's gonna be so great! I just hope you like it," he shared.

"Oh, I know I will. But I wonder what my dad will do when he finds out we're married. I know he'll blow a gasket. But it won't matter; we won't tell him until we are on the base."

"Try not to think about it. We won't have to face that for a while, not for a few months. The most important thing is we're married and you won't be going to California. Before you know it, we'll be on our way to Camp Lejeune . . . together . . . just you and me!"

We spent the day walking around Times Square and took in the sights of our ole haunt. Later that afternoon we went to the movies. Sometime before dinner we removed our wedding bands and headed home—me to Brooklyn and Frankie to the Bronx.

The following morning Frankie boarded the train back to Camp Lejeune and I went back to my old routine. Somehow I felt different; my world had changed. We were married. The ride home from work each night now seemed longer, and when the train would pull up to 72nd Street station, I'd race home, rush past my mother and head straight into the bedroom hoping a letter with the familiar handwriting on the envelope would be waiting on my bed. Although he used my maiden name to address the envelopes, he began each letter with "my darling wife." He told me he'd applied for housing and for spousal allotment.

I wanted to shout out to the world that we were married. I wanted to use his name. I wanted to tell everyone how happy I was. I wanted to share the news that I'd soon be leaving for North Carolina. Still, I held to our plan—keep our marriage a secret until the right time.

BUSTED

With our secret locked safely in my heart, I went to work each day as though nothing had changed. However, concentrating on work tasks was easier said than done. Frankie was all I thought about. I wanted to see him again, soon. When he called and told me he'd be home the following weekend, I could hardly keep my heart from jumping out of my chest.

The days that followed felt like an eternity. And when he called to tell me he was on his way home and would meet me for lunch the following day, I could barely focus.

As promised, we met for any early lunch. We wanted to be alone, yet there was no way to fulfill that desire. Once again, we resumed our usual routine: walking through parks, going to the movies, or riding the trains through the city. When we were alone, we wore our wedding rings.

"Here, hold onto this," he said and handed me our marriage certificate. "Put it in a safe place. The barracks isn't the best place to keep important documents."

I wasn't exactly sure where "safe" might be. The only safe place was to keep it with me at all times. After carefully folding the bulky certificate, I somehow managed to tuck it in my wallet.

The following day was Friday, and I'd taken the day off from work. We decided to walk to the Belt Parkway. Sitting on the benches and watching the water beat up against the rocks was always peaceful. Frankie shared good news: the housing wait was not long, only two months. We continued to mull over the best time to tell my parents, before leaving for North Carolina or after we arrived on base. Frankie leaned towards telling them in person, but I didn't want to face them. I was positive my father would go ballistic, and I honestly could not bear to see my mother upset.

I was reasonably sure that getting engaged probably triggered apprehension in my father's mind. I told Frankie he'd seemed edgy lately, somewhat cold. There was something on his mind, and I was sure it had to do with the engagement ring on my finger. Frankie told me it was probably my imagination.

When we returned from our walk, my father was home. He was sitting at the dining room table reading his newspaper, something he rarely did during the early part of the day. His normal routine during those short workdays was to tinker in the backyard or in the basement. But there he was sitting at the table. He shook Frankie's hand, and they chatted for a moment. On the surface things seemed fine, and yet I continued to sense something was wrong.

I knew my father's heart. I knew he had hoped Frankie would have disappeared from my life by now. The notion "out of sight, out of mind" was what he was counting on. Evidently he was unaware that absence makes the heart grow fonder! Deep down I knew my father liked Frankie—he was right for me, just not now.

I stood by the side of the table watching and listening and observing my father. Suddenly he reached in his pocket, handed me his bank passbook, and asked me to go to the bank and deposit his paycheck. Normally my mother did the banking.

"Where's Mom?"

"She went shopping. You go!" he shot back coldly.

Placing the check in my purse, we left the house not realizing I had left my wallet (with the marriage certificate tucked inside), where I'd placed it the night before—inside the drawer of my bedside nightstand.

When we returned home from the bank, we entered the house through the side door, walked into the kitchen and headed towards the dining room. My father was standing on the far side of the table, and rage is the word that best describes the look in his eyes. In his hand was our marriage certificate. I froze. For a moment it felt as though my heart might shop beating and I had to force myself to breathe.

"What is this?" he shouted angrily, waving the certificate in the air.

"It's nothing, Daddy. It's fake; we got it on Coney Island," I answered. "It's not real!"

"Yes it is. Look—this is an official New Jersey state stamp on a marriage certificate with your names on it!"

In less than one week our well-thought-out plan had fallen apart. He was holding the proof in his hands, and denying it further was futile. My heart was beating fast and for a moment I thought it might stop. Seeing the fury in his eyes and the anguish on his face felt as though a bolt of lightning had rammed through my body. I'd hurt him, crushed his heart, betrayed him, and he was traumatized. I'd broken a link in the family bond, one he valued deeply, and I suddenly felt disconnected.

It never dawned on me that my father might rummage through my bedroom drawers. I wasn't sure if he'd ever been in my room. Yet, I should have known; he had been acting peculiar. In light of what lay hidden inside my wallet, why I had absentmindedly left it home that day was puzzling.

For a moment longer he stood and glared at me. I was paralyzed, my mind went blank, and I could no longer think or speak. Suddenly he flung the certificate at us and headed out the back door. A surge of adrenaline began to rise in me and I knew we had to do something quickly. Acting solely on impulse, my only thought was to get as far away from him as possible.

"Let's get out of here," I said frantically.

"What? Are you crazy? We can't do that!" Frankie argued.

"Oh yes we can! Let's go, right now. I don't want to be here when this breaks."

Frankie tried calming me, but it was useless. I reached for his hand, and we headed towards the front door. We bounded down the red brick steps, through the wrought iron gate, and we began to run, aimlessly, heading nowhere in particular. Some of our neighbors were standing on their stoops and called my name, but their voices flew past us in the wind, whooshing by like birds in flight. My mother, on her way home from the market, also called to me, but I chose to ignore her as well.

Frankie continued to plead with me to go back and face the music that by now, without a doubt, was a full-blown symphony.

"Stop, please! Will you listen for a second? Your mom is home now and is probably upset. Let's go back and talk to them. We're married now—there's nothing they can do!"

"Talk? Are you kidding? My father doesn't know how to talk!"

I had my purse, my wallet, and the certificate, and nothing else mattered. With no real plan in mind, we ran past Indian Mary's Candy Shop, the YWCA on 15th Avenue, and PS (Public School) 112. Breathless, anxious, and uncertain of what to do next, when we reached New Utrecht Avenue and the train station came into sight, our minds cleared. We located a pay phone by the newspaper stand and Frankie called his brother Joey, told him what had just happened. Joey told him to head home and that he'd talk to their parents.

With my father's eyes and words fresh in my mind, we boarded a train packed with people rushing home from work. Every seat had been taken, and we stood holding on to the center pole of the train for the long ride to the Bronx. My insides were shaking and my hands were trembling. Frankie folded his hand over mine, squeezing it lovingly, and kept reassuring me that things would work out.

The next drama unfolded at his house—coming face to face with Dominick, his domineering father—someone I considered tremendously intimidating—someone who had little patience for anyone.

An hour later, Frankie opened the door to their apartment. It was dinnertime, everyone was seated around the table, and all eyes were focused on Frankie and me. The ambiance was eerily quiet, minus the lively chatter between parents and young children at dinnertime.

Mary, Frankie's mother, greeted us at the door. She looked nervous, teary-eyed. She kissed us, asked if we'd eaten, but we shook our heads. Neither of us had an appetite; food was the last thing on our minds.

Dominick ignored us and never looked up to acknowledge our presence. He chose instead to focus on his food, and the only sounds at the table were his. When he was done eating, he looked our way and broke his silence, but his words stung, like a swift slap to the face.

"So ya got married. I never imagined either of you were that stupid! Guess I was wrong."

Although I was grateful that he had not raised his voice, his tone was condescending—we were not stupid. I opted to ignore Dominick's harshness, as did Frankie. Shaking off his father's cynicism, Frankie explained our reasons for getting married, beginning with the move to California.

"That's a dimwitted excuse. I don't care if they're moving. How will you support her? Where will she live? It would have been much smarter to move to California, young lady, and wait to get married. Did that concept cross your minds?"

"Dad, if she moves to California, I'll probably never see her again!"

"How do you know that? Can you see the future?" he continued.

"So let's see, you have to be back on base by Tuesday, right? And what about you?" he asked me. What are your plans? Are you going home tonight, young lady?"

"No, she's not! She can't, not yet," Frankie shot back. "We haven't had time to work things out with her parents. This just happened a few hours ago. We were going to tell everyone once base housing opened up. That's not going to happen for two more months."

"Well, you can't stay here, that's for sure. Christ, didn't you think about what would happen if the news got out—like it did?"

"Dad, we didn't think he'd go through her wallet."

As time moved forward, one by one the consequences began to surface. I could not go home, we could not stay with his parents, and I had no extra clothes—not even a toothbrush. I wondered how I'd get to work on Monday morning. I thought about my siblings, probably frightened, and my mother,probably heartbroken. I honestly didn't care about my father's feelings, but cared deeply about hers.

Dominick lowered his eyes and stared down at his folded hands.

"Mary, call your sister Lilly. Tell her what happened," Dominick suggested. "Ask her if they can stay with her. Call Joey and ask him to drive them to Jersey." Turning to Frankie he added, "If Lilly says you can stay there tonight, consider yourselves lucky."

Mary looked relieved and ran to the phone to call her sister. Frankie had often spoken about his aunt. He shared that she lived with Walter, her lifelong mate, and they had no children. He told me everyone loved her, that she was sweet, and how Dominick disliked her for a myriad of selfish reasons.

Mary explained what had taken place with her sister, and when she was done, she handed the phone to Frankie. He listened for a moment and glanced my way as a look of relief crossed his face. Lilly had told him to come right over.

Before long Joey's car horn sounded from the street below. After saying goodbye to his siblings and thanking his parents, we ran down the stairs. Joey's black car was a welcomed sight, as was his smiling face motioning for us to get in.

"Hmmm, less than two weeks and things already went to hell. So much for keeping secrets! Hey, you guys didn't spill the beans and tell anyone I helped you? God, I hope not."

"No, no one knows a thing. Your part in this is safe." Frankie answered reassuringly.

"Exactly how did your dad find out?"

While Frankie explained what had taken place, Joey drove through the Holland Tunnel. A few minutes later we were driving through a lovely neighborhood of quaint homes, beautifully manicured lawns, and tall trees with long branches that reached out and touched in the center of the street.

Joey pulled up in front Lilly and Walter's house. We got out of the car, and Frankie knocked on the front door. A moment later, Lilly answered. Having delivered his special package, Joey greeted his aunt and Walter and went on his way.

Frankie, me, Aunt Lilly and Walter

I fell in love with Lilly and Walter the moment I met them. We were warmly welcomed, and the sound of their happy voices put us at ease. Lilly wanted to know what had happened, and we sat in their cozy living room and shared the details. She'd prepared a platter of fruits and nuts and a variety of sandwiches cut into bite-sized pieces just big enough for one Italian bite. The array looked appetizing and a far cry from the meatball and sausage sandwiches I was accustomed to eating. My stomach was still upset, as was Frankie's. Once I was able to relax, the knot in my stomach untied, and soon Frankie and I began nibbling at the tasty food she'd lovingly prepared.

Lilly and Walter's warm welcome, the food, the smiles, and their relaxing conversation helped to unwind our tangled nerves. The long day, with many twists and turns, was exhausting. It was close to midnight when Walter rubbed his eyes and announced he was ready for bed. Frankie and I wondered where we would sleep, and Lilly motioned for us to follow her. She led us to an upstairs bedroom with an adjoining bathroom.

Recognizing this would be our first night together, Lilly went out of her way to make us comfortable. The bedroom had two twin beds. She placed a bathrobe for Frankie on one bed, and on the other was a pretty nightshirt from Lilly's collection of feminine sleepwear. The lovely bathroom was colorfully decorated with various types of toiletries, including new toothbrushes and clean towels. Several items I would never have guessed would look pretty as bathroom décor caught my attention, especially the candles and fresh flowers. The room was lovely, and bore no resemblance to the tiny cluttered bathroom in Brooklyn.

"Well, goodnight, you two! You can push the beds together if you like!" she added teasingly. Lilly blew a kiss our way and closed the door behind her.

Except when I was little and spent time in Auntie Anna's house, I'd never slept away from home. I was never allowed to have sleepovers, and I'd envied my friends and the weekend sleepovers I was never allowed to partake in. As I looked around, it felt odd to be in a strange room with strange furniture and a husband that would soon cuddle close to me. On that night, our first night as man and wife, I decided to set aside the uncertainties of our future and the hurt I'd hurled on my parents. We were together, we were married, and it was all that mattered.

When I woke the following morning, thoughts about the previous day's occurrences immediately rushed into my mind. Frankie was still asleep. I wanted to wake him; I needed to hear him tell me that everything would be fine. I decided to snuggle quietly instead and watch the streams of sunlight filtering through the window blinds. In nearby trees birds were chirping, and I heard the rumbling sound of a train in the distance. The sounds of the world outside the room remained unchanged, and yet, in less than twenty-four hours, my world had evolved and would never be the same. As my thoughts drifted back to Brooklyn, to the day before, I wondered what was happening at the moment—if my mother was all right, if my siblings were okay.

When Frankie woke up, he pulled me close. I told him I was worried, and he kept reassuring me that everything would work out. We needed to take it one day at a time, one issue at a time. With him close, and his words in my heart, my world felt safe.

By the time we showered and dressed, a familiar and inviting aroma of coffee had wafted upstairs to greet us. Sitting at the kitchen table, I suddenly felt comfortable, at ease. Lilly had prepared a delicious breakfast, but as I ate, the memory of my mother's coffee eggnog took center stage in my mind and briefly erased the happy moments of the morning.

Later we sat in her cozy living room. Lilly was aware I'd need clothes, at least one change of clothes. "You need some things. I'll take you shopping!" she announced cheerfully.

Later, we went downtown. Lilly helped me pick out a few outfits. She was as generous as she was sweet, and I hardly knew what to say or how to thank her.

"Consider this my wedding gift," she said as she reached to hug me.

Later that day, I called my sister and asked her to pack some of my work clothes and meet us downtown. I was anxious to see her and find out how things were at home. She was only fourteen years old. I was worried. If my parents discovered she'd met with us, they would be angry with her as well.

At the train station, we waited and watched until we spotted her running towards us. I asked how things were at home and she told me they'd cried for most of the night. I wanted to chat a few more moments, but I was anxious for her to get home, hoping there would be no repercussions.

Lilly and Walter went out of their way to make us comfortable that weekend. They assured us that we could stay until issues with my parents were resolved. I could travel to work every day, just as I traveled to work from Brooklyn. She told me she'd drive me to the train station each morning and pick me up at night. She also told us Mary had been talking with my parents.

On Monday morning, Frankie needed to get back to Manhattan for his trip back to the base. Our bliss-filled weekend was behind us, and the inevitable changes that were about to take place—those I would have to confront alone—were front and center.

Walter offered to drive Frankie to the city, and I began fighting off tears long before it was time to say goodbye. Standing by the curb, he hugged me, reminded me not to worry, and slipped into the car. Frankie waved as the car pulled away. A moment later he disappeared down the street, and all I was left with was an empty feeling, as though he'd not been in my arms moments earlier.

Once Lilly and I were alone, she told me Mary had something to share . . . a surprise . . . something good.

"Your mom and dad want you to go home. Mary told me they were very calm and they asked her to bring you home. Mary told them you were afraid, but they assured her everything would be fine. Your mom told her if you return home now, they have a plan they'd like to discuss. It sounds promising. I suggest you hear them out. Dominick and Mary will drive you home tonight, and you can talk to them."

"I hate going home without Frankie," I said tearfully.

"I understand, but I think you'll be more than pleasantly surprised at what they have to tell you."

Lilly refused to share what my parents had in mind. She thought it would be better for them to tell me. I was nervous about going home. I felt safe in her cozy home; I wanted to stay a few more days before any further changes pummeled into my life.

Lilly looked at me and said, "My dear, you need to listen carefully and trust me. Strike while the iron is hot. If you don't go home—now—they may very well withdraw their offer."

I hardly knew Lilly, yet after that wonderful weekend in her home, I trusted her and reluctantly agreed to go home. After dinner, Dominick and Mary picked me up for the drive to Brooklyn.

Frankie and I had worn our wedding rings that weekend. Now, on the way home I could not stop twirling mine; a constant and comforting reminder that we were married. Yet I was terrified. I wanted Frankie with me. Sensing I was upset, Mary kept talking to me and tried calming my nerves.

The drive back to Brooklyn was every bit as frightening as the train ride to the Bronx a few short days ago. When Dominick pulled up to the curb, I glanced at the house but felt oddly disconnected. Although the trees, the flowers, the black wrought iron gate, and the red brick steps were the same, the house looked different. But in fact nothing was different. I had changed.

Dominick beeped the horn, and a moment later my mother was standing by the front door. She greeted Dominick and Mary but never spoke to me. And when I looked her way, she looked sad. She of all people was undeserving of any hurt.

It had been three days since I was last in that room where my father had confronted us. So much had happened; a lifetime of events had taken place in so short a time span.

My father was sitting where he always sat at the head of the table. His eyes were lowered, focused on his folded hands. The room was quiet; no one spoke. For a few moments it felt as though time had stopped. I wasn't sure where the conversation would begin, where it would lead, or how the drama would end.

Mary and Dominick greeted my father. He nodded politely but never spoke. Suddenly, my mother broke the silence and got right to the point.

"Are you pregnant?" she blurted out coldly.

At first, I was stunned at her baseless assumption. "No, of course not!" I shot back sarcastically.

"We answer to a lot of people. Do you know what everyone will think if we tell them you got married without our permission?"

"Just tell them the truth—you're moving to California and we want to be together. What's wrong with that? Tell them you would never have given us permission to get married."

"But you didn't ask us. You never told us you wanted to get married," she added.

"Of course I didn't ask. Daddy never wanted me out of the house—remember? Why would he have us given permission to get married?"

Dominick and my father listened to the banter but were noticeably quiet. Mary changed the subject and began discussing where Frankie and I would live, as well as the monthly government allotment. She explained that housing would be available by Labor Day. And when she was done my mother spoke.

"Listen to me—your father and I want you to stay home starting tonight. We want you to get married in church, but you're not to tell anyone you're already married, not one person. *Capisce* . . . understand? We'll have a small reception here at the house. If you don't agree, then you can leave tonight, and the door will close behind you. If you agree, we will explain that you and Frankie have our permission to get married and you won't be coming with us to California. One more thing—take off the wedding ring. And—your sister will not be your maid of honor. Understand? That's your punishment!"

"You'll never get a chance like this again," Mary interjected. "I think they're being fair. I'm sure Frankie would agree."

I had expected a far different scenario to unfold that night—loud shouting and screaming and my father pounding his fist on the table. His demeanor took me by surprise, and the proposal sounded like a reward.

For a few moments I sat quietly digesting the plan, then looked at my mother and nodded approvingly. Once I agreed, the mood lightened up. After coffee, Frankie's parents went on their way and my father went to bed. My mother and I were alone. The house was quiet, and I thanked her for letting me come home. I knew I'd hurt her deeply. For a while, we sat at the tiny table in the kitchen and talked. I could tell she was relieved. I was home, and she was happy I'd agreed to a church wedding.

After we tidied up the kitchen, I kissed her and made my way through the house towards my bedroom. The items I'd left on my nightstand remained untouched. I crawled into bed, letting the warmth and familiarity of the room I shared with my sister fold over me. As I lay in bed, I thought about Frankie and about my new life in North Carolina. I mostly thought about the events that transpired earlier and a church wedding in a beautiful white dress. However, I was positive their small-minded network of friends and family would nonetheless assume the worst of the situation.

Joey was right; things had a way of working out. When Frankie called the next day, I explained what happened. He was delighted, and we decided it was best if he didn't come home during this time. Things would be uncomfortable for him.

My attention turned to plans for a wedding minus the usual Italian fanfare. The first item on my agenda was going to church and speaking to the priest at Our Lady of Guadalupe. Father McGuire listened while

I explained what had happened. The look on his face told me he was less than thrilled. When I was done speaking, he asked if the marriage had been consummated. Although I had no idea what he meant, I answered no, and his eyes widened in disbelief. When he was done questioning me, he checked his calendar and told us Sunday, September 1st at 3 o'clock was available for a wedding—Labor Day weekend, less than two months away.

At home, my father continued to ignore me. I kept out of his way and avoided him as much as possible. I wanted to talk to him, but there were no words to make him understand. He was hurt, and only time would lessen the pain.

Two weeks later, my father, sister, and brother Joe left for California to check out a job opportunity as well as a place to live. Thankfully, my father had also taken the nucleus of our family's tension with him. My mother and I were now able to talk openly. She was more relaxed, and her mood had changed considerably. Actually it was fun being alone with her and Tony. We shopped for invitations (to be mailed immediately) as well as a dress, a photographer and flowers.

Not being able to have my sister as my maid of honor weighed on my mind, yet I had to let it go. Since MaryAnn and Joe had introduced me to Frankie, I asked MaryAnn to do the honors, and she gladly accepted. A few weeks later, she surprised me with a bridal shower, something I totally didn't expect.

One month later my father and siblings returned home and told us the job opportunity was with the Pomona Tile Company. He was far more relaxed, but he continued to ignore me. At this point I no longer worried about his feelings. He seemed more relaxed, and I remained focused on what was expected of me. Before long I'd be away from all the drama.

Once again I found myself counting down the days, and thoughts of Frankie consumed every waking moment. I missed him. At night I'd lie in bed wondering what life would be like living in small quarters, one no bigger than the bedroom my sister and I shared.

Frankie shared the exact same feelings in his letters. His words were now more intense and focused deeply on wanting me with him. On the radio "My Blue Heaven" by Fats Domino was number one on the *Hit Parade*. Frankie sent me the words to the song and told me he imagined coming home from work every night to our blue heaven.

When whippoorwills call, and evening is nigh,
I hurry to my blue heaven,
I turn to the right, to a little white light,
That leads me to my blue heaven.

I'll see a smiling face, a fireplace, a cozy room,
A little nest that nestles where the roses bloom!
Just sweetie and me, and baby makes three,
We're happy in my blue heaven.

COME FLY WITH ME, LET'S FLY, LET'S FLY AWAY

September 1, 1956

On the night before the wedding, I crawled into bed, and I turned on my portable radio. It would be a long night, and I hoped I could fall asleep quickly. After tuning in to my favorite music station, just as I'd done in the past, I tucked the radio under my pillow and listened to love songs until I fell fast asleep.

The morning of September 1ˢᵗ arrived long before dawn. I remained in bed feeling nervous and anxious. My mind quickly shifted forward to later in the day, to the moment Frankie and I would board the train to Camp Lejeune. Going home to Camp Lejeune with Frankie set my heart racing.

Surprisingly, two months had flown by quickly. There had been so much to do, but now every detail was in place, and all that was left was to get married. As I made my bed, I gazed around the room, locking the scene into memory and promising myself to never forget the pretty green and white bedroom with my sister fast asleep at the far end.

Like most mornings, I was drawn towards the wonderful aroma of coffee brewing in the kitchen. Knowing this would be the last time my mother would prepare coffee eggnog for her eldest daughter, I hesitated; it felt strange—this was our last morning together, and I did not want to watch her preparing my breakfast. I didn't want anything to mar the happiness I was feeling. I wondered if she was feeling the same way. The last thing I wanted was to inflict any further hurt in her heart.

During breakfast, we quietly chatted about the day, and soon I was on my way to an early Mass. The morning sadness in my heart followed me to church, lingering within me through the service. After Mass, I made my way down the church steps, grateful the sun had fought its way out of the fall clouds and was following me home. With the sun on my back, my heart felt light, and all was right in my world. I was happy.

By the time I arrived home, folding chairs had been lined up against the walls in the dining and living rooms. My mother decided to serve a cold buffet for the reception, nothing fancy by Italian wedding standards, yet suitable under the circumstances. Platters of cold cuts, cheeses, breads, and cookies from Romano's Bakery would soon be arranged on the table resting against the window.

Hanging on my bedroom door was my wedding dress—pretty, but nothing special or extravagant. While I was at church, my mother had pressed out the wrinkles and placed the veil on my bed next to the lace purse.

At one o'clock I slipped into my dress, touched up my makeup, placed the veil on my head, stepped into my shoes, and waited for the photographer to take "home shots." By 2:30, the limo pulled up to the curb. Neighbors had gathered on stoops to watch my mother help me walk down the front steps and through the hedged archway to the limo. Although my father and I had exchanged few words, I knew he was prepared to walk me down the aisle.

After the short drive, the driver pulled up to the front steps of Our Lady of Guadalupe Church. Friends and family had already gathered inside, and the pews were filled with folks speculating about the reasons behind the quick wedding.

My father and I waited in the church vestibule for the organ to sound the wedding march. And when the familiar melody rang out, he wrapped my arm in his, and we began walking down the aisle, past the people seated in the pews, the friends and family I'd known all my life.

As we walked down the aisle, my eyes were focused on Frankie standing at the foot of the altar alongside his best man, his brother Joey. When we reached the railing, my father lifted the veil from my face, kissed me and whispered, "*Spero che Dio ti benedice* . . . may God bless you." Turning to Frankie, he placed my hand into his. At that moment I felt my father's heart in mine, and I knew he loved me in spite of the humiliation I'd brought into his life.

As was customary, I walked over to the statue of our Blessed Mother, placed a rose at her feet, and offered a short prayer. When I was done, I walked back to Frankie, and we knelt before the priest. The bands of white gold we'd used in June would be used again. And as the angelic sound of the Ave Maria began to fill the air, we exchanged vows. The ceremony was brief. When it was over, Frankie kissed me, and hand in hand we turned and walked back down the aisle.

After a shower of rice on the church steps and a photo session at a nearby studio, we rushed home to a house jammed with people, some who'd never met Frankie. My parents had never mentioned to friends and family that I was seeing someone special. As I introduced Frankie, many of the men asked about the base. The women were mostly interested in where we'd live. Some asked how much money I'd get from the government. Others could not hold their curiosity in check and asked why we didn't wait until my family moved to California before getting married. I knew most were suspicious, and I resented having to explain. We mostly smiled and said, "Believe it or not, we just wanted to get married before they move to California!" By this time we were both more than ready to head to our home, to North Carolina.

BYE-BYE BROOKLYN

The train for North Carolina was scheduled to leave in the early evening. At five o'clock, I changed into the light blue suit I'd picked out for the trip (women during this era always dressed up when traveling), placed my wedding dress, veil, and the lace purse on my bed. (Someone would inherit the ensemble, possibly a cousin in Sicily.) For the last time, I glanced around the room, never wanting to forget the lovely ambiance my mother had created. After placing *la busta* (our wedding money) into the luggage, I slipped into my heels, reached for my purse, and closed the bedroom door behind me.

I hated goodbyes. I wished we could sprout wings, fly above everyone and wave like small planes do—dipping one wing, then the other, and then flying away. Saying goodbye to my siblings, my family, my friends, and Frankie's family was difficult.

My cousin offered to take us to Grand Central Station. My father sat up front, and Frankie, my mother, and I slipped in the back of his car. As we pulled away from the curb, I waved to everyone gathered in the front yard. For the last time, I glanced at the pretty white house with a million memories of my family and my childhood tucked within its walls. Soon another family would breathe the same air. And if they listened closely, they would hear echoes of my family. I'd been looking forward to this moment, yet now I felt sad knowing I'd probably never see the house again. When they moved, we'd be living on opposite sides of the country. Many years would go by before I'd see them again. My throat tightened, and I fought hard to hold my emotions intact. Brooklyn, my family, my friends, and my childhood years, filled with love and music and laughter, would be but a memory.

In time I would reach back and take comfort from the warm memories of my childhood years in our house on 72nd Street. I would remember the parents who showered me with endless love, who had given me all I ever needed and made my childhood years so safe, so happy. I knew the essence of their love would linger in my heart forever.

This was it—the moment I'd dreamt about for two months—Frankie and I leaving for Camp Lejeune together—bittersweet moments—saying goodbye to my parents while looking forward to what lay ahead. As we drove, my mind wrestled with ways to thank them for being so devoted and so forgiving.

We arrived at Grand Central Station with little time to spare. After parking the car, we raced through the terminal towards the designated platform.

It had been many years since I'd seen my mother in tears—not since they'd received the telegrams announcing the deaths of Camillo and Mario. This pain was different, this was hurt I'd inflicted, and there was little I could do to bring back the happy smiles we had shared when I was young. We embraced and I told her I was sorry. I promised her I'd write and I'd call every week. I asked her to be happy for me.

Fighting back tears, I turned to my father and hugged him. I'd forgotten how safe it felt in his arms, and I felt forgiveness in his embrace. As strict and stubborn as he had been, he was my daddy. He kissed me and then he turned to Frankie, shook his hand and embraced him.

Frankie and I stood on the steps of the train. I turned to look at them, noting how sad and small they appeared from afar, like two abandoned children. We waved and finally turned to step inside.

Sleeper cars were unavailable, yet it hardly mattered; we just wanted to go home. We settled comfortably into seats by a window. The drama was over; the wounds, though not forgotten, were mending. We could relax now and chat about the events that led up to that moment and how happy we were to be on our way home. Soon the sad goodbyes would settle into the quiet corners of our minds.

The past months had been emotionally exhausting. Now, on a train packed with travelers, we felt alone in our own world. We held hands. We felt married. As the train rumbled through the city, the sound became a lullaby easing our weariness, lulling us into a peaceful sleep.

Several hours later, we awoke to the sound of the conductor's voice shouting, "Next stop, Virginia!" When the train pulled to a stop, we stood up and stretched. Noting there was time before we'd be on the move again, we decided to walk through the terminal.

As we stepped off the train, my eyes scanned the strangeness of the terminal. It was much older and much darker than Grand Central Station, gloomy in comparison. The setting looked like a scene from an old movie. Voices with peculiar-sounding accents filled the air. Frankie had mentioned that Virginia marked the northern edge of the South. I suddenly realized we were in the midst of southerners with strange accents, traditions, and customs—a way of life far removed from my life in Brooklyn.

The second dissimilarity from the North were the words posted on signs above the restroom doors:

Restroom—Female—BLACKS
Restroom—Female—WHITES

"Amazing, huh? Yeah, southerners march to the beat of a different drummer. When we get on the train you'll see more of the same. Blacks have to sit in the back. I haven't seen any signs of segregation on base, or at least it's not blatant."

After a short walk, we reboarded the train and settled back into our seats. In eight hours we'd be in New Bern, North Carolina. We cuddled as close as we could, and Frankie continued to tell me about the South, focusing on the warmth and friendliness of the people.

Once again, the whining hum of the train lulled us back to sleep. We slept from exhaustion, waking in the morning with the sun beaming through the window to welcome a special day—the day when I'd see just how tiny our home actually was.

I looked out of the tiny train window and noted the landscape had drastically changed—all signs of city life had disappeared. Except for the scant signs of life around a scattering of shoddy shacks, the setting looked desolate and barren as far as the eye could see. The area had the distinct look of a Martian landscape I'd seen in science fiction movies. Frankie told me we were rolling past cotton fields. The only cotton I'd ever seen came in a ball or in the fabric of a garment. I had no idea that cotton grew in such a pitiful environment. The harvested fields left nothing more than barren twigs.

The train continued to rumble through the bleak countryside until we arrived in New Bern, North Carolina, the last leg of our rail travel. The remainder of the trip would be by car. I nervously waited as the train slowly pulled ahead and stopped by a platform in front of a small outdoor structure. This time the setting resembled that of an old western movie.

We stepped off the train, gathered our luggage and walked to an open area by the curb. Frankie had made arrangements with his friend Don and his wife to pick us up. Although I'd never met them, their names were now familiar, as were their personalities. Don was easygoing and Dana was very friendly and well familiar with military life. Frankie had assured me I'd like her, but warned me she was not like my Brooklyn friends. She was a southern gal, not shy but definitely not rowdy. Both were from Nashville and spoke with a deep southern drawl.

"Can't wait for you to hear them say *y'all*," Frankie teased.

Although Frankie had been touting their gracious southern personalities for months, I had reservations. I wondered if I'd fit in, if we'd hit it off—if they'd find my Noo Yawk accent, my Brooklynese grating! Yet I was hopeful. I trusted Frankie's judgment. Besides, they'd probably already become accustomed to Frankie's Bronx accent.

Suddenly a car began to approach and Frankie waved them to the curb.

"Hey y'all, welcome home!" shouted a pretty blond lady in the passenger seat.

Dan looked exactly like Frankie described her: blonde, petite and always wore a smile. And the sound of that charming southern accent was something I was already getting accustomed to and loving.

Don and Dana immediately got out of the car and quickly introduced themselves. Both radiated warmth—just as Frankie had described them—and I knew at that moment that I would welcome and enjoy their friendship.

I'm not sure what Dana thought when she caught sight of me. She was wearing shorts, a t-shirt, and sneakers. I was dressed like any other traveling New Yorker, in a suit and high heels. To someone who'd never lived in a big city, my outfit probably looked weird. I could tell she was sweet, never condescending, and I imagined visiting her home and feeling very comfortable, someone who probably sent you away with cookies in a take-home bag!

"How was the trip?" asked Dana. "Bet y'all are plum tuckered out!"

"Yeah we are," answered Frankie. "It was a long ride. We slept sitting up and we definitely need some sound sleep. But first some grub. You guys hungry?"

"Yes we are. We were waiting for you," answered Don.

While Don drove to a nearby restaurant, Dana began asking questions about the wedding and the trip. The more I heard the sound of that sweet accent, the more I was drawn to her and the more I relaxed. She described Knox Trailer Park and shared tidbits about life on the base. It was strange; I'd never met anyone like her. Frankie had described her perfectly. She was a far cry from my rowdy Brooklyn friends, those whom I was already missing, especially MaryAnn.

After lunch we headed home. While the guys chatted, Dana continued to describe life on base and Camp Lejuene. Soon we were driving though Jacksonville, North Carolina, a small town in the middle of nowhere. It boasted a strong military presence with pawnshops and jewelry stores on every street. Don drove through the town towards a major highway. When I read the words on a large brick wall that read: CAMP LEJEUNE HOME OF EXPEDITIONARY FORCES IN READINESS, I knew we were home.

I'd never been on a military base. I'd never seen a main gate with uniformed guards saluting and waving cars into the compound. As Don drove through the bustling base, he pointed to various buildings—the barracks, the PX, the commissary and the hospital. Groups of men wearing what Frankie described as "fatigues" were marching in cadence, and others were performing calisthenics. It all looked peculiar yet exciting.

He continued to drive until we came upon a heavily wooded area with a two-lane road carved down the center, a stark contrast to the energy we'd noted in other areas of the base. It was akin to something out of a child's fairy tale, a place where Hansel and Gretel might have once walked on their way to the gingerbread house. He drove until we came to another guard shack with one lone Marine standing at attention. Adjacent to the guard shack was a sign that read: Camp Knox Trailer Park.

For this Brooklyn gal, the setting didn't look real—it looked peculiar, nothing like the Brooklyn neighborhoods I was familiar with. I'd never seen a trailer or a trailer park in my life. Yet the ambiance looked familiar;

Frankie had provided very vivid descriptions. The trailers were small and some were really small. They were parked at various angles and painted in vivid pastel colors of pistachio green, baby blue, and pale peach like my June wedding dress. What I found most charming were the groups of mothers walking with babies in strollers and children riding tiny tricycles on wide sidewalks. The park could have easily been named Camp Candy Land.

Although Frankie had described the park in great detail, he neglected to tell me we'd be living in the center of a densely wooded area, close to a swampy river that ran along the furthest edge of the park. Soon Dana was pointing to their home. After a few more turns, Don pulled up in front of a light green trailer with the number 750 posted on top of the front door.

"Home sweet home!" shouted Don as he pulled up to the curb.

Frankie helped me out of the car and reached for the luggage. I was nervous and it showed on my face. Dana noticed and got out of the car. She hugged me, reassured me that I'd do fine, and added that she was but a breath away if I needed her. But I was not convinced.

"Say, y'all must be tired. Get some rest and we'll stop by later. I know y'all won't be cooking tonight. We can go to that cute place for dinner. You know the one, Frankie—the Italian restaurant! And we'll take y'all to do some grocery shopping," she added. The sound of her southern charm resonated easily in my heart.

"Sounds great. Thanks for picking us up! We should be ready by five," said Frankie, waving as they pulled away from the curb.

I could feel my stomach churning, yet I squeezed out a smile as Frankie reached for his keys and opened the screen door. Posted on the inner door was a sign that read: WATCH FOR SNAKES BEFORE STEPPING DOWN. Frankie laughed and tore the sign off the door. Although the note looked official, I thought it was a joke, someone jesting with a city girl. All I'd ever seen were squirmy worms, tiny lizards, and caterpillars. Frankie had not mentioned anything about snakes! Once I realized the note was not a joke, I was horrified.

"Honest, it's not that bad! Don and Dana will back me up. None of us have ever seen a snake! There are snakes in the river, but they don't travel on land. I'm not kidding!"

There was so much to learn about my new life. I was where I wanted to be, and there was nothing to be upset about. Setting aside my apprehension, I watched Frankie put the luggage into the trailer, and when he was done, he smiled and kissed me, then helped me step inside.

Although he'd prepared me well and I had immediately recognized the park when we arrived, I was taken aback by the interior. I was dumbfounded. The wall across from the front door where I was standing was almost in my face. Frankie kept smiling, waiting for a positive reaction, yet I was speechless. The trailer was much smaller than I'd imagined. He was correct: it was no bigger than the bedroom I'd shared with my sister.

To the right of the front door, at the far end of the trailer, was the couch. Directly across from the front door, against the far wall, was an area with barely enough room for a doll-sized table and two small chairs. To the left of the table was a counter, then the sink, and a stove. Miniature cabinets above the sink and under the counter had barely enough space to store more than two dishes and two glasses and a few small pans. There were two tiny drawers in the lower cabinet for silverware and dishtowels. Cookware would have to be stored in the oven.

Across from the stove was the refrigerator with a small food pantry on top. From the size of things, I knew we could not buy and store much food. To the left of the refrigerator was a narrow hallway with a closet on one side. Facing the closet was the bathroom—home to a tiny shower, a toilet, and a medicine cabinet. The sink was directly in front of the toilet, and I had the wildest vision that one could easily brush their teeth while doing their business.

The bedroom was located at the furthest end of the trailer. Directly under a window was a double bed that fit snuggly up against the wall. Next to the bed was a small end table with two drawers. Across from the foot of the bed was the back door. With no room for a dresser, I wondered where I'd store the items in my luggage.

"Are you okay?" he asked.

"Of course I am."

"I said it was small, but it's cozy, right?"

"Yes it is! I'm okay Frankie, honestly. I'm just wondering where we'll put everything!"

Frankie laughed. "Everything will find a place; it does for everyone. You'll see!"

I kept reassuring him that I was fine—and happy. I tried to smile, and not to look troubled. Between the note about snakes and the size of my new home, my feelings were difficult to disguise, and all Frankie's attempts to make me laugh failed miserably. While he continued to apologize, our home's tremendous size issue needed to be addressed quickly.

Frankie jumped in the shower and I plopped on the bed, staring at the wooden ceiling and thinking about the situation. I had some serious concerns. Where the heck am I? I wondered. We don't have a phone, a television set, not even a radio or a book. It didn't look as though I could hop a bus or a train and go to town. And I seriously wondered if the note about snakes had any validity. Was he afraid to admit it? I thought about my bike, my typewriter, and my mystery book and record collections. Where would I put it all? I would have to write and tell my mother not to send a thing except for tennis shoes, shorts, and summer blouses.

One thing I was sure of—we needed a radio. I would have sold my soul to be listening to the Platters singing "My Prayer." I wondered if I could find a place for my record player and my record collection, but from the looks of things, probably not. I knew we had to find room for a small radio. I made a mental note to call my mother and ask her to carefully pack my records and take them to California. Sadly, and for reasons never made clear, my records and record player never made it to California.

I was still lying on the bed, brooding silently, staring blankly at the wooden ceiling barely eight feet above me, when Frankie stepped out of the bathroom.

"Just wanted to tell you that I didn't make the bed. Dana did. She came by with sheets and a blanket, but we'll need some pillows. Talk about southern hospitality!" he added with a smile that stretched from ear to ear.

Bed sheets and blankets and pillows had not once crossed my mind. and I began to feel guilty. Frankie was deliriously happy. He'd planned well for my arrival, but here I was, nervous, anxious, and seriously lacking any excitement. However, he'd already adjusted to the tiny trailer. This was all new to me and in sharp contrast to my spacious home in Brooklyn.

"That was sweet of her," I said, hoping my voice did not reveal my concerns. "I'll thank her later!"

I collected my thoughts and set them aside. Frankie began to rummage around looking for a safe place to hide the wedding money. Most was in cash. I began to unpack the remaining items. Much to my surprise, I managed to find a home for two towels, two dishes, two coffee cups, as well as silverware, an old coffee pot, a small skillet, and a spaghetti pot. One thing was sure, there wasn't room for any shower gifts; they would have to travel to California. I placed the pretty nightgown MaryAnn had given me at my wedding shower on our bed and decided to chuck my sour attitude. We were together and worlds could collide for all that mattered.

I wondered about my beautiful blue traveling outfit—if I'd ever have an occasion to wear it again. I placed the suit and shoes in a small bag and stored them in the bottom of the closet.

At 5 o'clock Don's car horn sounded. I could not wait to get outside and stretch, hoping that going to dinner would greatly improve my mood.

We slipped into the back seat, and I immediately thanked Dana for making up the bed. She reached back, took hold of my hand, and smiled.

"Hon, it was the least we could do," she responded sweetly. "It's our wedding gift! You know, y'all remind me of myself! We got here right after we got married, and I freaked when I saw the trailer. I cried for days. But we found a place for everything. I was so upset and I wanted to go home to my mamma and the big house. But everyone here is friendly, and that helps. Y'all are gonna love it here, you'll see!"

Dana's quaint accent and her dripping-with-sweetness personality had a soothing effect on me. I felt as though I'd known her for years. She was right; I was missing home, the large white house, my adorable bedroom, and my siblings. I mostly missed my mother, my music and my friends.

The more she chatted, the more I relaxed. Actually, it felt good to be away from all the Italian drama. Don drove to a cozy Italian restaurant with red-and-white checkered tablecloths and several uniformed men enjoying dinner with their families. I'm not sure if it was the familiar food or the novelty of friendly southerners, but suddenly I felt fine. Calmness fell over me and I felt relaxed in this world of new experiences

After dinner, we drove to a shopping center. An eye-catching marquee with the names of various stores, including a market, had my immediate attention. Don parked the car, and we entered a gigantic market. I'd never seen anything like it, not in Brooklyn. The size was overwhelming. Everything anyone could possibly need under one roof—what a concept!

"God, how do you find anything, Dana? I've never seen so much stuff in one place!"

"Oh, this is a small store!" she said. "Wait till you see the PX and the commissary!"

I had no idea what we'd need. Luckily Dana led the way, strolling up and down every aisle confidently. Don and Frankie lingered behind, chatting as they walked. She kept tossing items she knew we'd need in a large cart, and I wondered where I was going to put the things she was selecting.

It was late when they dropped us off. We unpacked the groceries, stored the cold items in the refrigerator, and stacked the staples in the tiny pantry. Much to my surprise, we somehow found a place for almost everything, except for several homeless items left on the couch. Although I was still feeling anxious, by the end of that first night, I felt so much better.

When we were done, I showered, slipped into the pretty nightgown and slid into our cozy bed. Frankie turned off the tiny light on the nightstand. The moon was nearly full and shone brightly through the tiny window above our bed. I felt happy; we were home together.

An expensive honeymoon to an exotic island would wait for another time. The next few days in our little home was pure heaven. We spent endless hours talking, exploring the neighborhood, and walking through the woods and along the riverbank. Someone had given us a cookbook, and we began experimenting with recipes. It was then I discovered that Italian food was my only true forte.

Nestled between sunsets and sunrises, those first days and nights were paradise, as though our guardian angels had dropped us into a love nest.

I was aware that in a few days, Frankie would be returning to his military work world. And when the sound of the alarm clock announced his workday had arrived, it would be a wake-up call for me as well—the dawn of a new chapter in my life. For the very first time, I would be totally alone in a strange place, and I was completely unprepared.

With the sound of the alarm, Frankie quickly snapped out of bed. While he showered and shaved, I made coffee in our tiny percolator. And when he was ready for the day, we sat at the kitchen table, sipped coffee, and talked about things I could do during the day.

"If you get bored, walk over and see Dana—do some girl stuff together."

When Don's car horn sounded, Frankie kissed me and said he'd be home to help with dinner. He told me he'd think of me all day and asked me to think about him.

"I'll be thinking 'bout ya and how cute you look in fatigues *all day long!*" I said teasingly. "And see, I already know the lingo!"

From the tiny window above the couch, I watched until Don's car disappeared from sight. I felt strange in this quiet world. I needed some noise or sounds other than my own thoughts. Being without a radio and music made me feel off-center. It was even more troubling than the size of my living quarters. Music always lifted me; it was energizing. Frankie assured he'd bring home a radio, and I made up my mind to stop whining.

By mid-morning, the items left on the couch had been put away and everything was where it needed to be. By ten o'clock, the bed was made and everything was in place. I sat on the couch and wondered what I'd do for the remainder of the day when a knock at the door startled me. The sight of Dana's smiling face staring back at me chased away the doldrums; she was just what I needed. She told me to put on my shoes and she'd show me around.

Dana was a breath of fresh air and just what the doctor ordered. We walked up to the recreation hall, then to the post office, and then sat on the benches by the river. She told me about the park and added gentle gossip about the neighbors. When we were done, she invited me over to her place for lunch. Watching someone as young as Dana preparing lunch in her home awakened me to the reality, the nature of the role I'd accepted. I was no longer in my mother's home with her caring for my every need.

As promised, at 4:15 p.m. Frankie arrived home with a radio, and I quickly learned that having a radio and not having one was one and the same. There were only two stations broadcasting. One can imagine my disappointment when Frankie tuned in to the first station and all we heard were faint voices behind the annoying sound of static. On station number two, someone was strumming hillbilly music on a guitar. No rock and roll, no country music, no Elvis—nothing that held any possible interest. Music—or the lack thereof—was the one issue that strained at my serenity, yet I knew that somehow I'd have to come to terms with it.

By the end of the first week, I'd acclimated to the trailer and a world without music. Things had gone smoothly in spite of the strangeness of my new life. However, I'd gone through every outfit—some had been worn twice. Although Frankie had taken his soiled uniforms to the base laundry, a mound of dirty clothes, including the same two towels that we'd been using all week, lay in a mound in the closet. I remembered my mother changing bed sheets once a week. I remembered how she sorted laundry and washed our clothes in the basement. I remembered the washing machine. I stared at the pile of clothes and wondered how and where the women dealt with laundry . . . in the bathtub?

By the time Dana stopped by, I was close to tears. She listened, smiled, tore the sheets off the bed, gathered the stack of clothes by the closet, and plopped them into the laundry basket purchased during that first shopping trip.

"I'll carry the laundry—you get the soap and some nickels and follow me!" she said gleefully.

Dana walked towards a building with a large sign above the door that read: LAUNDRY ROOM. I had no idea there were public machines for laundry. The only familiar part of that scene was outside the building: clotheslines and bags of clothespins attached to a pole by the door.

By afternoon, the clothes had been washed, and the towels and sheets were happily flapping in the afternoon breeze. Later, I thought about my mother and how easily and lovingly she managed the preponderance of laundry for a large family. I made the bed and folded the towels—an amazing accomplishment for a new and inexperienced housewife!

By the second week, things began to fit better. Weather permitting, Dana and I would walk to the post office every morning and in the afternoon as well. Once a week she'd drive the guys to work and we would go downtown or to the commissary to shop. Buying fresh chickens in the chicken store or soup greens at the open markets in Brooklyn were now distant memories. Making shopping lists became my new way of life!

Dana introduced me to many of the wives we passed on our daily walks. I wasn't sure if it was my imagination, but in time I noticed some of them were avoiding me. They barely raised their eyes to greet me when we crossed paths. Dana told me it was strange behavior for southern gals and not to take it personally. She promised to get to the bottom of their peculiar behavior.

When a newlywed couple moved in across from our trailer, Dana suggested we welcome the new Marine wife to the neighborhood.

A petite, dark-haired young girl named Joan answered the knock on her door and invited us inside. She told us she was from Philly. Joan had an accent that sorta matched mine, and the familiarity of her Northeast flair made me think about home, my friends, my family.

Joan joined our walking group. In time I noticed the same faces that chose to ignore me were now greeting her. I shared this behavior with Joan and explained how unfriendly everyone was towards me. She was rather surprised and told me some of the housewives had already stopped by to welcome her, the same gals that had shied away from me.

A few days later Joan shared something she'd heard from one of the housewives in question. Laughing her way through the saga, she told me the housewives were afraid of me.

"They heard you're Italian, from Brooklyn, and that you probably belong to a gang and carry a switchblade. Get this—they think you have Mafia connections!" she added.

"Ya gotta be kidding! This is crazy," I blurted out.

When Frankie came home that night, I shared Joan's discovery.

"Hey, forget about them. Pick your friends and stand tall. They'll figure out you're not a mob wife. Who cares anyway? Most of these women are hillbillies with little education. Consider the source! Look at you—they're probably envious!"

I could not set it aside, and Frankie was no help. Taking matters into my own hands, I decided to topple their assumptions and lead those who feared me out of the darkness. I was hell-bent on making them aware I was not a gang member, nor did I carry switchblades in my purse. I began knocking on doors and introducing myself. At first they were startled, but once they heard my voice and looked into my eyes, their fears dissipated. And in time our walking group grew considerably larger.

With many friends to fill my days and Frankie in my arms at night, I was happy—we were happy. I also learned there were strong currents of change that might lift me from the comfort zone I'd settled into and rock our boat. I learned that life on base was unsettled the majority of the time. Marines were often transferred to bases far and wide, sometimes abroad. It had to do with training, the threat of war, and the inevitable duty rotations that often took place at a moment's notice—a reality that set me back on my heels.

Don and Dana were the first to leave. I'd known them six months when Don received his orders. By then the four of us had become very close: I felt as though I'd known them a lifetime. Saying goodbye was difficult. Dana had helped me through those first difficult days and weeks, and I knew I would never forget either of them.

As the days for their departure drew closer, watching Dana's demeanor taught me a lesson. She was at ease, and although she was sad about leaving her friends, she was looking forward to a new adventure. Her attitude helped me come to terms with transfers and relish friendships for the time we were together.

A touch of heaven

THANKSGIVING 1956

Be it war or special training, something was bound to disrupt the gentle peace and tranquility of our lives. It happened one afternoon when Frankie came home and announced he had weekend duty—Thursday through Monday of Thanksgiving week. We were newlyweds and this was our first Thanksgiving. Not being together did not settle with me.

"I really think you should go home for Thanksgiving. Your folks will be moving soon. This is a perfect opportunity to see them again. You can fly home on Wednesday and be back on Sunday. I don't think you should be alone for four days. Most wives go home; the park will be deserted."

As much as I wanted to see my family, I could not fathom being away from Frankie. His idea did not score any goals. Adding to the anguish was my fear of flying; the mere thought of it made my knees buckle. However, Frankie was convincing, and (reluctantly) I called home with the news. Frankie borrowed a car, and on the Wednesday morning before Thanksgiving, we left for the airport in New Bern. I cried as he drove to the airport, and my tears continued throughout the flight to La Guardia Airport.

My father met me at the airport sporting a warm smile. I could tell he was back to his old self; his embrace was warm as bread out of a toasty oven.

Thanksgiving Day was wonderful. My mother cooked turkey and lasagna; however, she did not serve mashed potatoes Americano style. Later MaryAnn and Joe stopped by to say hello and goodbye. Joe had signed up with the Army and would soon be leaving for Germany. As more friends and relatives stopped by, the house exploded with familiar sounds—my father's voice in song, the aroma of my mother's home cooked meals, and music and laughter—just like the old times!

On that last morning at home, the aroma of pot roast and onions braising on the stovetop had awakened me. Before long I would sit down with my family for an early *pranzo* and enjoy a togetherness that would not be repeated for many years. The moments of that day would leave a lifelong imprint on my mind—the last meal in our dining room in our cozy house on 72ⁿᵈ Street.

My mother fussed over the last details of Sunday dinner. Around noon, we were all seated in our usual places and all eyes were focused on my mother as she placed a large platter of pasta marinara in the center of the table. Knowing a new chapter in our family book was about to unfold, I gazed lovingly at the scene in that dining room and I embraced the melody of their voices. In a few months, they would move away and leave behind an ocean of memories. We would never again gather around that table in the dining room of the house we'd called home for so many years. And that extraordinary feeling of love and well being we had enjoyed through the years would rest gently as a fond memory never to be forgotten.

Saying goodbye was far more difficult than when I'd left in September. When it was time to leave, I hugged my sister and my brothers and fought back the flood of tears threatening to cascade down my face. As the car pulled away from the curb—for the last time—I glanced at the beautiful white house (the house my father painted every four years) the tall trees in front of the bedroom windows, the red brick steps, the homes bordering the avenue I walked along each day, and I silently promised myself to never forget the tapestry of life my parents had fashioned for their children in that home.

By the time we arrived at La Guardia Airport, I was trembling, and as I kissed my parents goodbye, I began to sob openly. I cried as the plane lifted off the runway. I cried as it began to cut through the puffy white clouds. I cried as we glided through the bright blue sky, and I never stopped crying until the plane landed in New Bern and I was staring into Frankie's bright blue eyes.

HAPPY DAYS

That winter, we decided to purchase a television set. Being entertained at night sounded like a great idea. We selected a portable model at the local Sears store. Much like what happened with the radio, our excitement was short-lived. There were only two channels, and both stations were on the air only part of the day. The programs were early talk shows, and the discussions were about tobacco and agriculture and local news. With no movies, no real news, no Dick Clark, the television set became an insignificant matter.

With the passing of time, the more we became familiar with each other, the happier we became. Love had entwined our lives like vines on a trellis. We were devoted to one another. Frankie didn't need "time with the boys," and I didn't need to buy the latest fashions. We were content just to be at home. We were in love, each day more than the day before and less than the next.

Frankie liked to dabble in cooking. Although he didn't have a picky appetite, he had his favorites and disliked fish. I was mostly familiar with Italian foods and struggled with American meals. Frankie taught me how to prepare his favorite meal—pasta with lima beans—and I loved that meal as well as he did. Some of the accomplished young cooks in the neighborhood also stepped up to the plate and taught me many basics of American cooking.

During the quiet times, while Frankie read a book or rested on the couch, his tenderness folded over me like a warm blanket on a cold night. I felt safe. And when he laughed or teased me or sang in the shower, the sparkle in his voice would reach deep inside me and energize my love for him.

Although we were young, we quickly learned the importance of expressing love. Frankie loved to snuggle, and I loved that part of him. He was never condescending, always looked at the bright side, and always had something sweet to say or share. At times I'd catch him looking my way, and I read love in his blue eyes—the windows of his heart. Pleasing Frankie came easy. We cuddled every chance we had, and I baked his favorite cakes and pies and cooked the meals he loved best, and he was always ready to help with chores. Worries and problems were not part of our lives. We hardly ever fought—well maybe once, and we spent two days making up. We were best friends—we were soul mates.

Perhaps it was Frankie's magnetic smile and jaunty personality that drew people close to him. Our circle of friends grew considerably. Some stood out above others. Within this special group of friends were Frances and Robert. We met them shortly before Don and Dana had been transferred. Frances quickly became part of our walking group, and Robert and Frankie became close friends. When Don and Dana left the base, Frances and Robert filled the void created by their absence.

They were both born and raised in Charleston, South Carolina, and had the deepest southern drawl I'd heard to date. Robert planned to make the military a career. He was a sergeant, a rank Frankie was working towards. Frances was a true southern gal with an effervescent smile and a warm heart to match her charming personality.

The following summer, Frances and Robert took leave and invited us to join them for a trip to Charleston to visit her family. Frankie and I were excited about our first real vacation. Just as we'd imagined, it turned out to be an incredible four-day adventure. We stayed in her parents' home and enjoyed southern hospitality in all its glory. Her mother, a flamboyant southerner with a Carolina drawl thick as golden honey, loved to cook, and introduced us to many of her favorites: southern fried chicken, grits, okra, biscuits and gravy, and southern style mashed potatoes.

Visiting our southern cousins was a memorable experience. We returned home rested and refreshed, with a greater knowledge of the South's colorful history and a lifetime of fond memories. Most memorable was the gracious hospitality of a southern family and the countless artifacts in Charleston's Historical Civil War Museum.

After our short but memorable vacation, Frankie and I returned to our normal routine: getting together with friends on weekends for leisurely car trips to Wilmington and other recreational areas, watching movies under the stars in the outdoor theater on base, and eating at the "It Drive-In" restaurant after paydays for yummy hamburgers—a twice-a-month treat we always looked forward to.

While I was busy settling into military life, my family moved to Montclair, California, purchased a new home on Orchard Street, and secured jobs for both parents close to home. My father was employed with the Pomona Tile Company, and my mother found work in a local dress factory. My siblings had easily adjusted to California and were attending local schools. Many of our cousins from Long Island also moved to California and settled in the same town. Some lived a stone's throw from my parents' house, and everyone loved life in sunny California.

My parents' circle of friends was larger than I'd imagined. Among this group of friendships was Sam Digati, "Mayor Sam" of Pomona, California. Along with his wife and children, Sam lived a few houses down the street. Sam's children were the same ages as my siblings, and the two families enjoyed a warm friendship.

Knowing they had acclimated well to California was reassuring. Now, more than ever, I was happy I had not joined them on their adventure. They'd adjusted well to their new life, and Frankie and I could not be any happier. Things do have a way of working out.

VIEQUES, PUERTO RICO

I had long recognized that a significant part of Frankie's happiness was tied to being a Marine. His focus was on earning the next rank. He spent endless hours studying, and he proudly earned the rank of E5.

By the beginning of the second year, I came to understand the dynamics of the Marine Corps and the training geared towards war efforts. Often training meant extended periods of time off site. For those stationed at Camp Lejeune, training maneuvers were often held in Vieques, Puerto Rico and lasted three to six months.

I found it curious how the Marines and their wives regarded the extended training. The men always looked forward to it, and their wives used this time as an opportunity to go home, visit friends, and enjoy their families. Frankie and I did not fit into those molds; we could not fathom any time apart from each other. Vieques became our nemesis, and we hoped that Frankie's name would somehow get lost in the shuffle.

I could always tell when training had been scheduled. Frankie would come home, and the dreaded Vieques training date list would take center stage in our conversation. Our discussion inevitably led to whether I should stay on base or go home. I always opted for staying on base. A trip home meant flying to California. Frankie did not want me to be alone, not even for the shorter three-month training. One thing was certain: at some point Frankie would be leaving for Puerto Rico. There was no escaping this eventuality.

It was ironic how things played out. Perhaps it was mere luck, or else someone from above was watching, someone who knew our destiny. By the beginning of Frankie's fourth year in the Corps, his name had not yet come up on the list. And as his discharge date drew close, we held our breath knowing the other shoe had to drop and soon. When the last scheduled Vieques cruise date within his enlistment period was announced and his name was absent, we celebrated; Frankie had beaten the odds.

During Frankie's entire four-year enlistment, to the amazement of his peers, Frankie escaped going to Vieques. In hindsight, I believe someone up above was granting us as much precious time together as possible!

THE PEDAL TO THE METAL

During spring of the second year, we decided to buy a car. Depending on friends to shop had gotten old, and we never went anywhere alone. Having spent very little of our wedding money, purchasing a car was clearly a sensible expenditure.

Due to the ongoing transfers, Marines often purchased cars from one another. Used automobiles on base were plentiful, although most were too pricey for our budget. Frankie called his brother Joey for advice. Once again Joey stepped up to the plate. He told Frankie he knew of a car, and the price was right—only three hundred dollars. He bragged about the car, told us it would make a perfect *first car*, and offered to make the trip to North Carolina for a front door delivery. It sounded ideal. Although buying a car *sight unseen* was not wise, we made a deal, and Joey told us he'd drive it down that weekend. The wait seemed like an eternity, and Frankie and I were on pins and needles for days.

My only relationship with cars had been the red-hot 1955 Ford Thunderbird convertible my friend Carol Pappas received for graduation, a sparklingly red car that had the vibe of a beautiful racehorse. Carol was my Greek friend from work, someone proud of her ancestry and even prouder of her new car. It was the dreamiest set of wheels I'd ever seen. I had to admit I was a bit envious.

On many evenings of that first school-free summer, Carol would pull up to the curb in front of my house, beep the horn of her proud ride, and wait for me to come bouncing down the path and slide in next to her. With the top down and the radio blasting at full volume, we would laugh and sing, and she'd rip through the streets of Brooklyn for a jaunt down the Belt Parkway—during that last glorious summer in Brooklyn.

"Frankie, did Joey describe the car? What about the color? I hope it's red!"

Other than the brand—an older model Plymouth—Frankie had few details about this car. Joey's assurance that the car was in good condition was all that mattered to Frankie. I was hoping for more . . . a red car would fit the bill nicely. More importantly, a car meant independence, and our conversations revolved around the places we could visit.

It was late Saturday afternoon when the beeping of a car horn signaled Joey had arrived. We practically jumped over one other to peek out the window above the couch.

Neither of us expected to see a car remotely resembling *classy*; however, the sight of our first car made our jaws drop. We were speechless and I felt like crying. The car, parked by the curb, looked like a turtle on wheels!

Our first car

"Oh crap, it looks like a pile of junk!" Frankie whispered under his breath.

We did not share our feelings with Joey. After all, we'd accepted the deal. It was hard to fault Joey, who'd taken the time to drive it down. To make matters worse, it had a manual transmission. I'd been dreaming about learning to drive, but that dream was suddenly shattered. I was not about to learn on a stick.

Joey continued to brag about the car, the great price, and that he'd encountered no problems on the drive south. With his assurance the car would give us a few good years of service, we thanked him, paid him, and after dinner drove him to the bus terminal for his trip home.

Once the bus disappeared down the deserted North Carolina highway, we turned to each other and laughed, wondering how odd we'd look on the base, home to far more stylish cars. But for now, the car was ours. It was at that very moment when the tone for our life with the car we had already named *the turtle* was set. The car would not start . . . our life with the turtle had begun with a loud thud.

The majority of cars on base were stylish, and many had automatic transmissions, including Don and Dana's car. Dana had assured me that learning to drive was easy. I'm sure she would not have uttered those words had she seen our car.

Frankie was confident that with his help I'd be able to learn to drive, yet my excitement dwindled with each passing day. The car had a laundry list of problems and had seen far better days. We were never able to hop in the car and drive away. It was completely unreliable, a transportation nightmare on its last leg.

The endless car problems brought major grief in our lives, and Frankie spent endless hours poking around under the hood. We feared being stranded on a lonely stretch of road, so we never ventured far from home. All the leisurely and romantic weekend drives we'd dreamt about were now on hold.

The humdrum color only added to our disdain for the turtle. Baby blue bored us to death. Some of Frankie's friends suggested a facelift, and with their help, the car was painted a dark shade of gray, almost black. Yet the new color did nothing for our spirits or for the car's reliability. It now looked like a dark turtle on wheels and remained stubbornly unreliable.

Despite all our car issues, Frankie decided to teach me the mechanics of the stick shift, and setting aside my negative feelings, I decided the time had arrived to learn to drive.

Only someone with a good nature could take on this driver-training project. As for me, learning to shift and parallel park in the Plymouth was a tall mountain to climb. Although my complaints and grumblings were endless, I was vigilant and practiced every night and on weekends. Although we shared the same frustrations with the car, including the cumbersome stick shift, Frankie never grew tired of my prickly patience. At some point, he decided that I'd learned as much as I needed to know about driving and told me I was ready to take the test. As far as I was concerned, my shifting and parallel parking skills were still very shaky.

On the day I was scheduled to take my driving test, Frankie had to jumpstart the car, and the sticky clutch was stickier than usual. It was the last straw, and I came close to changing my mind about the taking the test. With gentle prodding, Frankie convinced me the car would start and I'd do fine.

I was tense and nervous that morning, but after passing the written test, I was more at ease—until the instructor asked me to wait in the car. A moment later I watched as he began walking towards me and looking over the car apprehensively. I wondered what he was thinking. After he entered the car, he opened his pad and instructed me to start the engine and beep the horn. Thankfully the car started, the horn worked, and somehow I passed the test with no problems. The instructor looked relieved. As he exited the car, he told me he was going to pray the car died before anyone got in its way.

Frankie was proud of me. "Just think about it!" he said. "You fought the fight and passed the test. I'm proud of you—c'mon, give yourself some credit."

Although I had my license, I never drove the turtle. Aside from the sticky clutch and the car's unpredictability, I mostly hated to be seen in it, even when Frankie was driving.

All of our friends were aware of our disappointment with our car, especially Joe and Hilda. Six months after I'd taken my driver's test, Joe received transfer orders and decided to sell their car. They were well aware of our car problems, as well as our love for their red Chrysler convertible with an automatic transmission. When Joe and Hilda quoted a price—one too tempting to ignore—we didn't blink; we accepted. And although we were disappointed that Joe and Hilda were leaving, we could not deny that the day we purchased their car was one of the happiest days on that base.

The shiny red Chrysler was in amazing condition—not a dent, not a scratch, and best of all—no shifting! We were thrilled! I can honestly say we loved that car far more than we hated the Plymouth. She was a classic beauty, and we loved every red and silver speck of her body.

Stepping on the gas and pulling forward without needing a jump-start was pure heaven.

Weekends were fun. We never imagined a car could be so pleasurable. We would wake up early on Saturday morning, eat breakfast, and plunge into our agenda of washing and shining the car. Special care was given to the silvery chrome, the cloth top, and the leather interior. Weather permitting, we'd put the top down and go on long drives with our friends. It felt wonderful—like bending the bow, taking aim with an arrow, and hitting your target!

Our baby

AND THE CRADLE WILL ROCK

Frankie and I lived in a rainbow world of peppermint candy and chocolate ice cream—children living in an adult world. Most of our friends lived in the same world, although most were parents or soon-to-be parents. No one discussed birth control; albeit not many varieties were available back then, and no one seemed particularity concerned about conception.

It was only a matter of time until we would join the ranks of parenthood. When I missed my first period, I just wondered what had happened. When I missed the second month, Frankie made an appointment with a doctor. I had no clue about the dynamics of a woman's cycle, the male contribution, or the connection between my period, the egg, and the sperm.

When the doctor told us the due date was November 3rd, we were flabbergasted. We were pregnant and neither of us had any knowledge of pregnancy. As I'd done in the past, I would depend on my friends to fill in the gaps.

I continued to look forward to the morning walks with friends. One morning Frances knocked on the door and was surprised when I asked her if 'spotting' was normal. She panicked, immediately got hold of Frankie, and called an ambulance. In her frenzied state, while stepping out of her trailer, she fell down and broke her leg. When the ambulance arrived, Frances and I rode to the hospital together, knowing someday we'd laugh about that day and our doubled-up ambulance ride to the hospital.

Although I'd heard other women make references to miscarriages, in my mind, losing a baby was an anomaly, a rarity. As I lay in the hospital bed, the attempts made by the doctors to stop the miscarriage did not register. Later, when the doctor told us I'd lost the baby—we were stunned, unprepared for the sorrow that settled over us. After a short hospital stay, Frankie took me home. We cried and clung to one another, grieving deeply as the unexpected sadness quietly settled in our hearts.

It wasn't a huge surprise when the following year I learned I was pregnant and the baby was due on November 5th. Having been through a miscarriage, I was apprehensive. Frankie always looked on the positive side of life, and his peaceful demeanor always calmed my apprehensions. Once the fourth month came and went without an incident, I relaxed as well.

Since neither of us had a clue about the developing fetus, friends and Dr. Barnes became our mentors. The miracle growing inside me remained a wondrous mystery, and my lack of knowledge about pregnancy was obvious from the questions I'd ask.

As the days and weeks moved ahead and I grew in girth, we looked forward to the monthly doctor visits. During one of my early visits, I asked Dr. Barnes if the baby was breathing.

"Does it breathe through the belly button?" I asked.

He smiled and assumed I was jesting, but the look on my face noted otherwise, and he asked me to repeat my question.

"Have you read any books on the subject? What about your mother—has she discussed this topic with you?" he asked.

I laughed when he mentioned my mother, and I told him the subject of sex at home had been strictly forbidden. He shook his head disbelievingly.

"Tell you what, you are a good candidate for the Navy prenatal classes," he explained. "All your questions will be answered during the sessions!"

I could tell he was relieved when I agreed to sign up. I was excited about the classes. By the end of the first session, words such as the egg, the sperm, the fetus, the uterus, the fallopian tubes, and the birthing canal were imbedded in my mind. I learned the fetus was the term used for the baby, and the baby takes its first breath after being born. Dr. Barnes was pleased when I reported that my questions were being answered.

The classes were nothing less than amazing, especially the scenes of live births on a large screen. Much like a kindergartner sharing color drawings with parents, I'd rush home and share what I'd learned with Frankie.

Waiting nine months seemed like an eternity, but somehow we managed to glide through each month effortlessly. Frankie was attentive to all my pregnancy issues—my breathlessness, the unceasing indigestion, gas, hiccups, a belly larger than my chest, crumbs on my cleavage, and not being able to see my feet. And when stretch marks made their unsightly appearance, he told me he loved them as well.

I tried not to place too much importance on old wives' tales; however, I remembered my mother sharing one such fable with her pregnant friend: "Never raise your arms above your head or the baby will strangle!" Deep down I knew there could not possibly be any truth to this tale, yet I carefully avoided reaching over my head.

Frankie and I treasured each magical moment; the day-to-day nuances seemed like tiny miracles, especially that first flutter. And the kicks and endless hiccupping made us smile. Eating guilt-free ice cream and Frankie's attentiveness made up for any discomfort. With great anticipation, we were looking forward to the day the most important person in our lives—our baby—would be born.

Being away from home, I wasn't honored with a baby shower, nor were they commonplace events on base. According to the schedule I was given in my prenatal classes, the seventh month was the deadline for purchasing a baby layette.

One trip to the PX and we were all set. Considering the limited space in that trailer, a portable crib fit perfectly in the bedroom next to the bed, although it blocked the exit door. A day's supply of diapers could be stored in a cloth holder hung on the outside of the crib, blankets and baby clothes were stored under the baby bed, and baby care products were arranged neatly on top of the nightstand. It turned out to be just as Dana told me that first night—everything finds its place.

By October, Dr. Barnes was more than pleased about my weight—only nine pounds, a weight gain not acceptable these days, yet a prudent accomplishment during that era.

Although I'd attended all the prenatal classes, the labor process remained ambiguous. While young mothers shared their horror stories about labor and delivery, I listened and waited impatiently for that first bone-chilling stab of pain or the warm puddle of water to make an appearance.

HURRICANE HELENE

Due to the cold ocean waters in the North Atlantic, most storms lose force on their trek northward, so hurricanes in Brooklyn were a rarity. Only one storm broke the norm. It happened when I was approximately ten years old. Like most hurricanes, it began as a rainstorm, but as evening approached, the storm intensified. We hunkered down, excited by the sound of powerful winds and pounding rain. The storm raged through the night. My father's biggest concerns were for the 100-year-old tree in front of our house and the blueberry tree in the center of our front lawn. Thankfully both escaped the storm's wrath. By morning the sun was shining and we began walking through the storm-ravaged neighborhood. While many large trees were strewn across sidewalks and streets, some had fallen on homes. Luckily our trees and our house escaped harm.

Eastern North Carolina is a major target for hurricanes. I was in my eight month when a feisty storm named Helene came huffing up the coast. When it was over, it was classified as the most intense storm of the 1958 season.

As the storm's intensity increased, the base was placed on alert.

Everyone at Camp Knox was advised to prepare for a possible evacuation.

Storm calculations predicted the storm was due to arrive in Camp Lejeune the following day. The pounding rain on the tin roof and the howling winds made it difficult to sleep that night. In the morning, we packed and prepared for a possible evacuation. When Frankie left for work, he told me he'd be home by mid-morning. By ten o'clock, MPs were cruising up and down the streets and announced an evacuation was

197

eminent. When Frankie came home, he tossed the overnight bag into the back seat and helped me into the car.

The winds were fierce, and merely getting into our car was worrisome. The storm could have easily torn apart the cloth top and tossed us into the open tempest. Since the trailer was not cemented into the ground, the winds could have easily flipped it over. Traveling in our car to safety seemed like the lesser of two precarious situations.

We rode in a caravan to an evacuation site readied by the Red Cross. There were approximately two hundred evacuees, and everyone was given a flashlight, pillows and blankets. Cots were set up on one side of the room, with a makeshift kitchen area with long tables for meals on the other side. Along with two other pregnant women and their husbands, Frankie and I settled on cots close to the nurse's station located in a secluded corner of the large room. We were assured that, in the event of an unexpected special delivery, they were well equipped.

Once the doors were secured, everyone settled in by their cots. Before long the sounds of voices and laughter from children reverberated through the large room and drowned out the clamor of the violent storm outside. In some strange way, there seemed to be safety in numbers. Certainly God would not bring harm to such a happy crowd!

The Red Cross had readied a variety of food—sandwiches, fruit, cookies and milk for lunch, and coffee in large urns. For dinner they served hot dogs, potato salad, corn, and plenty of fruit. The foods were not particularly healthy, but it was fun on that stormy night.

That evening, the storm had greatly intensified. The howling winds and pounding rain on the roof of our safe house kept sleep at bay. By 10 o'clock, except for an occasional cry from a frightened child and the flickering restrooms lights, the room was dark and silent. As the storm thrashed about, Frankie and I lay snuggled side-by-side on separate cots for another long, sleepless night.

By morning the storm had puffed its way north, and we were awakened by the wonderful aroma of strong, hot coffee. A breakfast of oatmeal, orange juice, and sweet rolls had been prepared. Soon the men began opening the large doors to check on their cars. We worried about our car; a cloth top could be helpless against a powerful storm. We also wondered how our trailer had weathered the storm and what damage we'd encounter on the way home.

Thankfully our little car had weathered the storm beautifully. On our way home we noticed many large trees had been tossed on cars and houses and across many streets and roads. The storm had caused major damage, and we were expecting to see the same destruction at home.

Camp Knox looked like a war zone. Many of the beautiful pines were no longer upright. Fortunately our home escaped harm, although one large tree had fallen on a trailer directly across the street. We were mostly thankful that I had not gone into labor and that no one was hurt.

AND BABY MAKES THREE

After what seemed like an eternity, Frankie and I welcomed the month of November and looked forward to meeting the baby we already loved. In many ways we were prepared, and yet in some ways we were not. The horror stories I'd heard about labor were suddenly front and center in my mind. I was both skeptical and apprehensive. Being tired and anxious and ready to hold the tiny wonder that lay within me in my arms, great pain and discomfort would be worth it.

During our last visit to Dr. Barnes, we were told the baby was over seven pounds and labor could begin at any time. He also told us about another option—inducing labor. He told us the baby's weight was sufficient enough to make it a safe procedure.

"Sometimes a baby needs a gentle nudge to get them to leave their comfortable nests!"

Just as he'd done in the past, he explained the process and suggested we give it serious thought. Dr. Barnes also recommended long walks.

"Get plenty of rest. One way or another, your baby will be here soon," he added. "Hopefully you'll go into labor without any help!"

The weather decided not to cooperate. Pounding rain all weekend made walking impossible. By Monday morning, I was ready to give the baby the gentle nudge Dr. Barnes suggested. After calling him with our decision to induce, Frankie placed my bags in the car and we headed to the hospital.

When we arrived, Dr. Barnes was already waiting, and I was immediately assigned a room. After I was prepped for delivery, Dr. Barnes broke the water and told me to walk until I felt some discomfort.

Frankie and I walked up and down the corridors, visited the nursery, and marveled at the precious babies with scrunched up faces in blue and pink bassinets. The reality that the baby growing inside me would soon be sleeping in a tiny bassinet in that nursery was mind-boggling.

Before long, the first contraction struck with a punishing force. The nurse checked my vitals, sent Frankie on his way, and started an IV. I quickly realized the excruciating pains described by other mothers were not in the least bit exaggerated. Dr. Barnes added a "cocktail" to the IV, and his smiling face was the last thing I remembered.

Four hours later, I awoke to the sound of a familiar voice and my name being whispered in my ear. It was Frankie urging me to wake up. I felt him close by, and I could feel his hand in mine. As I began to focus, I could see his blue eyes looking into mine, and the sparkle told me we had been blessed with a baby.

"Can you hear me? We have a baby, a pretty little girl!" he whispered. "She's beautiful. It's unbelievable! I can't wait until you see her!"

There are few more intensely moving moments in life than when you meet your newborn baby for the first time. Frankie had already experienced that moment. He'd seen her. He knew what she looked like, if she was healthy, how much she weighed. He'd already met our new love.

"She has lots of dark hair," he said. "Not sure about her eyes—they're still closed and puffy. I can't believe it—she's so beautiful!"

Frankie wanted to stretch out beside me, but he decided to tell the duty nurse I was awake. Although I was still groggy, the excitement in his voice was a shot of adrenalin. Frankie's enthusiasm was always contagious.

A few minutes later, a smiling nurse carrying a tiny bundle with a pink cap on a tiny head came bouncing into the room. The moment the nurse placed her in my arms, I cried. I cried because she was healthy. I cried because her eyes briefly opened and she looked into mine. I cried because the aroma of our newborn baby was intoxicating. I wanted to hold her forever, but I shared her with Frankie and watched as he gently kissed her pretty pink cheeks.

I wanted to see more of her, and I began unwrapping the layers of coverings. I needed to see her tiny toes, her tiny ears, and precious little round bottom. We wondered what the black crusty bow on her tummy was all about—one more question for Dr. Barnes!

We named her Theresa Marie, after St. Theresa the Little Flower; my confirmation name. She was a precious little flower, and we immediately nicknamed her Teri.

Dr. Barnes asked if I planned to nurse. I'd never seen a nursing mother. I wasn't aware that women still breast-fed their babies, except in third world countries. It was something I perceived as archaic, and I answered no. Mixing formulas into sterilized bottles was all I've ever seen in my childhood home. Breastfeeding seemed barbaric.

My hospital roommate's baby had been born just a few hours before Teri. We began to chat, and soon a nurse arrived and placed the baby in her arms. I watched as she lowered the top of her nightie and placed the baby to her breast. I'd never seen a baby nurse before. Both baby and mom looked so content. When the nurse left, my roommate smiled and asked me to reconsider nursing. She looked so happy. While her baby nursed, she filled me in on the benefits of mother's milk. Suddenly it seemed so natural, so beautiful, so endearing. When the nurse returned, I told her I'd reconsidered and wanted to nurse. She smiled at me, told me I'd made a wise decision and that she would make arrangements for a lactating nurse to visit.

By the beginning of the third day, I was up to speed on nursing and ready to go home. Frankie had taken a two-week leave. He had gone shopping, and our tiny abode was ready to welcome its newest resident.

From the very start, one could best describe me as a nervous mother. When Teri cried, I cried. When she didn't nurse, I worried and fretted. I wanted my mother. I desperately needed her comfort and advice. I wanted her to meet her first grandchild, but she refused to travel. She suggested I bring Teri to California, an idea that greatly angered me.

The first two weeks were unsettling. Teri wanted to nurse often, but we were instructed to feed her at four-hour intervals—not any sooner. Teri introduced me to projectile vomiting. It didn't take long for paranoia to set in. I assumed something was wrong. But Teri had her own schedule—small meals and catnaps. Frankie had his hands full consoling me, pacing the floor with Teri in his arms, hoping she would sleep for longer periods of time. To make matters worse, the anger towards my mother began to fester.

As neighbors began to stop by, the young but experienced mothers quickly came to my rescue. Their suggestions were priceless: stop listening to the doctor's senseless advice, including my baby bible: Dr. Spock's famous book of outdated information.

"Feed your baby when she gets hungry—every two hours, sometimes sooner," they advised, and I listened.

It took a few more weeks before Teri began sleeping and eating for longer periods of time. Life was on track, and we were finally enjoying our new baby.

To my great disappointment, the projectile vomiting continued, and Dr. Barnes suggested I place her on formula. Thankfully, the formula also improved her sleep pattern. Once I settled into the formula preparation process (now easier than when my brother Tony was born), I began missing the closeness of a nursing baby.

When Teri was two months old, Frankie's mom and Aunt Lilly came to visit. Although they were forced to stay at a local motel, having them with us was a real treat. With seven children of her own, Mary was a tremendous help. We enjoyed their visit, and by the time they left, I felt like an ole hand at mothering. A few months later, Frankie asked his brother Chuck to christen Teri, to be her godfather. He gladly accepted and did the honors. It was great seeing him again and sharing our joy with him.

Christening Day: me, Chuck, and Teri

As the days gently folded into weeks and months, each day was filled with precious moments. Frankie came home every afternoon at 4:15, except now Teri was his priority. He was far more anxious to hold her than to help me prepare dinner.

"So what happened today? Did she do anything new?" he'd eagerly ask and wait to hear about our day.

To Frankie, any development was a spectacular event. And while he played with her, I'd share my day with Teri. When he was home, they were inseparable. He took her on walks or would play with her on a blanket under a tree. Sometimes I'd find them fast asleep on our bed, a sight that filled my heart with incredible joy.

Having her crib snuggled close against our bed was especially endearing. Sometimes we'd lie quietly on our bed and watch as she slept soundly in her crib. The sound of a newborn tugged at our hearts. One of my fondest memories happened many months later when we awoke one morning and found her standing in her bed watching *us* sleep.

One afternoon Frankie came home with a surprise. He'd gone shopping and purchased a baby walker. I wasn't sure about this apparatus. I'd never seen one before, and Teri was much too little to sit in it. I wasn't sure it was safe. But he was excited and figured out how to prop her safely into the seat. Her tiny hands immediately grabbed onto the front bar. Her feet were far from the floor, and all she could do was kick wildly in the air and giggle. Frankie would scoot her back and forth in the tiny area between the couch and the kitchen. Months later, when her toes finally touched the floor, she began thrusting forward on her own.

Around five months of age, Teri's first tooth made its appearance, as well as a stubbornness and determination to have her way. She was ready for cereal but wanted no part of metal or plastic parts in her mouth. The doctor suggested making the nipple hole larger and mixing the cereal with her formula. She could then drink this concoction easily from the bottle she loved passionately! We did and Teri was happy.

We had no idea how wonderful life would be with a baby. Each day, packed with new adventures, was a miracle. At night, after she fell sound asleep, Frankie would tell me how happy he was with our little family. On some nights, with only the gentle light of the moon shining in that tiny bedroom, we would stare at the tiny heart in the crib by our bed, knowing we were truly blessed.

Years later I would remember those wonderful months, the deep happiness we felt in our hearts, and I'd wonder if it was only a fleeting illusion of passing time.

BACK AT THE RANCH

As with all things in life, one moves on, and I let go of the angst towards my mom. Calling home remained a weekly priority, one that now included all the adorable niceties about life with Teri, and in turn we were brought up to date about their lives. We learned how everyone had settled in comfortably in California, and everyone was happy. My mother spoke kindly of their Italian friends. And from her words, I imagined that neither she nor my father missed Brooklyn. I was happy and proud of them. I learned my father now had a car and a driver's license—an amazing accomplishment for a man who barely spoke English.

Lena and Giuseppi Scarcella

My siblings were maturing by leaps and bounds. During one of our conversations, my mother told me my sister Rose had married a Navy Corpsman and was living on a base in Bremerton, Washington. The news came as a complete surprise. Rose was only fourteen when I left home. It was difficult to imagine her as a military wife living away from home. I hoped she'd be able to travel home when we arrived in California.

Rose attending Beauty College

My mother told me Joe had a job in the local market, as well as a girlfriend. She shared her concerns about Joe's relationship with this girl and told me the teachers were concerned as well.

Pat and Joe—forever in love

And last but not least was Tony. I learned that Tony was very happy and had many friends. Keeping with the family tradition, he loved music. Luckily, Tony was still young and was not adding drama into their lives.

Young Tony, maestro in the making

It made me happy to hear that everyone had acclimated well and were enjoying a less stressful life, a good life, a far healthier lifestyle. At times I felt detached and homesick.

For my father, living in California was a godsend. He felt great, was thankful for his job, and was especially thrilled with the mild climate, one that closely emulated the weather in Sicily. I imagined he missed living close to the ocean, as well as his beloved fish market, but my mother assured me he was very happy. His only disappointments were his failures at wine making. Without the coolness of a wine cellar, the grapes that grew abundantly close by could not ferment properly and inevitably turned to vinegar.

Frankie and I knew so little of California outside the word pictures my mother had created. Her euphoric descriptions about the weather, the flowers and trees, and the beautiful snowcapped mountains fueled a desire to begin planning for our trip to the Golden State. A few months before Frankie was due to be discharged, we contacted the Automobile Club for maps. As much as Frankie loved the Marine Corps, he never spoke about reenlisting. In hindsight, had he reenlisted and requested a transfer to Camp Pendleton, our lives would have taken a different path.

Mom and Dad and California grapes

Although my mother had painted a vivid picture of this warm and sunny place they now called home, I had a gut feeling she was not as enamored with California as the rest of the family. I sensed she missed her beloved *Brukolino*. How could she not? She was no longer able to hop on a bus, a train, or the trolley at will. Although they owned a car, she did not drive and had to wait for weekends to shop with my father. I sensed she probably missed her independence, including our shopping jaunts to Fulton Street.

She described their new home on Orchard Street as very modern, with tiny rooms in comparison to our spacious Brooklyn house. She told me the backyard was large and my father had planted fruit trees as well as his beloved basil and mint plants. She described the lemon orchards barely a breath away from their house and told me during springtime the fragrance from the blossoms would drift through the neighborhood, as did as the voices of fruit pickers singing cultural melodies.

I learned that Montclair, California was located thirty miles east of Los Angeles, close to the foothills of Mt. Baldy, a winter ski resort in the San Gabriel Mountains, and the snowcapped mountains could be seen from their front door.

When I was a child, I was often roused from sleep by a frightening and recurring nightmare, one in which I was tumbling into a large crevice and drifting aimlessly into a dark void. My screams would awaken my mother. To calm my fears, she would assure me there were no earthquakes in Brooklyn. That nightmare haunted me through high school. After Frankie and I got married, the daunting dreamscape vanished, only to reappear on our way to California. *A premonition?* I wondered.

COUNTDOWN TO D-DAY

As each day fed seamlessly into the next, the time to leave for California was quickly approaching. Our thoughts and conversations were mostly about the trip, traveling with a baby through the blistering heat of the Mohave Desert. At times, I'd feel melancholic. I would glance around to what had been our home for three years, and I began to imagine that in spite of the size, I would miss our cozy trailer.

The countdown was on, and we spent many sleepless nights wondering about the trip, about life in California. Frankie bought a small towing trailer, and the Auto Club mapped out the trip from Camp Lejeune to Montclair. Every night we'd review the route, noting the motels on the way, jotting down the phone numbers to make advance reservations. Never having stayed in a motel, the trip now seemed like a grand adventure. The thought of crossing the Mississippi River was especially captivating. Its history had always captured my imagination.

By August, Teri would be nine months old, eating solid food, and possibly walking. We gave serious thought to the diaper situation. Although disposable diapers had evolved worldwide, word had not spread to the base, and we were not aware. Tossing soiled diapers along the way was our only option.

While pondering about our trip and waiting for August to arrive, on an early June morning we were startled by a firm knock on the front door. It was not the friendly knock from friends and neighbors. Frankie peeked out the window.

"Hmmm, there's an MP with a kid outside!" he whispered and cautiously opened the door.

"Good morning. We found this young man wandering around. He said his name is Joseph Scarcella, from California, says he knows you, but he doesn't have any ID. Can you identify him?"

"Oh my God! Yes, he's my brother!" I screamed, stepping in front of Frankie to claim him.

Satisfied that the young man's story was legitimate, the MP left him in our charge. One can only imagine the shocked look on our faces. It took a few moments longer to sort out what had just happened—my 16-year-old brother was standing on our doorsteps, three thousand miles away from home. I barely recognized him. Joe had grown taller since I'd last seen him. He needed a shave, and his hair was darker and much wavier. I could hardly believe my eyes. Joe had grown up—he was a man.

We were anxious to know what was going on, why my parents had sent him to North Carolina, how he had made his way across the country. Joe stepped inside, and after a few hugs, we learned that my mother told him we needed help on our trip home and bought him a ticket.

"Well, I'm glad you're here, but this makes little sense. I never told her we needed help. Why didn't she tell me she was sending you?" I asked.

"I think it has more to do with my girlfriend Pat. Mom's been trying to break us up. She thinks we're too young!"

"But this is wild! How did you manage to find your way to the base with no ID?" Frankie asked.

"When I got off the bus in Jacksonville, I hitched a ride to the base. The guy let me off by the front gate, and I walked over to the guard shack!"

"Hitched a ride? That so dangerous," I admonished. "You're lucky you made it safely. What the heck is wrong with Mom?"

I could not stop looking at him. It was a strange sight to behold: my brother, three thousand miles from home, sitting on our couch.

"What about this girlfriend?" I asked. "Mom said the two of you are always together and even the teachers were complaining. Is she exaggerating? What's going on?"

"Well some of her story is true. Mom's worried because we spend a lot of time at Pat's house. Her mom doesn't mind when we watch television in their living room. I can't invite Pat to our house to watch TV. Mom and Dad would not understand. So Mom's solution was to put me on a bus to North Carolina. She's hoping I'll forget about Pat, but that's not gonna happen!"

Suddenly the sound of a tiny voice calling "Momma, Momma" startled Joe.

"Hey Joe, that's your niece!" I said.

Joe stood up, smiled. I could tell the tiny voice had startled him. He followed me into the bedroom, and when he saw her, he called her by name. Teri looked my way as though she needed permission to look at him.

"Hey little girl, meet your Uncle Joe!" Much to my surprise, she returned his smile, and when he reached out to her, she went to him willingly.

After breakfast Frankie and I turned our attention towards making Joe as comfortable as possible. His backpack found a home under the dining room table. Other than the worn sofa he was sitting on and food, there wasn't much more we could offer. Thankfully Joe didn't seem to mind and told us the trailer looked like a fun place to live in.

Frankie and I soon realized how much we loved having Joe with us, and Teri loved her uncle as well. It didn't take long to realize that having another person on a cross-country trip would be advantageous.

Joe loved our red car, thought it was cool. During the day we'd put the top down and drive around the base or downtown. Joe was easy to please, went with the flow, and didn't seem to mind the hot, humid weather or the armies of hungry mosquitoes.

By the time August rolled around, we were packed and ready for our long-awaited trip. With three years of wonderful memories packed in our hearts and a trailer hitched to the back of our car, we were ready to embark on our cross-country adventure.

The goodbyes to my family and friends at Thanksgiving were still fresh in my mind, as were the farewells to the many friends we met and loved for short intervals of time, those transferred to other bases. I now found myself avoiding goodbyes like the plague. When friends left, I'd cry for days. Now it was our turn to say goodbye. I'd asked everyone not to show up that morning, yet some ignored my request, others stood by their front doors and waved as we drove past. I knew I'd probably never see any of them again. I was sure I'd miss the many wonderful friendships we'd made.

Towing a fully packed trailer, we began the long journey. Frankie was the main driver, Joe rode shotgun, and Teri and I settled comfortably in the backseat. For the last time, we drove past the guard shack and down the road that led us away from the base. Once we left Jacksonville, the sadness of our goodbyes fell away.

The Auto Club had mapped out the shortest route—west to Tennessee and Arkansas. In Oklahoma, we would link up with the mother road—the historic US Route 66—and continue westward.

We drove during the day, and in the evening we stopped at motels where we'd made reservations. The Mohave Desert was still days away, and worries about the heat were only fleeting thoughts. Our focus remained on getting to California no matter what obstacles or problems we encountered along the way.

On our journey, we marveled at the uniqueness of each state. Many sights remain with me today, especially the grace and beauty of the weeping willow trees in Louisiana—how relaxing I imagined it would be to sit under their long, sweeping branches on hot summer days. I marveled at the historic Mississippi River, the navigation route for barges and steamboats, the river that inspired the fictional writings of Mark Twain. Suddenly history came alive. Nature had worked incredible wonders in the Ozarks by carving deep valleys with scenic rivers and lakes, and cozy log cabins had been built to enjoy the peaceful ambiance. When we reached Texas, we drove past oil wells and windswept prairies. We witnessed native prairie inhabitants, as well as herds of buffalo grazing on a sea of grasses and wildflowers.

It was in Amarillo, Texas when the glow of a happy trip came to an abrupt end. The car overheated, and the charm of all the new sights we'd enjoyed along the way instantly vanished. Frankie pulled into a local gas station, and the mechanic told us we needed a new fuel pump; however, a replacement part for that model car would have to be ordered. And after listening to the engine, he told us the transmission was also failing, probably due to the weight of the trailer.

The news watered down our enthusiasm. Base mechanics had looked over the car before we left and replaced what was needed. Every detail had been attended to. No longer surrounded by the trustworthy Marines, we wondered if the mechanic was being honest. Still, the car had overheated, and we had heard a strange sound while driving.

We eventually concluded that most likely the weight of the trailer had damaged the transmission.

Not far from the gas station was a small motel. We checked in, turned on the air conditioner, and considered our options. Only one made sense: purchase another car and continue on our trip. Thankfully, most of our wedding money was still in the base bank, but all our dreams of using the money for a down payment on a house would have to be put aside.

We decided how much we could afford for this unexpected expenditure, and Frankie and Joe went to a local used car lot. While the salesman called the bank to verify our account, Frankie picked out a car, one that could pull the trailer with ease.

Keeping in mind that the destination was the goal and not the journey, we dismissed the sadness about leaving behind our beloved red car, lunged forward, and never looked back. The following morning, we were back on the road with a newer car: a `55 Chevy. Although it was a stick shift and pale beige color did nothing for me, I looked at the positive side; we no longer needed to worry about the blistering desert heat of the Mojave—air conditioning would keep us comfy.

We left Texas and headed west towards New Mexico, the land of enchantment, a uniquely beautiful state with a rugged landscape of mountains, canyons, cliff dwellings, and exotic plant life. It was in New Mexico where I was introduced to the magnificent Saguaro cactus, an all-too-human shaped plant, each with a personality of its own. The scenery was mesmerizing, rich with Indian and southwestern culture and soil so red it looked unreal. This was our first taste of the west, and the stunning portrait of color and history has remained with me through the years.

By the time we reached the Mojave Desert, all of Joe's warnings regarding the blistering heat turned out to be true. It was murderously hot. And if there was any beauty to behold, we never came across any such sight. I was expecting sand dunes, like those in the Sahara, but there were none—only dried up scrubs and tumbleweeds. While seeking coolness, we enjoyed a brief respite as we drove in the shadows cast from low mountains. However, Frankie remained cautious, and from time to time he would turn off the air conditioning. An overheating problem in the desert would have been disastrous, especially for Teri.

After four days of driving, we were thrilled when a highway sign read: WELCOME TO ARIZONA. We were almost home. When we arrived in Yuma, Frankie drove into the last motel on our list. After showering, we ate and slept soundly knowing the next day Teri would meet her grandparents.

CALIFORNIA DREAMIN'

On the last day of the trip, we woke up before dawn, enjoyed an early breakfast, filled up the car with gas, and forged onward. Sometime after lunch the sight of a large sign in the distance caught our attention. Frankie drove faster until the sign became clearer: WELCOME TO CALIFORNIA. California, a place we knew little of and yet a lot of. The sign resonated like a splash of cold water on our hot faces. Joe told us that in approximately two hours, we'd be cruising down Orchard Street just in time for dinner.

California welcomed us on that first day with a flawless sky, brilliantly tinted in the deepest shade of blue I'd ever seen, a color so vibrant that looking up for more than a moment was mesmerizing. We had driven across many mountains, yet the brilliant shades of red and gold painted on the San Bernardino Mountains now held my complete attention. Soon we were driving past quaint homes with perfectly manicured lawns, gardens splashed with colorful flowers, and streets lined with tall palm trees. It looked like a scene out of a movie. California was beautiful, just as everyone had described, and I dared not blink fearing I'd wake up and we would still be in North Carolina or Brooklyn.

While driving past the tall mountains and through the quaint towns with romantic street names, I fell in love with California. Via Santa Maria, Camino de la Luz, Via Santa Margarita—Spanish names that easily rolled off my lips. Nothing resembled Brooklyn with its numbered streets and unemotional names—42nd Street, Canal Street, Fulton Street, and Wall Street. California planted itself deep in my heart. This was home. This was where I wanted to live.

Joe called home and told them we'd be there in a few hours. And when at last we arrived in Montclair, my eyes locked on the larger-than-life marquee of an outdoor drive-in theater that claimed the full corner of an intersection. There were no drive-in movie theaters in Brooklyn, and in comparison, the outdoor movie screen on the base now seemed pathetic. On the backside of the projection screen was a magnificent multi-hued scene that captured the essence of old California and the southwest, a vibrant work of art.

I'd written "Orchard Street" on countless envelopes, but when I caught sight of the words on a street sign, my heart began to pound. And when we drove past the lemon groves my mother had described, I knew we were home. Joe directed Frankie to make a u-turn and park in front of the mint green house across from Monte Vista Elementary School. Except for the color, it looked like every other house on the street. Frankie pulled up to the curb, and Joe reached over and beeped the horn.

They were expecting us, probably watching out of the large front window. And when the front door opened and my parents appeared, I could hardly believe my eyes. They were beautifully tanned and looked far healthier then the last time I'd seen them. It didn't take long for Teri's name to echo through the air . . . *Theresa, Theresa* . . . as she would be called. Right behind them was Tony, much taller, very tanned, and absolutely adorable.

Mom and Dad awaiting our arrival on Orchard Street

Tony and friend

There is no such thing as a subdued greeting in the Sicilian culture. I'd already envisioned the arrival scene and how it would play out. My mother quickly opened the back door of the car. With no seat belts to tangle with, Teri was immediately in her arms.

"Theresa, dami un vasso . . . give me a kiss," she bellowed out in her native Sicilian dialect. Teri obliged, reaching over to kiss her grandmother and then her grandfather.

Teri had never been around emotional people. I worried that a sudden avalanche of emotions might be overwhelming and she'd be frightened. Surprisingly, Teri seemed to enjoy the rush of excitement.

While my parents took full control of their granddaughter, Frankie and Joe reached for our bags, and we walked up the curved path into the house. They'd never sent pictures of the house, and the only images I'd conjured up in my mind came from their descriptions. Seeing the house in person was a surprise, clearly one-third the size of our Brooklyn home but in the modern style of the early sixties.

With Teri in her arms, my mother led the way to a tiny bedroom where a bed and a crib had been set up. Soon we were back in the dining room—a familiar scene with an added attraction: a highchair for their first grandchild and Italian cookies and milk waiting to be enjoyed. Hearing all the familiar voices warmed my heart. I realized how much I had missed everyone. Our separation was over now, we were together, and I was happy. Only one person was absent—my sister (and her family), and I hoped she'd visit soon.

The dining room, although smaller than the one in Brooklyn, was warm and colorful, filled with a familiar energy. So much had changed, yet many things remained the same—my father seated at the head of the table, everyone speaking at the same time, my mother busy in the kitchen, and the aroma of her cooking stirring everyone's appetites. As I drank in the ambiance, I suddenly felt safe and loved, as I did when I was young. A feeling of joy and love of family fell over me, something heavenly, like a gift from an angel refreshing me with a breath of a new life.

It was no surprise that the commotion had traveled to the home of their neighbors Louise and Bob. They'd been caught up in the anticipation of our arrival as well. The curbside clamor rallied their attention, and after allowing us time to settle in, Louise and Bob knocked on the back door, and my mother invited them inside.

Bob and Louise were the first Californians we'd meet. They were charming. Although they didn't understand the Italian language, they somehow understood my parents and accepted the warm friendship this colorful Italian family offered—as well as my mother's tasty meatballs and all the pasta they could eat. In time Louise and I became close friends.

I loved the quaintness of the little house with modern gadgets and appliances, especially the kitchen with a built-in oven and cook top, Formica counters, an automatic washing machine, a stylish refrigerator, and a garbage disposal, the latter an appliance I was completely unfamiliar with. My mother bragged about her new automatic washing machine, a far cry from the wringer-type machine she'd used in Brooklyn. My mother had been lifted out of the dark ages. I'd never been in a house with two bathrooms and an area in the back called a patio! Their tiny house was cozy, colorful, and contemporary.

A knock on the door sent Joe scrambling to the front of the house. One moment later, Frankie, Teri and I were introduced to a very pretty young lady, Joe's girlfriend Pat.

Over the next days and weeks, an endless stream of friends and family stopped by to meet us. It was clear their friends in California outnumbered those in Brooklyn.

With each passing day, California's charm settled deeper in our hearts. We loved everything about the west, especially the dry Santa Ana winds that turned Teri's cheeks into ripe red apples and dried the dampness out of bones. The beautiful snowcapped mountains visible from the front door created a fascinating attraction, and the fruit trees, mint-lined paths, and sweet basil in my father's garden had the familiar appeal of his Brooklyn garden. We would have to wait for springtime to hear the fruit pickers singing in the nearby orchards.

New words entered my vocabulary: patios, freeways, and garbage disposals. But the biggest surprise was parked in the garage—my father's car. I wondered how he could possibly have passed the driver's test and was now driving down streets and highways. It was a chilling image!

Teri acclimated easily to her new surroundings—the endless commotion and her doting grandparents. She especially loved her Uncle Tony, who never tired of playing with her. And when Teri wasn't with her uncle or sitting on my father's shoulders, my mother engaged her with a platter of cookies or a bowl of refreshing ice cream.

Although Teri was eating table foods, she was picky. I'd only fed her foods she enjoyed, but now the tide had changed. My mother began coaxing her to taste various foods. Teri made it clear she had no intention of eating unfamiliar cuisine, and no amount of cajoling or bribing helped the situation.

Theresa, mangia . . . eat! But Teri would stubbornly turn away from the spoon in her face. My mother remembered a food she'd fed to her own children—a blend of pastina, egg, spinach, and plenty of butter— and Teri loved it. My mother was content; she'd reached her goal of having nourished her grandbaby.

I had never heard about our relatives on the west coast until I arrived in California. I quickly learned about Eva, a cousin on my father's side. Along with her husband, three sons, and a daughter, Eva and her family came to visit on that first weekend. It was easy to draw Eva into my heart. She was full of life, with enough energy to send an army into battle. Eva possessed a delicious blend of East Coast Italian and Californian all rolled into one great lady. Eva became more of a sister than a cousin. In no time, we developed a close friendship.

Eva's visits were warmly welcomed. She was generous, extremely considerate of my mother, and always arrived with fully cooked meals when she visited. It was Eva who introduced us to homemade cream puffs, a delicious delicacy enjoyed by all.

Among the neighbors on Orchard Street was Sam, mayor of the nearby town of Pomona. Sam was a large man in girth with a heart to match. It was he who'd secured the job for my father at the tile company. Unfortunately, after six months, the company went out of business, and my father was out of work. Because my father had so few skills, Sam was unable to fit my father into another work opportunity close to home. However, when a position became available with Devoe & Reynolds Paint Company in a town thirty miles east of Montclair, my father reluctantly accepted. By the time we arrived in California, my father was already familiar with the long drive to work on intimidating freeways. He was not pleased with either his work environment or the daily drive.

When it was brought to my attention that my father's sole task was to clean out massive paint vats—a task far more dangerous than the dock work he'd had in New York—I was horrified. California OSHA work laws had not yet been implemented, and the company provided little protection from the damaging effects of paint fumes. Other than a mask, no other protective gear was made available, and the ventilation system did not adequately eliminate paint fumes. When he was later diagnosed with diabetes, the doctor informed us that most likely the paint fumes played a part in damaging his pancreas.

In spite of his situation, my father adjusted to his work environment. He loved California more than he disliked the drive to work and his job. For my father, life in California was worth any struggle. He lived for the weekends when he could dabble in the backyard or gather a bounty of wild vegetables on the nearby hillsides. When in season, the cactus apples and prickly pears now in abundance were always on the table for an after dinner treat.

At the opposite end of the spectrum was my mother's work environment. Through their network of Italian friends, she found work in a dress factory close to home. Each morning, before he left for work, my father drove her to the factory. Her gregarious personality had always been a magnet that attracted people to her. The women she worked with found her endearing and drove her home each night.

As the newness of our arrival in California settled down and the flurry of visitors lessened, Frankie filed for unemployment and began looking for work. Although we weren't paying for rent or food, our finances were tight. Unemployment checks would not arrive for many more weeks, and we were living on remnants of savings. The unexpected car expenditure had left us little to fall back on.

Frankie was confident. He'd been assured his training as a tool and die maker would guarantee a great paying job. Unfortunately, Montclair and the surrounding areas were pint-sized communities with no need for his job skills, and Sam had no connections in this field.

Frankie had something else to fall back on. He'd graduated from the New York School of Printing, a highly acclaimed technical institution. Turning his focus towards printing opportunities, he placed applications with newspapers and print shops. However, the printing environment had evolved since he was last in school, companies were now utilizing computers, and his skills were obsolete.

After spotting an ad in the *Los Angeles Times* for a position with a book binding company, he applied and was offered a job in development. Frankie was excited about the opportunity to learn a new skill, albeit the pay was less than adequate. It also required a move to Los Angeles. My mother scraped together enough furniture, and we moved into a cute apartment close to work. He was young, and with the opportunity to train and climb the proverbial ladder, Frankie was happy.

Within the confines of our apartment, we were happy. Yet Los Angeles was cold and unfriendly, unlike the ambiance at Camp Knox and the long list of charming friends we dearly missed. With only one car and no one to watch Teri, I remained a stay-at-home mom. Neighbors kept to themselves and no one stopped by to greet us. When the sun went down, the doors in our apartment building were closed shut, and all the lights went out. My days were long. I saw no one, nor did I have an opportunity to speak to anyone. I never heard the cheerful sounds of children playing, nor did I see women passing by with babies in strollers. It didn't take long before the unfriendly environment began to wear us down. We were not building a life; we were merely surviving.

Every night Frankie and I would reminisce about the friends at Camp Knox. Weekends were chillingly quiet, luring us to pack up on and head to Montclair. Being home with my parents was comforting.

And when it was time to leave on Sunday afternoons, we dreaded the ride back to Los Angeles.

There was no disguising our feelings. Our lonely existence in Los Angeles held no appeal. We didn't fit in. Sensing we were not happy, my mother suggested we move back to Montclair. Frankie and I discussed the tedious drive to work each day, and he insisted he would not mind. Although the distance was not far, the freeway bottlenecks made the drive an unpleasant start and finish to each day. With his nod of approval, we happily accepted their invitation, and we moved back into the tiny bedroom on Orchard Street.

During a conversation Frankie had with his mother, he shared his feelings about working and living in Los Angeles. He told her his salary was not the best. A few days later, Dominick called and told Frankie about a position with the Carnation Milk Company where he was employed, and he described the new milk delivery route in New Jersey. Frankie learned that the pay was great, triple what he currently earned, and the benefits were a definite plus. Since the book binding company did not offer benefits, Dominick suggested jumping at the opportunity—immediately—and moving to New Jersey.

Neither of us wanted to leave California. The Golden State had carved a place deep in our hearts. But money was steering the ship, and the new job with a great pay was a deal maker. Living close to MaryAnn and Joe and all our old friends was an undeniable benefit as well, one that took on a life all its own.

With Dominick's influence, Frankie was hired before we left California, and he resigned from his job in Los Angeles.

We knew that leaving California and ripping Teri away from my parents would break their hearts. They would miss her, and she would miss them as well. So would Frankie and I. Having absolutely no say in the matter, they stood aside in stunned silence. My parents did not deserve this disappointment. They'd opened up their home, their hearts, and at times their pocketbook. Yet their generosity wasn't enough. Frankie needed and deserved a good paying job.

We sold our car, and with the money we booked a red-eye flight from Los Angeles to La Guardia Airport. With heavy hearts we promised ourselves to someday return.

A few days after we arrived in New Jersey, Frankie began working. Mary and Dominick were now living in New Jersey, and for a short time we lived with them. I found a part-time job as a checker in a grocery store, and it didn't take long to scrape together enough money to buy a car and new furniture and to move into an adorable apartment in New Milford, a breath away from Lilly and Walter.

Surrounded by old and new friends, including MaryAnn and Joe, life in New Jersey resembled what we'd enjoyed in North Carolina. And in our stylishly decorated apartment, life was great. We were busy, we had money, and we were incredibly happy.

Yet beautiful California was never far from our minds. It was all we talked about. There was no denying how much we missed the warm sunshine, especially after the blast of cold during the first winter season and the snowstorm that buried our car for many days.

Towards the end of our first New Jersey winter, Frankie complained of not feeling well. We blamed the weather. Neither of us had acclimated well to the cold. He told me he felt tired and had little energy. Although he was eating well and taking vitamins, an intimidating malaise had taken hold of him. Although he had to force himself to get up each morning, he refused to see a doctor. We imagined things would change in the spring.

After the cold chill of winter fell away, the relentless malaise remained. The warmth of summer brought little relief, and we began to fear the coming winter. Convinced the years in the South and the time in California had thinned his blood, our focus turned westward. We were convinced the warm sunshine would take care of the problem—reactivate the strapping energy he had always enjoyed.

Dominick was not convinced a warm climate would cure his tiredness and told us we were crazy to give up the life we were enjoying. But Frankie was not feeling well, and we made up our minds to return. California was in our blood, in our future. Dominick promised to inquire about milk delivery routes in Los Angeles. With the possibility of working with Carnation on the west coast, plans for another cross-country trip began to take shape. Our friends told us we were making a mistake, yet it seemed like the right thing to.

The drill of a long distance car trip was still fresh in our minds, only this time it was minus a trailer. Bekins Van Lines packed our belongings, and my mother sent my brother Tony to help. With only the bare necessities in the trunk of our car, we set off on the northern cross-country route to our beloved California.

This time the trip was uneventful. And at the first sighting of the San Bernardino Mountains, the familiar feeling of being home fell over us once again. This was where we wanted to live.

We found an adorable apartment on Canoga Street in Montclair close to my parents' house. Frankie had been forewarned that a milk route with Carnation would take time, possibly months. He checked in with the book binding company in Los Angeles and applied at local newspapers as well. Sadly, the book binding company was not hiring; neither were the newspapers. But Frankie kept in touch with Carnation and things looked hopeful.

We both filed for unemployment, and I checked with the local retail clerks' union for jobs as a grocery checker in the area. My experience in the New Jersey market was a tremendous help. I was told a large market was looking for a floater. I joined the union and was hired to work the grand opening for a new market in Brea, a small town twenty miles from home. I was excited about the job; the pay was fantastic and the hours were perfect, 5-10 p.m., four nights a week.

For a while, Frankie seemed fine and did not complain about feeling tired. However, after I arrived home from work one night, he told me he'd fainted. Although the fainting spell was troubling, we assumed it was due to stress. My mother was not convinced, and Frankie continued to refuse medical advice.

THE DEVIL STEPS IN

After the market's grand opening, an opportunity for permanent employment became available in a store in Los Angeles. I accepted the position, and we moved and settled in an apartment in Inglewood, California, a city southwest of Los Angeles, an area where Carnation had assured us that a route would soon become available. Although Los Angeles was not our favorite place to plant roots, we felt fortunate, things were coming together, and we made up our minds to accept life in a city not terribly far from family.

With only a part-time salary and unemployment, finances were tight but workable. We were looking forward to better financial health once he began working for Carnation.

With the arrival of fall, Thanksgiving was right around the corner. Eva called and told us she was bringing an entire Thanksgiving dinner to my mother's house—turkey, mashed potatoes and gravy as well as her decadently delicious cream puffs. We'd not seen Eva since we returned to California, and we were looking forward to a wonderful day with her family. After a fabulous dinner, including my mother's lasagna, Eva took me aside.

"Is something wrong with Frankie?" she asked. "His lips are gray. Gosh, I don't remember him looking so thin. He's lost a lot of weight since I last saw you guys. Has he seen a doctor?"

"No he hasn't. He hasn't been feeling himself. Eva, he won't see a doctor. Did my mother tell you that he fainted a few weeks ago?"

"Yes she did. Listen, you need to make an appointment with a doctor right away. Something's not right," she added. "When we first met Frankie, he looked healthy, his face glowed. Seeing him now has me worried. I don't want to scare you, but he looks ill."

I hadn't noticed the color of his lips, but I was aware of his weight loss, and I knew the strength and vigor he'd enjoyed in North Carolina was gone. Yet it was easy to blame the changes that had occurred in our lives since he was discharged on how he was feeling. The long-distance moves were exhausting, and difficulties finding work were stressful. Still, Frankie was only 22. What could be wrong?

Keeping my promise to Eva, I immediately made an appointment with a local doctor. Having balked at seeing a doctor in the past, I imagined Frankie would object, but he didn't. In hindsight, he may have suspected it was time for a check up.

The next afternoon, Teri and I waited in the car and watched as he walked into the doctor's office. Although Frankie was in the prime of his life, the fainting spell was worrisome. I made up my mind that he might be anemic. He just needed some vitamins and a job. Of this I was positive.

It seemed like an eternity before the office door opened and Frankie reappeared. As he walked towards the car, he kept his eyes lowered, and when I reached over to open the driver's door and our eyes locked, I could tell he was upset. His lips were pulled tight, and his eyes were missing that normal sparkle. He looked frightened, and the expression on his face made my heart stop.

"What's wrong, what did the doctor say?"

"A lot. He wants a biopsy taken."

"A biopsy? A biopsy on what?" I asked as a gush of panic suddenly began to rise inside me.

"Remember that lump on my shoulder blade? Well, it's bigger, and there are lumps running down my back. I didn't know about the new lumps, and I didn't want to tell you the one on my neck got bigger. Something else—I've been waking up during the night soaked in sweat. The doctor told me the sweats and the lumps are linked."

"Linked? To what?"

"He said it could be tuberculosis of the glands. And, well, I can't believe this, but he said it could be cancer. They won't know for sure until they get the results back from the biopsy."

Frankie looked traumatized. Cancer—the doctor had told him it could be cancer. This was not possible. Merely thinking the word sent shivers through me. I reached for his hand, but he didn't react. He was frightened, I could tell from the look in his eyes that he was, and I felt as though someone had tossed a grenade into the pit of my stomach.

Frankie turned the key in the ignition, took hold of the steering wheel, and drove away. When we arrived home, Frankie immediately went to bed. I quickly fed and bathed Teri and put her to bed as well.

In the past, I'd always enjoyed a few moments of quiet contemplation, but this night was different. The eerie silence in that apartment was disturbing, and the possibility that Frankie might have cancer planted the seeds of despair in my mind.

Later I crawled in next to him, and the first time in our married life we didn't share love words or say goodnight. We just cuddled close until we fell asleep. In the morning I awoke to the same nightmarish sense that something ominous was about to unfold in our lives.

A biopsy was scheduled for the following morning. Results from the tests would take two days—two agonizing days of waiting and hoping against all odds it was all a mistake.

During the days that followed, the mood in our apartment was restrained—subdued. We were both frightened, but we never shared the fear. Frankie hardly spoke, and I could not pull away from what the results of the biopsy might reveal.

When the phone rang and I heard the doctor's voice, I was thankful Frankie was asleep. The doctor suggested we stop by his office, but I insisted on knowing the results immediately.

He reluctantly agreed, and I held my breath as he told me Frankie had Hodgkin's Lymphoma—a cancer of the lymph nodes, spleen, liver, and bone marrow—and I felt the blood drain from my head.

"Hodgkin's disease? Cancer? Is it fatal?"

"Yes, it's cancer. In most cases it is fatal, but your husband is young and strong, and there are treatments. I recommend UCLA Medical Center. I'll call to schedule an appointment for more extensive testing. Your husband will need to know the diagnosis as well," he added sorrowfully.

The mind-numbing news had sucked the breath from my lungs. I slumped into a nearby chair, suddenly lost in a world where unimaginable consequences ruled. This could not possibly be happening, not to Frankie. Yet I knew tests don't lie. I was paralyzed, unable to move or think. Thoughts about my little friend in elementary school who'd died of leukemia suddenly came to mind, and I imagined nothing good would come of this as well.

I was scheduled to work that evening, the last place I wanted to be. My mind was locked on the doctor's words—cancer, Hodgkin's disease, fatal. What would I say to Frankie? I knew if he looked my way, the fear in my heart would spill out of my eyes. The last thing I wanted to do was frighten him, but finding words to mitigate the truth was impossible.

I made up my mind not to share the truth—not yet. How could I tell my soul mate that he had a fatal disease? I would have chosen to die rather than share the diagnosis.

I could feel myself trembling; my insides had twisted into a tight knot. Once dinner was ready, I called him to the table, and I sat Teri in her highchair. I fought to keep from crying. I tried not to speak; the tone of my voice might divulge the terror running through me. I carefully avoided looking his way—my eyes could reveal the panic brewing within me. Fighting hard to maintain my calm, I reached inward for strength and somehow managed to keep the news to myself—at least for a while.

After dinner I tidied the kitchen, kissed them both, and left for work. I needed to speak to someone, anyone, but we were alone in Los Angeles with no friends or family close by. At work, I knew no one well enough to share my problem with as well. However, that evening, one of my coworkers noticed the distraught look on my face. When she asked if something was wrong, and I shared the mind numbing details, there was no holding back the avalanche of tears that began to stream down my face.

We sat in the employee lounge, and as she held my hand, I shared the details of the doctor's diagnosis. I told her I could not fathom the thought of an illness he could not survive, nor my life without him. She tried comforting me, but there was little she could say. She told me Frankie needed to know the truth no matter how I felt about it.

"He needs to know how ill he is. It wouldn't be right to keep this to yourself." She also cautioned me to lace my words with love and hope.

On my way home from work, I tried sorting out what to say to him, but my thoughts were chaotic. I worried how this would play out, if he'd freak out when he learned the truth. While I struggled to find the right words, the fear inside me was escalating with each passing moment.

I decided it was best not to procrastinate. The following morning, I made coffee and decided to tell him immediately. Following our morning routine, I poured our coffee, placed the cups on the living room coffee table, and waited for him to sit by my side. When he sat down, using the softest tone I could muster up, I spoke.

"Frankie, the doctor called with the results."

"And?"

My throat tightened. I worried that my own fear would easily be revealed in my voice. I had to choose my words carefully. Frankie eyes were looking directly into mine, and I struggled to stay the course, maintain calmness, speak softly.

"He told me you have Hodgkin's disease. I've never heard of it. He said there are treatments."

Frankie listened, appeared puzzled, but he made no comment, nor did he query me about the disease. Thankfully I had maintained control of my emotions, purposely avoided using the word *cancer*. I wasn't sure if Frankie had ever been exposed to people with cancer in the past.

"You have an appointment at UCLA Medical Center for more testing tomorrow morning," I added.

He didn't react, and I wasn't sure what he was thinking. I knew if he called the doctor for details, the doctor would be forced to reveal the less-than-hopeful prognosis.

If he was afraid, or concerned, he kept it well hidden. We were both quiet; functioning like zombies and maintaining a happy mood around Teri was difficult.

When we arrived at UCLA, several doctors spoke with us. Their questions were focused on the timeline beginning with the appearance of the first lump. Soon a young doctor came into the room and introduced himself as the doctor assigned to our case. After more questions, he ordered a laundry list of tests to begin the following day.

Fearing I'd fall apart, I hesitated calling home. My emotions were raw, at a breaking point. Yet I knew I had to let my family know what had occurred. His family needed to be aware as well. I decided to call my mother from work, away from Frankie. When I broke the news to my mother, she gasped, and I cried. She asked me to move back home—immediately. I told her about the tests at UCLA Medical Center and that I needed to bring Teri to Montclair, to distance her from the nightmare.

After a week of tests, we were told the results would be available in a few days. I continued to avoid using the word *cancer* around Frankie, yet there was no escaping the word, as it kept reaching into the quiet places of my mind. I remained determined to keep the prognosis of impending death from his ears.

A few days later, UCLA called to schedule an appointment for the results. When we arrived, we were led to a large waiting room. Frankie was quiet. He looked drawn and pale and was still not sharing his thoughts. I'm not sure what kept either of us from screaming out in fear.

When a doctor walked into the lounge and asked us to follow him to his office, I sensed the tension in his voice, and the forced smile on his face made my heart sink into the pit of my stomach.

He motioned for us to sit down. His tone was poised yet strained. He began to speak of pointless matters—small talk—his attempt to soften the less than somber mood. He took his time as though he was seeking just the right words, but his facial expression gave him away, and I already knew the news was not good.

"Mr. Attardo, I'll get right to the point. The test results confirm the original diagnosis of Hodgkin's disease. I had hoped it would turn out to be something less severe, but unfortunately this is not the case."

We felt powerless, and an ominous feeling of despair fell over us. All hope of a mistaken diagnosis had been eliminated. I reached for Frankie's hand and squeezed it. When he squeezed back, I fought off the urge to cry and forced myself to breath deeply. Suddenly Frankie rose from his chair and told us he needed to use the bathroom. The doctor directed him down the hall.

Once Frankie left the room, the doctor turned to me and said, "Mrs. Attardo, I'm not sure how much knowledge you have about this disease, how much your doctor told you. I'll assume you probably know this is serious; the cancer has already spread. I'll be honest; he probably has less than six months to live. I've conferred with the hospital staff and they concur with the diagnosis. That said, I've gone ahead and scheduled a series of radiation treatments. They may help, but most likely it's too late. I'm sorry to tell you this, but you need to be aware, as does Mr. Attardo."

He continued to speak, but my mind had locked on his words— "he probably has less than six months to live"—paralyzing words that stunned me, and I had no questions for the messenger.

Oh my God, how could this happen? How could this be? This can't be happening. Is this a punishment for running off and hurting my parents? Oh God, please help him! We're sorry.

I felt as though I would pass out. The doctor came around from behind the desk and told me to take deep breaths.

"Doctor, please don't tell him he's going to die, *please*! I'll tell him. I'll find my own way. You can't possibly be sure. Maybe the radiation will work!"

He held my hand firmly and said, "By law I have to tell him."

Years later I would remember that doctor and the concerned tone in his voice, the sad look in his eyes. How very difficult it must be to tell a patient they will soon die. I wondered what he felt inside. Had he fallen asleep peacefully that evening, or did the tragedy of Frankie's diagnosis keep him awake? Did he hold his wife closer and silently give thanks for their good health?

"Please," I begged. "Please don't say a word to him. I'll tell him at home. I promise."

Frankie walked back into the room and appeared paler than when we arrived that morning. The doctor offered him a glass of water, but he refused the drink. The doctor explained the radiation process and what to expect regarding side effects. I wondered if the doctor would ignore what I'd asked of him. If Frankie asked any questions, he would be forced to speak the truth.

"Mr. Attardo, radiation has the capacity to destroy the disease and bring about a complete remission. So let's look at this in a positive way and begin treatments immediately. You're young and basically in good health. These are all good things to consider."

I was relieved; the doctor had respected my request. On our drive home, Frankie was quiet and kept his eyes closed. If he was worried or fearful he never let on. I wanted to talk to him, but I was trembling inside and could not sort out my thoughts. I thought about Teri, sweet little Teri. She was only two years old. What would I say to her when he dies? It would happen soon, according to the doctor. How long could I shield the truth from Frankie? I felt like I could never share the whole truth—that the cancer had spread, that the treatments would probably not help, and that the chances of surviving more than six months were not likely.

When we arrived home, he threw himself across our bed. I watched as he closed his eyes and quickly fell away into the world of dreams, hopefully somewhere peaceful, a place absent of diseases and the fear of death.

Later that night, during my work break, I called my mother and spoke to Teri. Hearing her sweet voice immediately brought me back to center.

LOVE RULES AND FAITH GUIDES

Fear makes the wolf seem larger than he actually is. In this case, the wolf was much larger than the terror embedded in every cell of my body.

As much as I hated leaving Frankie and going to work, I welcomed the solitude of the car. Lost in a draft of helplessness, knowing there was no escaping the devil cancer, the car become a refuge, the only place I could cry openly, where I could scream and not be heard.

But work was not a distraction from my fear. Concentrating on customers had become a challenge. It didn't take long for my manager to notice my demeanor. The last thing he needed to hear from a new hire was a problem at home such as mine. His objective was the assurance his employees would show up for work and leave personal problems at home. However, he was a kind and gentle man, and when he asked if something was wrong and I tearfully explained, he said he understood and told me he'd work around my problems. And he did.

The treatments were scheduled to begin immediately—three days a week for three months. Frankie's appetite was now poor, not hearty enough to maintain health and energy. The night sweats kept him from sound sleep, and the early malaise had been replaced by a debilitating fatigue.

On Friday, we drove to UCLA for the first treatment. A nurse led us through a myriad of corridors, deep into the bowels of the hospital. It seemed as though we'd walked a mile before arriving in an area where a large, blinking red light above a door was flashing at a feverish pace. And when I read the words RADIATION IN PROGRESS—DO NOT ENTER, I cringed.

I sat quietly in the waiting area and watched a nurse lead Frankie through the door below the menacing red light. My hands were clenched tightly, and my fingernails were digging into the skin. I wondered what Frankie was thinking. Emotionally, Frankie was strong but how could he not be terrified? I was.

Thumbing through fashion or glamour magazines held no fascination. With little to do, I began praying. I asked the Blessed Mother to stand by his side. I began praying for a miracle—a cure.

Blessed Mother, I've never asked for much, but I'm asking now, not for myself, but for Frankie and Teri. Please help him, hold his hand and give him courage. I'm pleading with you to ask Jesus to make him well.

The wait seemed like an eternity. I kept watching the nurses working behind the station and wondered how anyone could work in this ominous environment where death was a breath away. When the doors finally opened and Frankie reappeared, I noticed his parched lips. I reached for his hand, and we walked through the gloomy corridors, towards the front door, to the blessed California sunshine and fresh air. Once inside our car, I asked him about the treatment.

"What was it like?"

"Well, it was painless. But look at this," he said as he lifted his shirt.

The technician had drawn dark lines on his chest, neck, and back, targeting areas that needed to be radiated. I'd never seen anything like it before. It was frightening to look at, and when he told me in a few days the area would turn red and blister, I was frozen into silence.

Burned skin was the least of his problems. Within a few hours, he was seized by surges of vomiting. It continued the rest of that day and night and through the weekend. By Monday, his chest was a deep shade of red madness, and the debilitating effects of vomiting left him weaker. Although the vomiting eventually subsided, his appetite was now pitifully poor, and I had to remind him to drink fluids. Inevitably he became dehydrated and was admitted to the hospital.

I cried in fear of losing him. I cried because I didn't want him to know he was dying. I cried because I did not want him to suffer. And I cried knowing we would no longer enjoy the dreams we had planned for our future.

EXODUS

I was born with music in my heart. It was a vital part of my life, a euphoric escape. Frankie and I shared the same intense love for music. Like mine, his love of music encompassed many genres. I loved that part of him. Whether we were at home or in the car, the radio was always blaring loudly. It mattered little if we knew the words to a song or not; we would laugh and sing along enthusiastically.

It happens to most music lovers. You fall in love with a particular song, and it attaches itself to your mind for long periods of time. The tune becomes an obsession, and you find yourself humming the melody spontaneously, hoping the disk jockey will play the song again and again and again. Through the years, this scenario had often played out for both of us.

My world was different now, and a very popular was song was having a disquieting effect on me. The melody, though beautiful, was disturbing and always brought me down further than I already was.

The song was wildly popular, and disks jockeys aired it unceasingly. The moment I'd turn on the radio, it was there to haunt me, and when I tuned in to another station, it would be airing there as well.

I mentioned this odd occurrence to a coworker—how the melody made me uneasy, how it saddened me, and how I deliberately avoided listening to it.

"It's so weird. The song touches a nerve. I have to change the station immediately, but when I do, it's always playing on another station!" I continued. "It's creepy."

She asked what the title was, but I didn't know.

"It's a piano concerto by Ferrante and Teisher."

"Oh yeah, I know the song. It's beautiful—Exodus. It's called Exodus."

"Exodus?"

"Yes, like the Bible exodus. Do you know what it means?" she asked.

"Of course I do. I know the word and I know what it means."

The title, the meaning, even the tone of her voice when she questioned me was disturbing.

"I'm sorry. I know you're thinking the song is a premonition. It's probably just a coincidence."

On our way to the hospital one morning, Frankie did something he'd not done in a while; he turned on the car radio. And, as if requested, the daunting melody began to fill the air.

"That song gives me the creeps," he murmured. Frankie seemed agitated and immediately tuned in to another station.

After hearing his reaction, I was positive the song *was* a premonition. Soul mates often react in unison. I never shared my feelings regarding the song with him, and I'm sure he never knew the title.

MOTHER MARY

In a perfect world, harmony prevails, crime is unheard of, wars are fought on chessboards, doors are never locked, rainbows follow storms, and children never die before their parents.

One of the hardest things I had to do was tell Frankie's mother her son was terminally ill and was not expected to live.

Mary Attardo—"Mother Mary" as she was often called—was a living angel, 4 feet 10 inches of sweetness and love. Her life had not been that of a beautiful rose in a springtime English garden.

Mary's family included her husband Dominick and seven children, six males—Joey, Paulie, Frankie, Chuck, Tommy, Johnny—and last but not least a female, Mary, her namesake. Dominick was an authoritarian figure in the family, and Mary obeyed his every demand. Love for Mary came mostly from the children she adored. Most of the male siblings were born jokesters and loved teasing their mother. They would come up with a prank just to hear her laugh. She was an easy target and a great sport.

"Jesus, Mary, and Saint Joseph—stop it! I'm gonna pee my pants!" she'd scream and head towards the bathroom. Mary cherished their antics and regarded their pranks as acts of love.

A sick child is the ultimate pain for any parent. Bringing anguish of this caliber into Mary's life was the last thing I wanted to do. My mother had called to tell her Frankie was ill but had not elaborated on the severity of the illness. And never imagining the worst, Mary had not inquired any further. Frankie asked me to wait until after the treatments before calling home.

On the day Frankie received the last treatment, we packed up and left for Montclair. The following day, he called home and spoke to his brother

Tommy. Frankie told him he had Hodgkin's disease and described the treatments. When their conversation ended, Frankie handed me the phone.

"Tommy wants to say hello," he said and handed me the phone.

From the tone of Tommy's voice I knew he was upset. He asked me to call when Frankie was not around. The next day I called from a pay phone and shared the disturbing news about his brother.

"It's not good Tommy—its cancer," I said tearfully. "Cancer of the lymphatic system. The doctors are not hopeful. It's already spread, but Frankie doesn't know. They told me the treatments most likely will have little or no effect and he has approximately six months to live. And it's now down to three. Frankie is under the impression that radiation will take care of the problem."

I knew the news had stunned Tommy. "This is too weird," he said sadly. "When we were young, Frankie was never sick, and now this, the mother of all diseases."

Tommy's words "Frankie was never sick" triggered a memory, something Mary had shared with me when I first met her.

"Frankie's not like his brothers or his sister," she'd boast proudly. "He is never sick—never has been!"

Although he was constantly exposed to a myriad of childhood illnesses in school and from his brothers, he never caught colds, never had chicken pox, the mumps, or the measles. Not one childhood illness, or even a cold, ever put him to bed! Mary considered Frankie the healthiest of her seven children.

It was ironic that in light of his childhood healthiness, the king of illnesses had now come to mark a place in his life. It was as though all the diseases he'd never suffered had united and now marched on him in concert, like a plague.

I read that scientists were looking into the phenomenon of children who never experience normal childhood illnesses and later develop cancer. Scientists suspect the culprit is the immune system.

In one theory, scientists believe the immune system is destroyed in the fight to ward off childhood diseases and thus rendered ineffective against a larger enemy—cancer. In other theories, it is believed that childhood diseases prime the immune system and thus prevent cancer. Scientists continue to search for answers.

PROMISE YOU WON'T LEAVE ME

When someone you love is diagnosed with a terminal illness, a toxic feeling of helplessness and despair invades every cell of your body. You hope you'll wake up from the nightmare. But you aren't dreaming, and there is no escaping the brutal reality.

Waiting for the results of the treatments was agonizing, as was the daunting thought of impending death. If the doctor was correct, Frankie had only a few months left of life. He'd be gone by Teri's next birthday. The thought now provoked a gnawing resentment in every aspect of my life, even towards people I met each day. I envied those leading normal lives, those who went to work each morning. I resented couples that danced on weekends and those who made love every night. Although the sun continued to rise each morning, there was no light in our world. We'd been barred from all elements of normalcy, knocked off our axis, kicked into a black hole.

The day before our next appointment at UCLA, we packed up for the ride back to Los Angeles. I wanted to stay in the warmth of that tiny house with my parents close by. It felt safe when they were near me, just as I had felt when I was young, when no one was ill. My mother kept reminding me to be strong—to have courage. I had no courage. There was sadness at every corner, and a wrenching ache had nested in my heart.

Leaving Teri with my parents while Frankie received treatments ripped at both our hearts. Thankfully, she loved being with my mother. When it was time to leave, we would wave and blow kisses her way. These were tortuous moments that prompted spontaneous tears. I'd wipe the wetness away quickly, hoping Frankie had not noticed. I didn't want him to take blame for this sadness.

Teri was Frankie's best medicine, a beam of beautiful light in his life. He considered her a blessing and struggled to find the strength to play with her. Although she was very young, she observed the changes in him.

"Mommy, why does Daddy look so sad?"

I always assured her he'd be "all better" soon, and she always accepted my hopeful explanations.

My mother had been teaching Teri bedtime prayers. They prayed every night and would ask Jesus to make him well. When Teri and I were alone, we'd pray as well. Because most conversations between the adults revolved around Frankie's illness, in time Teri began to understand her daddy was sick.

Convinced that God was now the only answer, during quiet times I would silently pray. Reaching deep into my heart I pleaded with God, Jesus, his mother Mary, and St. Jude, the patron saint of desperately hopeless cases. I began asking St. Theresa, the little flower, to intercede for us. I'm not sure if it was self-hypnosis or merely a crutch, but I was soon convinced that God's blessing would come to the rescue.

Eventually prayer became my escape, the place in my mind where I found peace. I prayed from the moment I woke up each morning until I drifted off to sleep at night. I prayed everywhere—in bed, in the car, even at work. I prayed for a cure so we could return to the deliriously happy days of the past. I was convinced I could accomplish this goal and he'd return to his former self—healthy, full of energy and love, and with that same spark for life he'd had before the cancer—God willing.

FAUX PAS

It's ironic how life plays out. After diligently keeping the devastating prognosis from reaching Frankie's ears, through my own carelessness, the earth-shattering information suddenly was exposed.

After a quiet drive home from Montclair, Frankie immediately went to bed. It was still early evening, and I decided to write to my cousin in New Jersey. Except for Eva, I had not yet shared any details about the disease or the prognosis with any one else in our family. I began my letter stating the devil had stepped into our lives and Frankie was diagnosed with Hodgkin's disease—cancer. I held nothing back. I told her Frankie had less than six months to live, how frail he looked, how he was feeling, and how overwhelmed we all were. I added that Frankie was not aware that he had cancer and that it had spread. I shared how most likely the treatments would have little effect and no further treatments were available. The letter spelled out his fate.

It had been a long day; it was late and I was tired. Since I was not done writing, I placed the letter in an envelope, addressed it, and set it on the kitchen counter unsealed. In the morning, I would add my last thoughts.

Before going to bed, I tidied up the kitchen and sat on the couch to watch the late news. Suddenly Frankie walked into the kitchen. He told me he was thirsty and poured himself a glass of water. Seeing the letter on the counter, he picked it up and checked the address.

"Hmmm—you wrote to your cousin Roseann? What did you tell her?" he asked.

"Ya know, the usual stuff about Teri and you. And some girlie stuff. I told her that you weren't feeling well."

"What else?" he shot back skeptically.

"I told her what the doctor said, that you have Hodgkin's and that you'd received treatments."

When he was done with his drink, Frankie slid down on the couch next to me. In the past Frankie had never shown any interest in the letters I'd written. Perhaps the tone of my voice made him skeptical, but that evening, he was clearly suspicious.

He sat by me for a few moments then told me he was going back to bed. We kissed and I watched as he stood up, calmly walked back to the counter and reached for the letter. Seeing the letter in his hands sent shockwaves through me; my heart began to race. I walked towards him and reached for the letter. The last thing I wanted him to do was read what I'd written.

"Frankie, give me the letter. You can read it when I'm done writing," I said, desperately struggling to hold my panic in tow.

"I just want to read what you wrote. I'll give it right back."

The letter was clearly out of my reach, and I began to tremble. Frankie turned from me and walked towards the bathroom. I raced after him, but he dashed into the bathroom and locked the door behind him.

It was a moment of unthinkable panic. Dizzy with guilt, I slumped to the floor in front of the locked door and I began sobbing. Not one detail had been left out of that letter; I had not minced words. I'd used the word I feared most, "cancer." Soon he would know his destiny, that he had less than a few months to live, and that the doctors offered no hope.

I listened for sounds from behind the locked door, but there were none. When the door finally opened, he stepped over me and walked towards the bedroom. The look of fear in his eyes sent me into a tailspin of guilt, as though I'd caused the cancer. My heart was pounding, and I could not take a deep breath. Gathering all my strength, I stood up and watched as he fell facedown on the bed. He now knew how seriously ill he was—the hopelessness of it all—and I knew that he had not heard it from any of the doctors.

I climbed on the bed, stretched out on top of him, and felt his body quiver beneath me.

I'm not sure when Frankie fell asleep that night, if he ever found peace in slumber. From time to time he would turn quietly, and I would fold myself into him. That night was the longest night of my life.

Exhausted from the regrettable event of the previous night, when we woke the next morning, I made a weak attempt to soften the truth. I told him what I'd written was based on other patients and I reminded him that I had not yet completed the letter.

"Frankie, in your case, another doctor might have another opinion, tell us about other treatments."

I knew Frankie was not buying what I was selling. He never said as much, but the panic and fear in his eyes told me there was no point in continuing this charade, nor in concealing the truth.

My heart felt heavy. While he showered, I prayed. I prayed with all that was in me. I pleaded and begged God to make him well.

Later that morning, Frankie drew me into his arms and told me how much he loved me. It was then I noticed another small lump protruding from the side of his neck—a new lump. I knew if I could see the lump, he'd seen it as well.

The new lump spoke volumes and there were no words to mitigate the obvious—the illness was progressing. I wanted to talk to him, wanted to tell him he'd be fine, but my words were no longer believable, not that morning, not after he'd read my letter and saw the new evidence bulging out of the side of his neck.

When we arrived at UCLA, we held hands and walked towards the doctor's office. During the examination, Frankie told the doctor about the new lump he'd noticed that morning. When the doctor completed his examination, we returned to his office.

The doctor took his time before sharing any information. And when he finally spoke, he went right to the point.

"As evidenced by the new lump, the treatment has not been effective, and the original lumps have not shrunk," he said coldly, unemotionally, empty of all things human.

He looked directly into Frankie's eyes, waiting, anticipating a negative reaction. It was a surreal moment; neither of us spoke, as though we were waiting to be told of another treatment, a sliver of encouragement. His words had not yet registered, not until he cleared his throat and told us UCLA had no other treatment options.

He'd shared the cold realism and offered no encouragement. There was none. The facts were in the report on his desk, and there was nothing more to be said. What lay ahead was obvious; Frankie was being sent home to die.

The test results and the doctor's demeanor unraveled me down to my core. Yet Frankie continued to keep his feelings to himself. While driving home I silently prayed and asked God to open a door of hope. And when we arrived home, I called my mother. Somehow she always knew what to say and suggested we pack up and come home. It was obvious we could not continue to live in Los Angeles.

At work that evening, I spoke to my manager and told him we were moving back to Montclair. In the short time I'd worked at the store, he'd empathized with my nightmare and had cooperated on every level. I thanked him for his understanding and support. Before I left, he told me to check with the Pomona store and added that he'd speak to the manager about my situation and ask if there was an open position available.

ALL MY POSSESSIONS FOR
ONE MORE MOMENT

With help from my family, we moved back to the cozy house on Orchard Street, and once again we were surrounded by love and the positive input from my family. Having placed my complete confidence in God, I was convinced that He was not going to let us down.

Some elements in our lives were stable. After contacting the manager at the Pomona store, I learned that a position was available—a tiny light in the darkness of our world—and I was immediately placed on the schedule.

With only two months left on the sixth month marker, the cold truth made me shudder. Louise, my mother's neighbor, recommended getting in touch with a local doctor.

"Sending him home to die is unacceptable. You need to get another opinion." She recommended a local doctor—a man who in time became a friend as well as our family physician.

Dr. Kleinman was a large man in stature and spoke with certainty and conviction. Although he did not offer any outright hope, he did not send us away coldly. After examining Frankie, he suggested registering with the American Cancer Society, adding that he'd put us in contact with Dr. Powers, a local cancer specialist.

Following his recommendation, we registered with the ACS. What happened next was astonishing and provided what was now severely lacking—hope! A few days later, we received a call from Dr. Powers. He told us a drug for Hodgkin's disease was being tested on the east coast, and he'd taken the liberty to forward a referral letter to the hospital where the drug was being administered. He gave us names and phone numbers, and with his suitcase in hand, Frankie boarded a plane to New

York. Sadly, Teri and I remained behind. I could not jeopardize losing my job, our only source of income.

This would be the second round of a cancer treatment, except this time the outlook was hopeful. The experimental drug was called *Velban*, a periwinkle plant derivative—from the earth, natural, close to God. I was convinced this drug would provide the miracle we needed, the answer to my prayers. With the expectation of a positive result, a fresh wash of hope fell over me, and the knot in my stomach untangled.

The series of treatments took three months. While under treatment, Frankie enjoyed visiting with our friends and being home with his family. By the end of the third month, the drug had shrunk most of the tumors and Frankie was told they would continue to shrink.

Assured that the prayers I'd flooded the heavens with had been answered, I placed the nightmare behind me. Donning our Sunday best, Teri and I drove to the Los Angeles International Airport to pick him up. We spotted him immediately and ran towards him, struck by the sight of someone enjoying robust health coming our way. Frankie had gained back all his weight, his eyes were bright blue, and his lips and cheeks were flushed in pink. He kissed me and picked Teri up for a quick twirl around. He looked healthy and happy, full of vigor, and I suddenly realized that I'd forgotten how handsome he was.

He decided to drive home that day, something he'd not done in a while. Seeing him looking happy lifted our spirits. I felt refreshed, like flowers after a spring rain. Teri had her daddy, I had my healthy husband back, and the euphoria felt wonderful. An encouraging future was again in our hands.

We began doing things that young couples enjoyed. We rented an apartment close to where I worked. The apartment complex was small, only twelve units—two buildings facing each other and separated by a large grassy area where Teri could run and play with other children. All the tenants were young couples with small children. The apartment community had an ambiance close to that of Camp Lejeune. The only difference was Frankie's health and job situation. The Carnation Milk route had been placed on the back burner.

One month later, while enjoying the blissfulness of rejuvenated health, a new lump made a disturbing appearance. Not wanting to disrupt the energetic ambiance, Frankie kept this information to himself. Noting a change in his behavior, I questioned him and it was then he shared the earth-shattering news.

LEAP OF FAITH

The nightmare had returned with a vengeance, igniting an all-consuming fear and destroying the haven of momentary peace we were enjoying. Frankie was back to square one, and we turned to Dr. Kleinman for guidance. After examining the new lump, he asked us if we were familiar with the City of Hope. We were not. He described it as a research institution specializing in cancer research. He explained about clinical trials—unfamiliar and frightening words—adding how the trials often led to cures, or, at the very least, remission.

We learned that patients were only accepted at the City of Hope when conventional treatments were no longer effective. Frankie fit the profile. The only chance of beating the disease would occur at a research institution.

Filled with renewed expectations, the beacon of hope in our hearts led the way to the City of Hope in Duarte, California. A new opportunity for a cure once again was within reach.

Greeting all who entered the grounds at the City of Hope were the words carved into a wall close to the entrance: THERE ARE NO INCURABLE DISEASES, ONLY DISEASES WHERE CURES HAVE NOT YET BEEN FOUND—words that sent a surge of new hope into our hearts.

During the weeks and months and years that followed, whenever things were not going well, these words always filled me with strength and hope.

As we drove through the beautifully landscaped gardens with stately tall trees, walking paths, and gardens bursting with colorful flowers, the breathtaking ambiance beamed of life. We drove past small bungalows

251

for families to stay while loved ones received treatments and noticed plaques on trees with names of patients and contributors. It was lovely, so peaceful and beautiful, with a promise of hope for the eyes of the beholder.

We parked in a lot close to the main building and walked towards the front entry doors. The receptionist took our papers and asked us to have a seat in the waiting area. After a few minutes, a candy striper led us to the office of Dr. Colin Sinclair, a prematurely gray-haired man with a striking appearance. He welcomed us with a warm smile and shook our hands. Dr. Sinclair asked us have a seat, and I suddenly felt very much at ease. He glowed with self-confidence, and when he spoke, his tone was soft, like he was speaking with close friends.

He'd already reviewed Frankie's records from UCLA as well as those from the east coast. He shared the vision of the City of Hope, focusing on all types of cancer, including Hodgkin's disease, and reassured us a remission was a real possibility. He advised us to live life as though this illness was a passing anomaly that in time would fall away to be forgotten.

Hope had been rekindled and our hearts soared. Dr. Sinclair had renewed our confidence, and with this dynamic doctor at the helm, I was convinced the cancer did not have a chance.

The first scheduled treatment was chemotherapy, another frightening and unfamiliar word. The chemo of choice was Nitrogen Mustard Gas, an anticancer chemotherapeutic treatment.

After reading a description of Nitrogen Mustard Gas in a health magazine, I learned this compound had previously been used for chemical warfare purposes in World War II, a fact that numbed my senses. Dr. Sinclair had provided details about chemotherapy but never made reference to its origin. When I questioned him, he explained the gas had been re-calculated and classified safe for human treatment. Having placed my complete trust in the doctor, I never shared my uneasiness about the use of this drug on Frankie. There was no alternative.

Frankie was scheduled for treatment the next day. When we arrived, Frankie was prepped, and a technician took me aside and described the side effects as follows:

"His white and red blood cells and platelets will decrease and will place him at risk for infection, anemia and/or bleeding. He may have severe or prolonged diarrhea, violent vomiting, loss of hair, bruising in the area of infusion, ringing in the ears, loss of appetite, as well as a loss of taste buds."

The ominous list of side effects sent me into a tailspin. Frankie was dancing around death. I called Dr. Kleinman and was reassured that choice of drugs used was based on the impeccable experience of Dr. Sinclair and his staff. I came away from our visit with a clearer understanding that Frankie was in a frightfully serious situation and it was far better to receive the treatment than to be sent home to die.

That evening I sat by his bedside, feeling as though hell was about to rain down on him. After Frankie fell asleep, I watched the poison begin its slow journey into his veins. Around midnight he awoke and said he was nauseated. He began to vomit—relentless vomiting that continued until morning. He was monitored closely, and after twelve hours the chemo was replaced with a saline solution. By the next day, the vomiting began to subside, slowly, but the treatment and the nausea left him weak with exhaustion.

After seven days, he was able to go home, but he looked frail, as though he'd been through a war. One month later, tests revealed the treatment had been ineffective and the lumps remained intact, unscathed by the hellish gas.

Once his blood platelets tested normal, a series of treatments with various newer drugs were administered. Each subsequent treatment came with more debilitating side effects, and sadly none had any effect on the cancer. Dr. Sinclair continued to lift our spirits, expressing with certainty that one of the treatments would have a positive result. His confidence never failed to replenish our dwindling hope.

Through the course of treatments and the energy-draining side effects, Frankie was in the hospital more than he was at home. In spite of it all, he never complained or felt sorry for himself. Dr. Sinclair and his staff noted his accepting demeanor and at times were speechless—as was I.

As time went on, I became familiar with the dynamics of this hospital. I met other patients and befriended their families. While Frankie fought the battle, some patients would pass away. Although their deaths always set me back, I continued to pray for a cure and fought hard to stay on course. It became an emotional tug of war between hope and despair.

By the end of the first year, none of the drugs had proven to be effective. Frankie began to look frailer with each passing day. It was difficult for my mind to move away from thoughts that he was merely a testing mechanism for drugs. Dr. Sinclair always drew me back to center. On the surface, he appeared unperturbed and continued to reassure us that eventually one of the drugs would bring about that elusive remission. His stalwart confidence never failed to restore my hope and made it possible for me to put on a happy face in Frankie's presence.

At times it felt as though we were living in a place that God forgot. In the solitude of my car or in the company of friends, my family, or in church, I shed an ocean of tears. I reached out to hospitals in England and Germany. I wrote tear-filled letters to doctors, inquiring about alternate drugs for Hodgkin's disease, those not available in the United States. The responses were all the same: *The City of Hope is a highly acclaimed research institution, and the treatment your husband is receiving is the best to date.*

Although he looked frail and had grown considerably weaker, his training as a Marine was paying off—doing what needed to be done. I was proud of him—still a Marine, strong-willed in spite of the odds against survival. Living through this frightful nightmare with side effects designed by the devil, he continued to show no outward signs of despair.

I began praying with new vigor. Requests for prayers traveled far and wide. I began receiving prayer cards, holy medals, and promises for novenas from strangers all over the world. I wrote back to thank them, pleading for continued prayers. Eventually we received holy water from Lourdes.

In the shadow of these potential miracles, I clung to hope, and while Frankie continued to tread dark, deep waters, I remained resolute, convinced that Frankie would somehow beat the odds.

FATHER ALOYSIUS ELLACURIA

We'd met Betty and Bob at our apartment complex. They lived next door, and we quickly became close friends. Bob worked long hours but never failed to stop by to ask if we needed help. Betty would always bring me back to center when I was feeling down.

Betty shared information about a priest many believed had performed various miracles. His name was Father Aloysius Ellacuria, a missionary known for his gift of healing. Many believed his interventions had brought about miraculous cures. Father Ellacuria attracted the rich, the poor, the famous, those seeking a miracle from God through this holy man.

Together with Betty and Bob, we drove to Los Angeles and joined thousands of others who'd traveled far and wide to attend church services led by the holy priest. The hour of prayer was followed by benediction, and the congregation filed up the center aisle and knelt by the railing in front of the altar. Father Ellacuria moved slowly from person to person, placing his hands on each head, lifting a special prayer to God. When the holy priest placed his hands on Frankie's head, he hesitated, hovered over him for a drawn out period of time, praying deeply as though he sensed his illness and was soliciting special prayers from God.

We went home elated, confident that something positive happened that day. There was no doubt this man of the cloth had sensed something. He'd lingered over Frankie, prayed hard, harder than he had prayed for others at that altar.

We requested a private audience with Father Ellacuria. Our request was granted, and we met with him for the second time. This time we were able to describe Frankie's health situation privately. Once again Father

Ellacuria prayed over Frankie, asking the Lord to provide us with the needed strength to accept His Will.

We went home that day deflated; hope had slowed to a crawl. The priest's prayers had left me cold. He prayed—not for a cure—but for strength.

Yet God had a place in my heart, and I prayed that just possibly, in due time, the holy man's prayers would bring the miracle we desperately sought,

Once again it was not to be. That same week, we learned the treatment Frankie had just completed had failed to shrink the tumors, and our hopes once again came crashing to the ground.

GUARDIAN ANGELS

There were many people that crossed our paths during this time. They nurtured and comforted us with words and deeds and at times a shoulder to cry upon. They entered our lives mysteriously, casting aside time and money to provide any needed help. These were our guardian angels.

Betty and Bob were the first angels to enter our lives. Another angel friendship began at work. Her name was Karen. She worked at the Soup and Salad Bar, a small restaurant connected to the market where I worked—my favorite place to take breaks. Karen and I began sharing our lives, and eventually I told her about Frankie. Her husband Gary often stopped by for coffee as well. After Karen shared Frankie's plight with Gary, she told me they were prepared to help us in every possible way.

Along with Betty and Bob, the six of us become close friends. Whenever Frankie was feeling well enough, we'd get together for coffee and laugh away a few hours.

It was also at work where I met two more angels, special guardian angels named Geri and Kelly. They were an older couple, retired, and had no children, nor did they have any family in the area. In time they became a major part of our lives, especially Frankie's.

My friendship with Geri began on the day she came through my checkout line. She smiled, greeted me warmly, and I was immediately drawn to her. Geri looked and seemed so sincere. Soon she was coming through my line regularly, and her bubbly personality always brightened my day. Whenever the store wasn't busy, we would strike up a conversation, and we were sharing information. Eventually I told her about Frankie and Teri, and she told me about her life with her husband Kelly.

It didn't take long for Geri to tell Kelly about Frankie's illness, and each time they stopped by to shop, they never failed to ask how things were going. Kelly had taken time to educate himself about Hodgkin's disease, more than I expected anyone to do. I immediately felt close to them, but especially to Kelly. His compassionate manner was like a warm hug on a cold blustery day.

During one of their grocery shopping excursions, Geri and Kelly extended a dinner invitation. "Young lady, we won't take no for an answer, so don't disappoint us. I love to cook!" added Geri with a smile. "It gives me a chance to try out new recipes."

Their invitation was tempting, yet I had not shared all the morbid details of Frankie's treatments, the side effects, the endless hospital runs. I hated turning them down, but with little time to spare in our lives, my initial reaction was to refuse. After explaining the entire situation at home, they told me they understood.

"I understand he's fighting a war," Kelly said while jotting down their address and phone number on the grocery receipt I'd just provided. "But please tell your Frankie I want to meet him—and Teri too, of course. We have a cat she can play with. Tell Frankie that Geri makes a great pot roast—the best."

Frankie was unaware of this workday friendship, but I had a warm feeling about Kelly and Geri and decided that the time had come to tell him about this fascinating couple I'd befriended.

"Frankie, Kelly and Geri are so sweet, like grandparents. I know you'd love them!"

Being self-conscious about his looks, Frankie was reluctant to meet with them. The lumps on his neck stood out conspicuously, his weight was well below normal, and the last thing he wanted to do was make anyone uncomfortable.

After gentle prodding, Frankie eventually accepted their invitation. When I called Kelly and Geri with the news, they were ecstatic. That first dinner launched the beginning of a valued friendship.

Their modest home was located on a quiet street in Pomona, a quick 10-minute drive from our apartment. After a warm greeting at their front door and a quick tour of their modest home, I felt as though we'd known them a lifetime. While Geri introduced Teri to Sugar, their cat, Kelly and Frankie made themselves comfortable in the front room. From the warm tone of his voice, I knew Kelly had adopted Frankie. We were given an open invitation to weekly dinners, depending on how Frankie was feeling and when we were free, given our hectic schedules. Later that evening, we thanked them and agreed with Kelly—Geri's pot roast was the best. She even prepared a "to go" package of leftovers, enough for sandwiches and another meal.

Frankie had just completed a treatment, and daily trips to the hospital for blood monitoring were a priority. Kelly volunteered to help with transportation, thereby freeing me to spend more time with Teri and to better manage my work schedule. Frankie became Kelly's charge, and Kelly became a father figure to Frankie.

Geri quickly became my dear friend—a jewel. I began sharing my innermost feelings with her, things I could not share with my younger friends who were busy with husbands, jobs, and children. She had more time to listen to my heart. When I worried and cried, she had time to comfort me. She came to understand the hopelessness that drove my prayer requests, yet I suspected she looked upon my devotion to prayer as a denial of reality.

While the City of Hope continued to dip into a seemingly bottomless pit of treatments, Kelly stood by Frankie. He became acquainted with the staff, the treatments and side effects, as well as the ups and downs of rekindled hope and the inevitable downward spiral. The reality was obvious to Kelly; each failed treatment left Frankie noticeably weaker.

Kelly was a blessing. He was also a longstanding member of the prestigious Elks Lodge. He suggested that Frankie join the organization and explained how the benevolence of the lodge could be tremendously helpful. Frankie agreed and was soon initiated into Elk-dom. When he was feeling well enough, he attended meetings and enjoyed the friendly ambiance. The members quickly embraced their young comrade. Kelly had introduced Frankie to a new world.

Kelly never stopped thinking of ways to make our lives easier. He was keenly aware we were barely getting by on one income. Although my pay was adequate, working part-time meant scraping pennies.

He began seeking details about the origin of the illness—the tiny lump on Frankie's shoulder blade—and when it was brought to the attention of the Marine Corps enlistment doctors. He questioned why the lump was ignored by all the doctors Frankie had encountered in his life.

"And you're telling me none of these doctors, including the military medics, ever suggested taking a biopsy to see what the lump actually was?" Kelly asked.

"No, no one did!" Frankie told him. "They weren't concerned about it, so I never worried."

Kelly was convinced that Frankie might be entitled to military benefits and that the Elks Lodge might be of help. Many of the members had affiliations with the Veteran's Administration Board of Directors. Since this illness was not military-induced, Frankie was not convinced he was entitled to any benefits. It would be a hard-pressed connection, but Kelly looked at the situation from a far different perspective.

"You said the lump on your collarbone was there when you enlisted and you pointed it out during that first checkup. Correct? And you continued to make the doctors aware of this lump during all your checkups, including your last checkup before your discharge?" Kelly continued.

Frankie answered yes to all his questions.

"Something stinks. I think you have a case!"

The scenario was presented to the Elks Lodge members and they agreed, Frankie's unique situation had a better than average chance of approval.

Following Kelly's advice, Frankie made an appointment with the Los Angeles Veterans Administration. Having dealt with them in the past regarding his own health issues, Kelly knew the ropes. With Kelly at the helm, the Board was provided documentation from UCLA, the American Cancer Society, the hospital on the east coast and the City of Hope.

Kelly eloquently presented the facts, playing out the events leading up to the diagnosis. At the end of a question-and-answer session, Kelly confidently stated, "Had Mr. Attardo been treated sooner, the disease might not have progressed to this point."

The ducks were lined up and standing at attention. Six weeks later we were notified that an award had been granted, including college benefits for Teri's education.

Kelly's help was endless. He'd set aside his own personal health problems with emphysema to ensure Frankie got out of the house as much as possible. Long car rides and lunch at favorite restaurants became weekly events.

While Kelly injected bits of sunshine into Frankie's life, the health situation continued to worsen. The disease continued to aim and fire, and the gut-churning setbacks tore apart the veil of hope in my heart. Navigating through our world of uncertainty was emotionally draining. Almost two years had gone by, and Frankie had not yet responded to any treatments at the City of Hope. Dr. Sinclair's optimism was now shadowed by the reality that the prolonged treatments had probably damaged healthy organs.

And yet, Frankie's demeanor continued to amaze everyone. He was a rock, even after a treatment had not generated a positive result. Disappointment dropped off his shoulders like raindrops. He took each day as it came, always looking forward to the next day and the next treatment with renewed hope.

There were some exemptions from the cruelty of the treatments. Frankie never lost his beautiful hair or any of his teeth. Although he continued to take fastidious care of his appearance, sadly his diminished weight and the ashen look on his face were testimony of a losing battle.

With the opening of the Pomona Downtown Mall on Second Street, residents in the area welcomed the new, groundbreaking shopping experience. Conveniently located at one end of the mall was Freeman's Shoe Store, a rather unique establishment where Kelly was employed as a part-time salesman. The large store offered designer shoes at discount prices, and a continual flow of delighted customers was an every day event.

Most of the men employed at this store were retired military, most were disabled, and all possessed fun-filled personalities. The store was a great place to buy shoes or to visit for a few laughs. Kelly asked Frankie if he'd like to meet the guys, adding that it might be a great change of pace.

"I'm telling you these guys are crazy—pranksters, just like your brothers!" Kelly added for extra bait. In time Frankie agreed to go.

During one of Frankie's better days, Frankie called Kelly and told him he felt well enough to visit the store. Kelly was delighted, and I kept my fingers crossed that he'd feel well enough to enjoy the day. When he returned home later that day, he walked through the door wearing a wide smile, still feeling good, and anxious to tell me about the crazy guys he'd met. He sounded and looked like a child coming home from a candy store. It had been a while since I'd seen Frankie smile. Kelly's suggestion had turned out just as he'd imagined it would—a fun-filled day and a much-needed diversion to the nightmare of his illness.

It was obvious the guys at Freeman's had made a deep impression on Frankie, and soon he struggled to find the energy to visit the store. Mr. Freeman also had taken a special interest in this very ill young man and even suggested that a job might greatly benefit his emotional spirit. And when Kelly told us Mr. Freeman was tossing around the idea of asking Frankie to come to work on a "come in when you can" basis, we were taken aback by the kind offer.

Frankie was hesitant. He wasn't sure he had the energy at this point. But Kelly insisted he give it a whirl and reminded Frankie of Mr. Freeman's crystal-clear offer—come to work *only* when you feel up to it. Frankie decided to give it a try.

Frankie accepted the job but was never placed on the schedule. Whenever the treatments and side effects allowed, Frankie went to work. He quickly developed a love for the store and the guys. At times I could tell he was forcing himself to go. But once Kelly was at the door, the devil inside his body stepped aside.

The men at Freeman's embraced Frankie, as did Mrs. Freeman, a deeply religious and devout Jew. In time she told Frankie prayers were being offered at her synagogue and asked Frankie how he felt about being adopted into their place of worship—not a conversion, an adoption.

Frankie was deeply moved. "Prayers to God are prayers!" he told her. He thanked her and accepted a Jewish name—Isaac. Her compassion touched us both, and we were sincerely grateful.

It didn't take long for the guys at Freeman's to form a strong bond with Frankie. They quickly realized their problems were minor and extremely trivial in comparison. Before long they were pulling pranks on Frankie, and customers began asking for him. Just like the Elks Lodge, Freeman's was another B12 shot.

Frankie was not covered by insurance. Fortunately treatments at the City of Hope (back then) were gratis, except for blood transfusions. In the beginning, the American Cancer Society had covered all transfusion costs. When that option was no longer available, the Elks Lodge picked up the tab. When Frankie needed fresh blood—a person-to-person transfusion—calls for blood went out on the radio. It was astonishing how people with the same blood type would flock to the City of Hope. Their compassion opened my mind to the endless generosity of strangers.

We were tremendously appreciative for the government allotment as well. It had provided the much-needed breathing room for our financial situation. Yet we had remained frugal with our finances. Instead of buying a new car, we kept repairing the blue Ford we'd driven from New Jersey to California. But after endless trips to the hospital, it was clear that the car had seen better days.

Sometimes good things happen, and they often enter our lives unexpectedly and in odd ways. One afternoon, Karen and Gary stopped by in their shiny new black Ford and asked us to hop in. Riding in their slick-looking car with a new car smell was a real treat. The quiet hum of the new motor sounded like a tiger yawning after a long nap. I knew Frankie wanted another car—we both did. Watching Karen and Gary with their new toy stirred up old memories of our red car.

That night we talked about another car, revisited our budget, and realized the government allotment allowed us to afford a new car. Frankie was excited. He immediately called Kelly and asked if he had time to take him to car shop.

At the car lot, a new Ford grabbed Frankie's attention. He came home loaded with details, and I knew the fire to buy was blazing hot. The next day we drove to the car lot. Frankie walked directly towards the car he wanted, opened the door, sat in the driver's seat, and began checking out the latest gadgets and new technology. The car was a quantum leap from our old Ford, which was at that moment parked in nearby lot with a rope tied from the trunk to the bumper to keep it from popping open while driving.

Frankie got a well-deserved wish that night and drove home in a new Ford. That night we recaptured the euphoria with our red convertible, and for one evening our world seemed normal.

The following day, a call from Dr. Sinclair burst the happy bubble. The news stopped me cold and destroyed the magical new-car-owner experience. He told us Frankie's white cell count was dangerously high and insisted he return to the hospital immediately. I cried most of the day and through the night. The joy of the previous night was now a momentary gratification. He was back to fighting this wicked enemy.

What kept hope alive were the worldwide prayers offered each day on his behalf. We were armed to the nines, and Frankie was not alone in his war. God was always with us, and in the quiet solitude of a church, or our bedroom, or the car, or the hospital chapel, I would plead my case, and I never questioned who would win the battle. Praying fervently for a cure remained my focus. God would provide this miracle, and Frankie would live out a normal life.

Yet there was no escaping the fear and helplessness in our world. The words "Hodgkin's" or "cancer" would immediately flash into my mind before I opened my eyes each morning and would remain with me throughout the day, haunting me, nagging me until I drifted off to sleep at night. Sometimes the words would awaken me from a sound sleep.

In my mania during these most desperate of times—in my heaven-bent goal to help Frankie survive the perils of cancer—I'd pray before each meal and ask God to transfer the nutrients in the food I was about to consume to Frankie.

When treatments failed and a cure appeared to be inaccessible—beyond our reach—from behind the locked doors of our darkened apartment, alone and afraid, I would cry until exhausted. Yet, no matter how many setbacks, I would turn to God. I remained steadfast in my faith that He would fulfill this need. I accepted that Frankie had to struggle through a few more fiery hoops before God would cure him. In the end he'd be well, we would drive away in our new car, and the emotional scars of the illness would fall away like dry autumn leaves on a windy day.

Frankie's illness wasn't the only sadness in my life. Never being able to spend time with Teri weighed heavily in my heart. Each day was a struggle to balance work schedules and hospital runs, duties that left little time to be with her. There was no denying my frustration. I was perpetually running in all directions, and the three of us were hardly ever together.

One day, as I prepared to leave for work, I glanced at Teri as she watched television in my mother's living room. I desperately wanted to stay home with her that day, and knowing I could not, I felt desolate and helpless.

After kissing Teri goodbye and thanking my mother, my throat began to tighten as I turned to leave. By the time I reached the front door, tears were streaming down my face. I closed the door behind me and I began to cry.

My father was gardening close by, and after hearing my sobs, he rushed to my side and wrapped me in his arms. I told him I was scared,

Frankie was not getting better, the wellspring of drugs was running dry, and I hardly had any time for Teri.

"My world is upside-down, Daddy, I'm exhausted. He's not getting any better. Nothing is helping. It's hopeless," I cried. "And I can't help him, and neither can the doctors. Daddy, no matter how hard I pray, I'm scared that he's gonna die. I feel as though I've abandoned Teri. I hardly ever see her except to say hello or goodbye, and every time Frankie asks about her, my heart break—he misses her."

My father was taken aback by the desperation in my voice. He held on to me, but I began crying harder, trembling in his arms.

"What are you saying? Stop crying or you'll scare your daughter. You haven't abandoned anybody, especially Teri. She's fine; she's happy here!

"*Figlia mia, hai lavore da fare* . . . my daughter, you have work to do," he said. "And you're doing the best you can. Frankie is in God's Hands and there is only so much you can do," he added. "You may not know it, but you're an inspiration to everyone!"

The unhappy truth shattered my hope. I wanted to run. I tried breaking away from his embrace, but he drew me closer, and suddenly I remembered how safe it felt in his arms. He kissed my forehead and reminded me how strong I was and how my strength would help me through these dark days.

Perhaps it was the tone of his voice or his patient embrace—or both—but suddenly my mind cleared and my equilibrium returned. While driving to work, my heart turned to the Blessed Mother and I offered a quick prayer. Moments later, I reached down deep and found the strength my father assured me I possessed.

NEW YEAR'S EVE 1962

A few months before the end of the year, Kelly and Geri began promoting the Elk's Lodge annual New Year's Eve party. They told us the festive, black-tie event was a magnet for local dignitaries and Hollywood personalities. When we received our invitation, Frankie told me he hoped we could go. Since we lived moment to moment, attending the event would inevitably depend on how Frankie felt that day. However, I gestured towards the positive, set aside all my doubts and trepidations, mailed in our RSVP, and began looking forward to New Year's Eve and the party.

Frankie needed a new suit, and Kelly volunteered to take him shopping. In the past, Frankie loved buying new clothes. But things were different now. He was thin and would need to shop in the young men's department—something he greatly resented.

I needed something to wear as well. Not since high school had I shopped for dresses. Geri volunteered to help. We went to several stores, but our shopping excursions were frustrating. Most of the dresses didn't fit, and those that did were not exactly what she had in mind. After several exhausting trips downtown, she volunteered to sew my dress— something splashy, yet classy—a dress that would dazzle Frankie as well.

Geri loved to sew. She'd sewn all the outfits she wore and was looking forward to creating a beautiful dress for this special evening. A shiny, royal blue fabric with silver threads running through the design caught my eye. Geri loved it as well, said it was perfect for what she had in mind. With her help I chose a dress pattern, shoes, a purse and a fancy evening jacket to match the color of the fabric. Geri dug in and began to sew, and when she was done, I was astonished. The dress was stunning, one that would brighten that night, and I could hardly wait to surprise Frankie.

On the day of the event, I was thankful Frankie was home and not in the hospital. I'd been scheduled to work, Teri was at my mother's house, and Kelly volunteered to stop by and check on Frankie during the day. At work I kept wondering and hoping we would not be making a mad dash to the hospital instead of the ball. Frankie was looking forward to the evening as well, and I could hardly wait for him to see me in that beautiful dress. During my break I called Kelly. He told me Frankie slept during the day and was still feeling well when he left.

At 6 p.m. I clocked out and rushed home, leaving just enough time to shower and get dressed. When I arrived home and opened the front door, I was greeted with a wonderful surprise. Frankie was sitting on the living room couch, fully dressed and ready to leave. He smiled, stood up, and walked towards me.

Lately, shows of emotions—times when he felt well enough to indulge in a sweet kiss—had been scarce. This was one such moment, when we stepped aside from the gravity of our problems and shared a heart-stopping kiss and a quiet embrace.

As I rushed to get ready, I hoped nothing would happen to mar this night, this special evening that Frankie had been looking forward to for months. When I was done dressing, I walked into the living room and watched his eyes grow bright, brighter than the strand of rhinestones around my neck. The look on his face was the same one he wore on our wedding day and the day Teri was born—deliriously happy times that were never far from my mind.

Except on prom night and our wedding day, he had never seen me dressed formally. As he walked towards me, I could see his eyes had dampened, and I knew we would have both cried had it not been for the knock on the door announcing that Kelly and Geris had arrived.

We had never attended a gala event with men in tuxedos and women in lovely, long evening gowns. Even the prom wasn't as elegant. The event looked as festive as Cinderella's ball. Many members wished us "Happy New Year" and shared how pleased they were to see Frankie. Each time I looked his way, Frankie was smiling and I knew he was enjoying the evening.

Eleven o'clock on New Year's Eve is a special hour for Elks Lodge members. It is the hour when they pause to honor and remember those who have passed on. It was an especially somber moment for me. I reflected on the past year and wondered about the following year—if Frankie and I would be attending the next New Year's Eve party or if he would be the one being honored and remembered.

FIGHT, MY LOVE, FIGHT

Beyond a doubt, our lives were driven by the demands of the treatments. Frankie's life resembled a rollercoaster ride. There were ups and downs and loops and curves. At times it felt as though Frankie, Teri, and I were alone on this planet, existing in our own private nightmare. People around me were functioning on a different level, and I could barely disguise my envy of those enjoying normal lives, of families where illnesses had not twisted their lives into a formidable existence.

Whenever the nightmarish world we were tethered to got the best of me, I would turn to Dr. Kleinman. I relied on him. He had taken a special interest in Frankie, and I knew he would regularly call Dr. Sinclair for more technical details on his treatments. Recognizing the doctor's genuine concern, I leaned on him, and whenever I called to lament, he would invite me to stop by. He tried preparing me for what seemed inevitable to him, but I would not listen. I knew he regarded my prayers as crutches. He'd gently remind me that Frankie had never experienced a remission, except when he was given Velban, but that was short lived. He'd tell me Frankie was now vulnerable to infection and that I needed to understand and accept that fact—a fact I passionately rejected.

Somehow I always rose above the negativity; somehow I always felt better after speaking to him, especially the times when he'd speculate and put hope back on the mound.

"I honestly believe there is only one way to cure cancer," he explained one afternoon. "Cancer patients need to be exposed to a more virulent virus—something similar to the viruses thriving close to the equator." I snickered at his theory and asked if he knew where I might find such a virus without going to the South America.

Theoretically, his virus speculation had merit. I wondered if any research was being conducted in this area. When I mentioned the theory to Dr. Sinclair, he simply shook his head. He was inundated by many theories and was dealing with the reality of a difficult case. His patient had been weakened by the treatments, and there were few options left. Dr. Sinclair had scraped the bottom of what was once a bottomless pit.

Frankie was fighting another battle. He missed Teri, and she missed him as well. She had not forgotten her daddy and continued to ask about him. I would reassure her that he would be home soon, and she continued to accept my responses. Yet there was sadness in her eyes when we spoke of him. When Frankie was feeling well enough to be home, I'd bring Teri home from my parents' house so we could all be together. I was concerned that she'd be frightened; his eyes had sunken deeply into his face. Frankie looked very frail and spent his time on the couch or in bed. At this point, Teri fully understood how very ill he was.

Frankie loved his time at home. For a while we were a family, just the three of us. Teri would quietly sit in front of him, and he'd watch her play with her toys. Sometimes she would sit next to him and they would solve a puzzle. I could almost taste the sadness in his heart. I knew he would have preferred to be outside teaching her to ride her bike.

In August 1963, an anomaly seemingly unrelated to the cancer occurred. Frankie developed hiccups—persistent hiccups—loud and exhausting hiccups. They began while he was in the hospital recuperating from a treatment. The staff was sure the hiccups would quickly pass, but when they continued through the night and into the morning, Dr. Sinclair was notified. He left instructions on methods to stop the attack, but nothing helped. By the third day, the sound of unrelenting hiccups began to disturb other patients, and Frankie was moved into an isolation ward. A surgical option was available—cutting a nerve in the diaphragm—but Frankie was now too weak to undergo surgery.

The hiccupping continued through the week. Staff members stopped by and provided a myriad of solutions, but nothing helped. Dr. Sinclair's told me it was a matter of wait and see, and hopefully, the hiccupping would stop on its own. Yet the persistent hiccupping continued into a second week.

By the tenth day, things seemed hopeless. He was exhausted, and I feared the hiccups would end his life. By mid-morning, while several nurses attended to him, I waited outside his room. Suddenly, one of the nurses opened the door and told me Frankie's vitals had dropped, a situation that sets off a hospital code—an automatic call for a priest— and my already upside-down world took a frightening turn.

"A priest? Oh no, please, no. Don't send for a priest! Frankie might wake up and find a priest by his side giving him Last Rites. That would be terrifying!"

"The call is automatic," she explained. "He's already on the way. Frankie's exhausted. He won't wake up. Even if he does, he won't be alert enough to know what's going on or even care.

"Just stay close, hold his hand," she suggested sweetly. "Frankie knows when you're here by his side."

The last thing I wanted was a priest administering Last Rites to Frankie, yet it was out of my control. I called Kelly, then my mother, and returned to his room. I was alone, frightened, and in my prayers I asked God why it had come to this point. Why did Frankie have to suffer? I wanted to run, but I waited, held Frankie's hand, and the moment the priest entered the room, I froze. The priest blessed Frankie and asked me to clear the nightstand. As he set up the altar with holy water, anointing oils, and a crucifix, every sound in that room ceased. The setting did not seem real. The priest was poised to offer death prayers, and I felt as though I was in a gray and cold place. All I wanted to do was run home where it was warm.

Praying always brought me back to center, and I headed for the serenity of the chapel. I wanted to chastise God for not hearing my prayers. I wanted to unleash my rage at Him. Instead I prayed with renewed confidence. I asked God to take pity on Frankie and to cleanse his body of cancer and the hiccups. I prayed until I was exhausted. And when a burst of fresh confidence fell over me, I made the sign of the cross and returned to his bedside. Once again I was in the comfort zone of faith.

When I returned to his room, the priest had gone, and Kelly was standing by his bedside. Frankie was still asleep, but the hiccups remained, stoically, and Kelly told me to take a break, assuring me he'd stay close.

I decided to sit on the terrace outside his bedroom. His bed and the monitors could easily be seen outside from where I sat. I just needed a few moments to unwind and breathe in some fresh air. The star-filled sky made me feel closer to God. I closed my eyes and thought about Frankie's hiccupping and about the priest and his prayers. The likelihood that Frankie might die crossed my mind, but I set it aside. He would not die. I loved him, he loved me, he would never leave me—not now—maybe when we were old and feeble. It was a solemn promise we'd made to one another.

I began to pray, and I asked God for a sign that Frankie would survive—a falling star would suit me fine. I waited and watched the sky closely. After a while, disappointed that nothing extraordinary had occurred, I went back into his room.

After Kelly left, I settled into the chair by his bed. I dosed off but was awakened by the sound of two nurses rushing in. They told me Frankie's vitals were registering normal. Except for the elation in their voices, the room was quiet—the hiccups had vanished. I wondered if this was the sign I'd prayed for earlier. As always, any hint of good news sent my hopes soaring. How could I *not* believe this was the sign I'd prayed for on the terrace earlier?

Three months after the hiccup episode, another disturbing event occurred: Frankie came down with a virulent blood infection. We were at home when Frankie's temperature spiked to 104. Kelly and I rushed him to the hospital.

Results from numerous blood tests proved inconclusive; the infection was unidentifiable, and the doctors were baffled. Fearing he was contagious, Frankie was placed in isolation. Antibiotics were administered, although it was a guessing game. With no identifying markers in his blood, the doctors scrambled for answers, hoping he could fight off the nameless infection in spite of his weakened state.

Recalling Dr. Kleinman's virus theory, I immediately called him and described Frankie's current condition.

"Remember what you told me about the "bigger virus" theory? Do you think it has any merit right now, in his condition? They can't seem to identify the virus."

Dr. Kleinman asked a few more questions. He seemed elated but skeptical. His hypothesis had no backing; it was merely a theory. He told me to keep in touch and he would contact Dr. Sinclair for more details.

Frankie was delirious—oblivious of his whereabouts, unaware of the nurses and technicians entering his room dressed in isolation garments. While the infection raged, opinions were sought from other doctors and medical institutions. No stone was left unturned. Eventually his vital signs dropped low enough to trigger another call for a priest.

This time I did not wait for the priest to arrive. After calling Kelly, calling home, and calling Frankie's mother Mary, I went directly to the chapel. Recalling the encouraging results after the priest's last visit, I remained confident that Frankie would be fine. If the virus didn't obliterate or stop the cancer, the Last Rites would chase away this devil.

I prayed until Kelly came back and found me in the chapel. We chatted for a while and then walked towards Frankie's room. Frankie looked peaceful, yet the fever continued to rage.

Later that evening, I sank into the lounge chair by his bed and drifted off to sleep. During an early morning bed check, a night duty nurse awakened me and told me his fever had dropped to normal. I rushed to feel his forehead. It felt wonderfully cool, and I was convinced, once again, that God's Hand had played a part in his recovery. Yet the best was to follow.

Just as it had mysteriously appeared, after five horrendous days, the ambiguous virus had vanished without ever being identified. However, the battle necessitated fresh blood transfusions, and the need was aired over radio stations. After receiving two pints of blood, Frankie felt stronger and had a wonderfully healthy glow on his face.

Dr. Sinclair arrived early for his morning rounds and was beaming from head to toe over the outcome. He chatted with Frankie for a few minutes and then examined the areas where the tumors were normally visible. He hesitated for a moment, and his fingers dug deeper into the neck area and down his back. He looked puzzled, but he turned to Frankie and told him the tumors on his neck and back had shrunk—greatly. He was smiling widely, shaking his head in disbelief, and immediately ordered X-rays of the other problem areas.

The X-rays confirmed that most of the lumps had disappeared, and the news sparked a groundswell of excitement throughout the hospital. It spread like a wildfire. I was convinced that Frankie was cured—the mysterious virus had destroyed the cancer—an unmistakable answer to prayers and major kudos to Dr. Kleinman's theory.

Frankie's astonishing recovery was the topic of discussion everywhere. The hospital was inundated with many new faces. Many doctors traveled from afar to learn more about the events that led to this baffling recovery. Yet Dr. Sinclair seemed reserved. He regarded the mysterious recovery with some skepticism. Although Dr. Kleinman had shared his theory with me when I called him, much like Dr. Sinclair, he was unconvinced of an actual connection between viruses and cancer. For the doctors, Frankie's recovery was an anomaly.

Although he was painfully thin, the healthy glow on Frankie's face from the blood transfusions was uplifting, and he returned home with renewed energy. Frankie set a goal: eat well, gain some weight, and call Carnation.

But it was not to be. One month later, Frankie woke up with excruciating pain in his stomach. At the hospital, tests revealed the cancer had metastasized to his stomach, groin, and lungs.

With the sound of his moaning tearing at my heart, hope was placed on a back burner. Later that evening, the morphine kicked in and Frankie fell asleep. The blackness of doubt had drained every ounce of my energy. Once again I wanted to rage at God, yet I felt empty inside. Frankie was back to square one. Except now there was pain, gut-wrenching pain. We were living in a house of horrors; the battle had taken its toll. Frankie was barely one hundred pounds. His big, beautiful blue eyes now looked larger—much sadder.

I dialed Dr. Kleinman's number. The moment I heard his voice I cried, and he asked me to stop by his office. When I arrived, I sat by his desk, and he told me he just spoken to Dr. Sinclair.

"Are you aware that Frankie has been coded as critical?"

"No, I didn't know. Besides, what does it mean? Labels mean little to me, things can change by the moment," I answered dismissively.

"It means a lot, it notes his condition. You need to get a hold of yourself and understand where things stand. Frankie can't go on much longer. I know you don't want to hear this, but he is very weak, too weak to go on much longer."

"He'll jump back. He always does," I said tearfully. "This crisis will pass, just like the others, and he'll get better—he has to."

"No he won't," the doctor insisted. "It's impossible! If my virus theory had no effect, then I was unfortunately wrong, and nothing will turn things around. Listen to me, your job is to do what you've been doing—visit him, wear a smile, look your prettiest, tell him how much you love him. There is nothing more you can do. I know it's difficult but you have to prepare yourself and your daughter. Do you understand?"

"Prepare? Tell Teri her daddy is dying? No, I won't! He's not going to die."

"You may not be preparing yourself, but you are watching something that inevitably will come to pass."

With the doctor's words weighing heavily in my heart, I raced back to the hospital. Frankie was now sleeping; the meds had provided relief. As he slept, I watched the monitors and held his hands—now swelled from the edema that had infused most of his upper torso.

JFK—NOVEMBER 1963

Those of us old enough will clearly remember the event that unfolded on November 23, 1963. It is a day etched in our minds, the day President John F. Kennedy was assassinated. Each of us can easily recall where we were when we learned the president had been shot and the shock that filled our hearts and embedded itself in our consciousness.

Frankie was in the hospital on that day, and I'd spent the night by his bedside. By mid-morning of the next day, I needed to go home and tend to some neglected chores. I also needed to pick Teri up from school and take her to my parents' house. Kelly agreed to stay with Frankie until I returned. Knowing Kelly was with him always put me at ease. After assuring Kelly I'd be back as soon as possible, I raced to my car for the short drive home.

When I arrived home, I turned on the television for background noise and dug into my chores. Suddenly a bulletin flashed across the screen, and the trembling voice of Walter Cronkite read an official statement, *"Here is a bulletin from CBS News. In Dallas, Texas, three shots were fired at President Kennedy's motorcade in downtown Dallas. The first reports say that President Kennedy has been seriously wounded by this shooting."* At first the words didn't register. I turned the channel only to hear the same words repeated by other newscasters—Kennedy had been shot.

Preliminary reports were sketchy and flowed in slowly. The reports noted the President had been riding in a motorcade on Dealey Plaza in Dallas and was seated in the backseat of the car with Jackie when the bullets from an assassin met their target. The president had been taken to a hospital; his condition remained unknown.

Soon details of the moments prior to the tragedy began to surface—the ride down Dealey Plaza, the sound of three shots, and the president slumping in Jackie's lap. Reports noted that the shots came from the book depository building.

With the disturbing news trapped in my mind, I completed my chores and picked Teri up at school. When I arrived at my mother's house, I immediately turned on the television. The news reports now stated that the president's condition had turned critical.

There is nothing more evocative than the peal of church bells. And when the bells of Our Lady of Lourdes Catholic Church began ringing a mournful toll, the tone echoed that the president had probably passed away.

Until that moment, nothing had ever distracted me from Frankie's health, yet I could not detach myself from the horrible tragedy. I drove back to the hospital completely focused on the news blasting loudly in my car. At the hospital, Kelly was watching the news in Frankie's room. They were showing Jackie holding the President's bloodied head on her lap, the frantic drive to the hospital, and the heart-wrenching news that John Kennedy had passed away.

It was Friday, six days before Thanksgiving. In homes throughout the nation, everyone set aside their normal Thanksgiving traditions to watch the tragic events unfold. Reports soon shifted away from Jackie and turned their focus to the speedy capture of the lone gunman, Lee Harvey Oswald.

The moment-by-moment news accounts led to Vice President Johnson's swearing-in ceremony, yet every heart was with Jackie, our gracious first lady. In spite of the tragic event, Jackie maintained control of her emotions. Her demeanor was admirable and touched hearts all over the world.

Two days later, reporters followed Lee Harvey Oswald as he was being transported through the Dallas Police Headquarters en route to the Dallas County Jail. No one dared to stray far from their television sets. The world watched as cameras captured the moment Jack Ruby shot and killed Oswald. Live television resembled a Friday night movie.

On the day of the funeral, Jackie looked beautiful—a class act. As she bravely held the hands of her two young children Caroline and John-John, the world watched and shared her grief. Her poise touched everyone, especially during the funeral procession, when the horse-drawn caisson carrying her husband's coffin slowly made its way to the U.S. Capitol. I envied her composure and wondered if I could ever be as strong. Her bravado was admirable.

Tidbits of information about Jackie Kennedy's last moments with her deceased husband were later revealed; how she removed her wedding band from her left hand and slipped it on the President's finger.

Jackie's image remained with me. Whenever doubts about Frankie's recovery fell over me and I feared he would die, I thought of her. I promised myself if my prayers were not answered, I would emulate Jackie's dignity and demeanor. For Teri, I promised. Yet I never wandered far from my firm belief that Frankie would survive—he promised me!

AN IMPOSSIBLE DREAM

Long before the hiccup and virus episodes, Dr. Sinclair had begun to recycle treatments, combining drugs in varying dosages. These were desperate attempts to halt the further progression of the cancer, always with the hope of bringing about a desperately-needed remission. Frankie had been severely weakened by three years of continual treatments, and I was not surprised when we were told further treatments would be placed on hold.

Frankie was weaned off morphine and placed on a more potent medication. Once the meds were adjusted and he was no longer in pain, he asked me to take him home, and I froze. I did not want Teri to see him in this condition, but Dr. Sinclair came to his defense.

"He needs to be home. It's Christmas," he added. Setting aside my apprehensions, Frankie came home. Once again Teri surprised me and never questioned his frail appearance.

With Christmas only two weeks away, I set aside all my trepidations and began planning for the holidays. To a child, the season meant the baby Jesus, Santa, toys and a decorated Christmas tree. Teri deserved far more than she was receiving, as did Frankie. With him at home, I made up my mind to make this holy season special.

A week before Christmas, I came home with a tree. Lying on the couch, Frankie watched as Teri and I began sorting the colorful ornaments we'd purchased during our first Christmas in North Carolina. With Christmas music softly playing in the background, we sang and strung lights and hung decorations. When we were done, we sat on the floor admiring the snow scene under the tree, the tiny cardboard nativity scene, and the miniature town we created to replicate Bethlehem. Later

I dimmed the lights and turned up the Christmas music. With only tree lights illuminating the room, the apartment looked cozy, as though it were a happy home where a mommy, a daddy and their young child were preparing to celebrate the birth of the Christ child—and the arrival of Santa.

In spite of the vicious illness now a breath away from snatching Frankie from our lives, that night was peaceful. Frankie was quiet, wrapped in his own thoughts, drinking in the beauty of the moment. I wondered what was in his heart, what he was thinking. Although I held on to hope, I now found it impossible not to have doubts, not to muse about the agonizing reality that this might be his last Christmas.

On Christmas Eve, my father stopped by and asked us to come over for dinner. We accepted and told him we'd be there later. It was now a struggle for Frankie to leave the apartment, yet he gave it a hero's try. During dinner he became ill and we rushed home. Our days were no longer uneventful, and we spent Christmas Eve and Christmas Day alone in our cozy apartment.

On New Year's Day, 1964, Frankie woke up with severe stomach cramps, and I called Kelly. With Frankie slumped over in the backseat of his car, Kelly raced down the highway. X-rays revealed that the newly enlarged lymph nodes in his stomach and groin areas had grown larger, as did the lumps in the neck area. Dr. Sinclair's focus was now on Frankie's comfort, and his meds were adjusted to relieve the pain. Once the pain was under control, Frankie asked to go home.

Adding insult to misery were the lumps on his neck that had burst open and were oozing. I was frightened; there was no escaping this devil, and I braced myself for another bumpy ride. I knew I could never allow Teri to see him in this condition and was unsure of my own limits. I hoped I had the strength to care for him. I was also painfully aware that Frankie deserved to be home, among the familiar things he loved.

Frankie was able to go home but was clearly a shadow of his old self, bedridden, unable to walk more than a few steps. His beautiful, deep-set eyes were now deeper, and his boundless vitality was gone. The new meds seemed to be helping, but a few days later, he was stricken with gut-wrenching cramps. While Kelly and I prepared for another hospital run, Frankie insisted on staying home. It hurt my heart to see him in such pain. I wanted him to have whatever he desired, and yet, caring for him at home had become a challenge.

Dr. Sinclair preferred that the meds be administered in the hospital, but he honored Frankie's wishes and called in a prescription to a local pharmacy. He also prepared me. He told me the new meds were far stronger than the last painkillers, and most likely Frankie would become incoherent and could hallucinate.

Once the meds kicked in, I relaxed, grateful for little things like the sound of his gentle snoring during a pain-free slumber. Taking a deep breath, I thanked God he was finally resting comfortably.

Frankie settled into a comfort zone of sorts, although he barely ate and mostly slept. I relaxed, yet I wondered where this was headed, and I kept in close touch with Dr. Sinclair.

For a few days, the situation was stable—until the day I heard Frankie call my name in a tone that told me something was drastically wrong. I rushed into the bedroom and found him standing by the bed with a look of pure terror on his face.

"Look at this!" he said as he pulled up his t-shirt. This was the first time I'd seen fear in his eyes. I gasped at what I was seeing. He waited for me to offer a logical answer, an assurance that would mitigate the horror he'd woken up to.

I stood by the door, paralyzed at the sight of a massive lump protruding from his chest wall. He looked deformed. My knees felt weak, and I reached to steady myself on the back of the chair by the bed. I was speechless, and all I could do was stare at him until he dropped back onto the bed.

I sat by his bedside, horrified at the sight, incapable of providing any encouragement. All I could do was rub his back gently until he calmed down. A few minutes later I called Kelly, and then I called my mother.

"Mom, we're rushing Frankie to the hospital. I don't think I'll be back tonight." As the last word left my lips, my throat choked closed and I was no longer able to speak.

I felt lost, frightened, and I fought to hold back my tears. It now looked hopeless, and the panic I saw in his eyes had drilled into my mind. It deeply pained me to see the look of terror in his eyes.

As I waited for Kelly, I said a quick prayer but suddenly realized Teri needed some things, and I decided to make a quick run to my mother's house.

"Frankie, Kelly is on his way and the front door is unlocked. I have to bring Teri some things. I'll be right back, I promise."

The trip to my mother's house and back would take less than fifteen minutes. I was sure Kelly and Geri would arrive before I returned.

I remember the following event as though it occurred recently and not forty-seven years ago . . .

I quickly packed some of Teri's things, raced to my mother's house, and rushed home. As I approached the front door, I heard sounds. Assuming Geri and Kelly were inside, I walked in and called their names, but there was no response. The shades were drawn, the room was dark, and when I flipped on the light, I quickly realized the sounds were coming from Frankie. He was lying on the living room floor in a fetal position and sobbing openly. He was speaking, but his words were choked with tears, and I could not understand what he was desperately attempting to say.

I fell to my knees and tried pulling him close, but he was doubled over and rocking from side to side. I stretched out beside him, and soon the words he was muttering became clear. He was crying and praying and thanking God for bringing Teri and me into his life. He was pleading with God to lift the nightmare and keep us safe and in good health. He thanked God that he'd been allowed to live long enough to know the joy of being a father. He repeated his plea for our health and to keep us safe.

Fearing he was about to die in my arms, I drew him close. When he realized I was by his side, he folded me into his arms. We lay together in a locked embrace rocking back and forth. In between his prayers, he told me he loved me, thanked me for marrying him, for loving him, for taking care of him. I was frightened and begged him to stop praying. I begged him not to leave me, not then, not ever. I told him I loved him again and again.

"Frankie, I love you. Why are you praying this way? Remember the promises we made to each other? We said we'd always be together no matter what happened. You're scaring me."

Suddenly he became quiet and, taking hold of my face, thanked me for loving him again and again, over and over. He told me how lucky he was to have me as his wife and was sorry I had to suffer through his nightmare.

I did not hear the door open nor footsteps close by, nor did I hear Kelly's voice, nor did I see the tears running down Geri's face. I did not feel their presence as they watched us locked together on the floor, crying and praying as though we were the only two people on earth.

It took awhile longer to feel Kelly hand rubbing my back and to hear Geri's gentle sobs.

"What happened? Why are you both on the floor? Did he fall?" Kelly asked.

"No. I left to take some clothes to my mom's, and when I came home, he was on the floor praying."

While Kelly helped Frankie into the backseat of the car, I called the hospital. Soon we were racing down the highway. Frankie's head was resting on my lap. He was moaning, but all I could do was stroke his head gently. His emotional prayers just a few minutes earlier began to play over and over in my mind. I was emotionally exhausted and worried, and I wondered why in all of God's Goodness He would allow such horror to befall Frankie.

Kelly drove directly to the emergency entrance. The staff was expecting us, and Frankie was immediately placed on an IV drip. By the time he was settled in a room, he was sleeping peacefully.

After Kelly and Geri left, I sat by Frankie's bedside. The room was serenely quiet, and my mind drifted back to our apartment and the scene that took place before we left for the hospital. I knew then that time would never dim the memory of those heart-wrenching moments. His emotional words and feelings were burned into my mind and would return like echoes, always reminding me of that chilling afternoon.

Frankie slept through the night, waking the following morning for a few groggy moments of awareness and then falling back to sleep. While he slept, several young interns joined Dr. Sinclair for morning rounds. They spoke in muted tones and took turns examining the shockingly large lump in Frankie's chest area as well as the X-rays that confirmed the tumor. And when they were done, Dr. Sinclair asked me to stop by his office.

I knocked on his office door, and a barely audible voice asked me to come in. Dr. Sinclair was seated at his desk, and for the first time, his eyes did not immediately look up to meet mine. When he finally looked up, he asked me to sit down and began speaking.

"You've been with him every step of way, and you must know the treatments have not stopped the progression of the illness. However, we can't give up, not yet. I'd like to administer another treatment, and I'm hoping you'll agree. I'm referring to TBR."

Before he uttered the last word, I felt the earth shake below me. I had heard about TBR—total body radiation—a treatment that needed little clarification. I was also aware that this treatment was a final effort to stop the cancer, and I was solidly against it.

My hands were trembling. This was the first time I would disagree with him. "Dr. Sinclair, can you explain what good can come from giving him this treatment? He weighs one hundred pounds. It makes little sense to radiate his entire body," I said tearfully. "It will kill him."

"I understand your apprehension, but in all good faith, we can't leave any stone unturned."

My back was against the wall. I was not a doctor. Neither was I well informed on the subject. I based my argument on the conversations I'd heard in the waiting room from families whose loved ones had died after this treatment. Nevertheless I agreed—reluctantly—knowing full well the treatment would do little more than damage everything in its path.

Frankie would never be aware of Dr. Sinclair's last attempt to save his life. He was sleeping peacefully when the attendants carefully lift his frail body onto the gray metal bed in the center of a dimly lit and very intimidating room. He continued to sleep as they aligned his body to accept the beams of cobalt from a large tube that resembled a giant flashlight.

Thirty minutes later, an attendant rolled Frankie back to his room. Dr. Sinclair stopped by and tried rousing Frankie from his state of semi-consciousness.

While he slept, I called his mother, as well as the Red Cross. His brother Chuck was in the Air Force stationed overseas. That afternoon, Mary called my mother and told her she would arrive in the morning and Tommy was with her. Later that day, I was notified that Chuck would arrive as soon as possible.

I sat at Frankie's bedside and rested my head on his pillow. His eyes were shut, and I wondered if he could sense I was close by, if he was aware of my heart beating in harmony with his. I held his swollen hand and noticed his skin was taunt and shiny, stretched to the limits from the fluids. I spoke to him in my mind, and in a language that crosses all barriers, I begged him to fight, fight hard, and I reminded him of the promise we'd made to one another.

His sleep was restless, delusional, and he kept shifting in and out of consciousness. In some small way, knowing he was no longer in pain was comforting. But it was difficult to watch his arms thrash around aimlessly and to listen to his ramblings about past events in his life. He spoke of the movie we watched when he came home from boot camp. Other times he seemed to be praying. Frankie was already in a far more peaceful place.

The following morning, I sat in the bedside chair and watched the nurses change his bedclothes and sheets. Frankie never opened his eyes and was oblivious to the nurses sponging his face with a cool cloth and refreshing his mouth and the perfectly aligned teeth that he'd fastidiously cared for. I had not seen his lower torso in a while. When the nurse pulled down the top sheet and lifted his nightshirt, I froze. All that remained was a paper-thin layer of wrinkled skin over a very visible skeletal frame. You could easily count his ribs, his legs were pencil thin, and I was sure he now weighed less than one hundred pounds.

While Kelly drove to Los Angeles to pick up Mary and Tommy, we were notified that Chuck would arrive later than day. By evening we were all together, standing by his bedside. Mary placed her rosary in Frankie's hand. I watched and hoped the sound of their voices would bring him around. He had not acknowledged anyone's presence for days and was unaware his mother and brothers were by his side.

Once again a priest had been notified. Frankie would be receiving the Last Rites for a third time. I began to pray with a deeper intensity, believing against all odds the TBR would have an effect. I prayed for a miracle, hoping it would happen that evening with his family at his side. I continued to trust in God, believing Frankie would come very close to the gates of heaven before he was cured.

We remained by his side throughout the night, sleeping on chairs in his room and on couches in the waiting rooms. When we awoke the following morning, Frankie was in a deep coma. Father Fiore, the priest from Our Lady of Lourdes, had been driving to the hospital every day to administer Holy Communion. The guys from Freeman's and other close friends, some from the Elks Lodge, also stopped by. Feeling detached from the commotion of people coming and going, I stood by the door of his room and focused solely on the rosary beads twirled tightly around my hands.

I thought about Teri. I wanted her with me but dared not bring her to the hospital. Frankie would not know she was close by, and she would be frightened to see what was left of him. I wanted her to remember him strong, healthy, an active and loving dad that was once ready to run and play. If not that, I at least wanted her to remember how he looked on the couch on Christmas Eve.

Mary and I had visited the chapel to pray as soon as she arrived. She told me she'd been asking God to take him. She wanted to speak to a priest and ask if it was a sin to ask for this favor—if it was wrong to ask God to release him from all the suffering. I was stunned. I could hardly believe what she told me. While I prayed for a miracle, she was praying for death. Her words infuriated me. When Father Fiore stopped by that morning, she spoke from her heart and asked if it was wrong to ask God to take her son away from his pain.

"No, it's not wrong," he answered. "Asking God to free him of pain is kind. Just remember, God won't take him until his work on earth is done. I will pray that God provides you and your family the needed strength."

Mary turned and asked me to understand how she was feeling. But I could not. I wanted to run away from her. She was walking down a street of hopelessness; I was not.

IF YOU DIE BEFORE ME, ASK GOD IF YOU CAN BRING A FRIEND

On the morning of March 27, 1964, Tommy and Chuck stood by Frankie's bedside, speaking to him, hoping he could hear their voices. They joked as though he could hear them, and they spoke of the good ol' days in the Bronx, the pranks they'd pulled on one another, especially the ones on their mother. They hoped that maybe he could hear them and would open his eyes and respond.

Standing at the foot of the bed, Mary prayed silently, oblivious to the conversation between the brothers. Kelly and I stood alongside the bed as well, noting Frankie's shallow breathing and listening to Tommy and Chuck's banter.

After Dr. Sinclair completed his morning rounds that morning, he asked me to meet him in his office. And when I arrived, I was greeted by the somber look of someone about to share disturbing news. He asked me to sit down, then stepped around his desk and reached for my hand, and looking directly into my eyes, he began speaking softly, slowly.

"I'm going to be painfully direct. Although it's too early to tell if the TBR had any effect, I have surmised that it did not. Frankie has slipped into a coma, and his body is shutting down. He can't possibly live through the night."

With his mind-numbing words whirling around in my head, I sat in stunned silence. He confirmed my worst fears—none of the drugs had helped. He told me Frankie would probably pass away that night, yet that could not be. For a moment, I wandered away from hope. I questioned God and asked Him why my prayers had not yet been answered.

Dr. Sinclair's words had sliced across my heart. He began to share his feelings, his hopes, his disappointments, and then he touched on the treatments, how brave Frankie had been, his stamina to withstand the brutal side effects. He spoke as though Frankie was already gone.

Unlike in the past, Dr. Sinclair had nothing positive to share—no words of comfort, no words of encouragement, no words to keep us hoping. I could tell he was hurting as well; we had reached the street of hopelessness. Being young, Frankie's chances had been better than most. The doctor had made no bones about his fondness towards Frankie. He felt deeply about his young patient, wanted a happy ending to his pain-filled journey. I'd seen Dr. Sinclair attending Mass at Our Lady of Lourdes on Sunday mornings, and I knew he offered prayers for all his patients. I suspected Frankie was foremost on his mind.

Before going back to Frankie's room, I went to the chapel. My heart felt heavy. I tried to find the right words—new words to send singing to the heavens. And once again I asked God why He had not yet answered my prayers.

Kelly had been at Frankie's bedside most of the day. It was evening now, and he wanted to go home and bring Geri to the hospital. Standing by Frankie's bed and hoping Frankie could hear his voice, he said, "Hang in there, Buddy. I'm going home to get Geri. She wants to say hello."

I walked Kelly to the front door. When we reached the exit, he turned towards me and said, "Listen, I'm worried about you, really worried," he said. "Do you understand what's going on? 'Cause I'm not sure you do. Frankie won't live through the night. Do you hear what I'm saying?"

"Well, you're wrong—you're all wrong, including the doctor!" I snapped back. "He'll hit bottom and jump back. He always does, you know that. You've seen him do it!"

"No, not this time. Listen to me—you need to snap out of this fantasy world you're living in. Teri is going to need you, and you need to be strong for her as well as yourself."

"No, Frankie's not gonna die. Stop saying that!" I shot back.

"Well you're wrong. Frankie can't get better. It's not possible, not at this point!"

Kelly argued his point for a few more minutes. When I began to cry, he backed off, apologized for upsetting me, and walked towards his car.

I felt so alone, the only one who held out hope for a recovery. No one had any faith—not the doctor, not his mother, not Kelly. Yet my heart told me this was not the time to turn away from believing Frankie would recover.

I needed to get a hold of myself, sit alone for a few minutes, and separate myself from Kelly's confrontation. The waiting room was a few short steps from Frankie's room. I turned down the lights and settled into the familiar couch.

What's wrong with everyone? I wondered. *Death should not be Frankie's reward. I want him well. He has to get well, and I know he will.*

I needed to pray before returning to his room. *God, can You hear me? Are You listening? How much longer does he have to suffer before he gets well?*

Suddenly Mary walked into the room and sat next to me. Taking hold of my hand, she whispered, "I need you to promise me something."

"Promise you?" I questioned.

"Yes, promise me. I have to tell you something, but I need you to promise me you won't scream."

"Why would I scream?" I asked.

"Promise me," she pleaded.

"I promise—what is it?"

Looking directly into my eyes, she squeezed my hand tighter. Her voice was barely above a whisper. "It's Frankie," she said. "He's gone. He opened his eyes, looked around, took a breath, and he was gone. He didn't struggle; he went peacefully."

Suddenly the familiar world I lived in seemed off-center. I went deaf, into a silent world devoid of thoughts or feelings. Mary asked me to take a deep breath. Fearing I had not understood her, she repeated what she'd just told me, "He's gone. He looked up and took his last breath."

Mary took my hand and helped me to my feet. I glanced her way and noticed her blue eyes—the pretty blue eyes Frankie had inherited from her—were now wet with tears. Yet I remained quiet. I did not react. Her words had not registered.

As I waited for my world to right itself, as though in slow motion we walked past the nurse's station towards Frankie's room. One of his nurses rushed to my side and hugged me, told me she was sorry, yet I did not respond. It was ethereal; my mind made no connection to Mary's words or to the nurse's teary condolence.

The door to his room—normally open—was now closed, and the lights had been dimmed. Except for the muffled sounds from Tommy and Chuck's quiet sobs, the scene was motionlessness.

One nurse was standing by his bed. As I approached, she turned and embraced me. "We made no attempts to resuscitate him," she said. "It happened suddenly, and he went peacefully. Our hero did not struggle."

I stood by Frankie's bed, stared at the expressionless look on his face, and then glanced at the silent monitors. And it was then I understood. My eyes locked on the screen, and I hoped that maybe, just maybe, the lines and dashes and sounds would begin to record life again.

My throat was dry, and I still had not spoken to anyone. Standing by his bedside, I gazed at the stillness of his body, wondering what I'd tell Teri. I suddenly realized that God had abandoned me. Mary got her wish. Death had freed her son from his suffering.

I reached for Frankie's hand and kissed his cheek. He was still warm. I wanted his big, beautiful eyes to open. I wanted to hear him tell me he loved me. I could feel tears welling in my eyes, but I did not cry. It was as though the well had run dry.

Moments later, Dr. Sinclair walked into the somber atmosphere of his patient's room. For the last time, he checked Frankie and spoke to the nurses. When he was done he hugged each of us, repeating again how brave Frankie had been. He told us the results from the treatments had been recorded and in time would be instrumental towards a cure. I was sure this compassionate man had done all he could and I'd never forget him.

Later, we gathered in the waiting room. Kelly and Geri were waiting. We embraced, and our earlier confrontation was now a distant memory. Although my rosary beads were still tightly clutched in my hand, I no longer had any desire to pray. Frankie was gone, my prayers had not been heard, and the disease had won the battle. One thing I was sure of: Frankie had taken my heart and I felt cold, empty, and alone.

I did not cry that night, nor did I cry the next day or in the days that followed. I had already shed an ocean of tears.

~ ~ ~

It was early morning when we left the hospital. When we arrived home, my parents were waiting by the front door. I rushed towards them, into the safety of their arms, and we exchanged a few words. I needed to be with Teri, who was sleeping peacefully in the tiny bedroom, and I quietly slipped into bed next to her. Come morning I would tell her that while she was asleep, her world had changed.

This would be the first night I'd fall asleep without Frankie in my world. I would never again wake to find him next to me. I'd never again hear him softly breathing or find his arm draped over me in the morning. I would never again see him in his hospital bed fighting a ruthless enemy. Death had permanently detached us.

As I lay next to Teri, I focused on the words to tell her that her daddy was in heaven. I wondered if she'd ask why Jesus had not answered her sweet prayers. I needed to choose gentle words, words that would not frighten her. Teri had never been exposed to death, not even with animals. She had long ago accepted he was sick, prayed for him every night, but the word "death" never entered our conversations. She was expecting to see him return home.

Kelly was right; I was not prepared for this moment. How could I be? Until Frankie's last breath, I was in faith and honestly believed he would not die. I dreamt of the day when we'd move somewhere, away from the memories of his illness. We'd have more children, brothers and sisters for Teri, and live happily ever after. I'd dreamt he'd get well and the illness would be nothing more than a hiccup in our lives—a test from God. Yet death had had the final word, like a period at the end of a sentence.

After hours of tossing, the first light of morning began to filter through the window. I waited for Teri to wake up, and when she did, she smiled and I drew her close and kissed her. The moment I'd dreaded had arrived. Before I uttered one word, she asked, "Mommy, is Daddy coming home today? Is he all better?"

"No Teri, he's not coming home," I answered and drew her closer to me.

"How come?"

"Because he's not better. Because—well, because sometimes when someone gets sick—really, really sick, like your daddy—Jesus takes them to heaven and then they get better. Last night, Jesus took Daddy to heaven to be with Him. Now he's not sick; he's all better."

My words had flowed easily, spontaneously. Teri didn't cry. Instead she snuggled closer. She didn't appear to be frightened, but remained quiet. I wondered what she was thinking, how she'd feel about Jesus, and if she, like me, would believe her prayers had gone unheard and were all for naught.

Teri and I stayed in bed for the better part of the morning. She had accepted what I'd told her—her daddy was in heaven and was no longer ill.

The first day was a misty blur. I felt numb, as though I had drifted somewhere, above it all. Nothing made sense. By noon the phone began ringing and people were stopping by to offer condolences. Other than my family and closest friends, my mother was carefully shielding me from visitors. Teri was my only tangible reality, wandering in and out of the bedroom, always returning to lie down beside me for a few minutes.

On the second day, Geri drove me to Dr. Kleinman's office. Seeing him meant so much to me. He'd been an important part of this journey. When I entered his office, he hugged me. His embrace conveyed his private feelings for Frankie, the young man he'd known for only three years, someone who'd touched his heart. He sat on the edge of his desk, and I sat close by and looked directly into his eyes. And although he didn't say much, I knew he understood what I was feeling. And I knew that he too had hoped Frankie would, at the very least, enjoy a long remission. But now all he could do was praise Frankie's courage and tell me I'd done an amazing job. Before I left, he told me he would like to give me something to help me relax.

"It's a mild relaxant; you'll feel better," he explained. I agreed, reluctantly, and on the way home I felt somewhat disoriented.

Geri reminded me of the decisions I needed to make immediately: the church, the mortuary, an outfit for Frankie. The thought of picking out clothes for him took my breath away, as did the call from the hospital asking permission to perform an autopsy.

While the infinite rhythm of time kept moving forward, memories kept rushing back. I wanted time to stop, to rewind back to when Frankie was alive. I missed him and wondered how I would function in a world without him by my side.

After arrangements were made at church, we drove to the mortuary. I was not feeling well, and things appeared foggy. The word "funeral" had been the furthest thing from my mind. I had imagined instead a short vacation for just the three of us to an exotic place far away from the nightmare.

The somber-faced director greeted us, offered his condolences, and began asking questions. By this time, the doctor's shot had taken effect, and I could barely focus. I needed to lie down. Kelly took over and helped me sort through the countless documents needing my signature. When the director asked about interment and Kelly told him it would be at Fort Rosecrans National Cemetery in San Diego, I was puzzled—what and where was Fort Rosecrans?

By the time we'd left the mortuary, I could barely walk without help. When we arrived home, we walked directly into the bedroom, bypassing the dining room filled with people who'd stopped by to see me. Geri explained that I'd had a reaction to the shot the doctor had given me and that I needed to lie down and sleep it off.

I slept in a drug-induced state through the remainder of the day, stirring only at the sound of my mother's voice as she checked to see if I was all right. I slept deeply, into the evening and through the night, waking in the early morning to the sobering truth—the unthinkable reality that Frankie was no longer with us.

The following day Geri stopped by and drove me to the apartment to pick out an outfit for Frankie. I was still feeling groggy. When we arrived at the apartment, I opened the door and we went inside. The apartment felt so strange, so cold, so unwelcoming. The apartment we'd called home a few days ago was now a residence where Frankie no longer lived. As I glanced around, my thoughts rushed back to the night when Frankie's anguished prayers filled me with despair, and the sentiments he shared that night were now permanently engraved in my heart.

His essence was everywhere, in every corner, in every room. I thought about the morning when he stood up to show me his chest—the fright in his eyes, the frantic race to the hospital for the last time. I forced myself to focus, to move forward and pick out something he'd feel good about wearing.

In the bedroom, I sorted through his clothes. Frankie loved trendy fashions. He also liked the classic look for special occasions. I wanted him to look handsome and well-groomed. I knew he would count on me to make that happen. I selected his dark suit, a long sleeve white shirt, and his favorite tie—the outfit he'd worn to the New Year's Eve party. When I was done, Geri delivered the clothes to the mortuary.

A few days later, the City of Hope called with the autopsy results. As expected, there were no surprises. The cancer had metastasized, but the actual cause of death was listed as "pneumonia." Upon completion of the autopsy, his body was released to the mortuary. Three days later, we received the call from the mortuary. The moment I dreaded had arrived.

Mary, Tommy, Chuck, and my mother and I made our way to the mortuary, and when we arrived, a man dressed in a dark suit greeted us. He spoke softly and led us to a dimly lit room with a casket on the far end. As my eyes settled into the scene, I stiffened. I did not want to see his lifeless body in the wooden box I'd selected.

Although Frankie had lost over sixty pounds and was painfully thin, he was still strikingly handsome. I was not expecting to see my healthy husband lying silently in that casket. He'd been through a deadly war and lost the battle. However, the sight of the body in the casket made me shudder. His hair had been combed into a style he would never have worn, his face looked swollen, his jowls were puffy, and makeup had failed to erase the gray, chalky skin-tone. Frankie looked angry. In all my days and nights with Frankie, I had never seen an angry look on his face. During the darkest moments of that last year, he had never looked as angry as he did lying in that casket.

Perhaps the funeral director was aware there would be questions. And when I tore out of that room in search of answers, I found him standing close by. He politely asked if he could help and led me to his office.

"I don't understand why the body in the casket doesn't look anything like my husband. Kelly gave you his picture. What happened? Why does he look so angry?"

He spoke slowly and explained that Frankie was barely one hundred pounds, that his eyes and cheeks had sunk into the skull and there was little they could do to make him look more natural. There wasn't much left to work with.

"But you had his picture. He doesn't look anything like the picture. He looks angry! I can't let my daughter see him."

"The picture was taken before the cancer. Your husband suffered a tremendous weight loss. Trust me, it's very discouraging for us as well, especially with someone so young," he added sorrowfully.

"So there's nothing more you can do?"

"No, I'm so very sorry, I'm afraid not," he said.

"Then close the casket."

When we returned to the viewing room, the director spoke to everyone and repeated what he had just shared with me. When he was done, he apologized and left us to decide.

"I think the casket should be closed. I don't want to be alone in this decision, and I hope all of you agree. Teri will be here, and I don't want her to see him and remember him looking this way," I said.

Mary nodded yes. "I'd like to remember Frankie the way he'd want to be remembered."

Thankfully everyone was in agreement. Before they closed the casket, we took turns praying. Chuck and Tommy reached in and touched Frankie's folded hands, said a prayer, and quietly said goodbye. Mary bent down to kiss Frankie. (In a perfect world, mothers are not supposed to bury their children.) My mother was next, praying as she reached to touch his hands. When she was done, she turned, looked my way, and then left the room.

I was finally alone and knelt by the casket. For a moment I wondered if he could see me or read my mind. I began to speak to him, and I told him it hurt to know I would never be able to look into his eyes, eyes that would never enjoy the sight of a fiery sunset splashed across a late afternoon sky. I would never again hear him tell me how much I was loved. Without him by my side, I would never be able to enjoy coffee on lazy Sunday mornings or to take a late afternoon walk on a beach. How would I ever be able to marvel at the beauty of the moon and stars brightening a dark night or the sound of a train rumbling past in the distance? Once again I reached out to God and asked Him why He had taken this man from my life. And for the last time, I kissed Frankie's cheek and told him how much I loved him.

We rode home in silence, absorbed in our own private grief. It hurt deeply to see Frankie looking angry, yet I knew his warm, loving smile was tucked away in my heart.

The following afternoon we arrived to find the casket had been moved into a spacious room. Colorful sprays and bouquets of flowers had been delivered and were standing guard next to the casket and along the walls. Frankie's picture had been placed on top of the closed casket.

Taking Teri's hand, we walked past the beautiful flowers to the closed casket. Although I had already explained about death and the casket, I wasn't sure how much she understood. We knelt together, and I told her she could talk to her daddy in her mind. I reassured her that he was listening and watching, but he could not answer. To a five-year-old child, no matter how well prepared she might be, I was sure the setting was perplexing.

Frankie had many friends. His beautiful smile and warm demeanor were magnets, drawing you close, wanting his friendship. I was not surprised when the room began to fill with the familiar faces of friends and family and neighbors, including men from the Elks Lodge and from Freeman's Shoe Store.

Many moments touched me deeply that evening, yet one stood out above the rest. It occurred when Dr. Sinclair and several of the City of Hope nursing staff entered the room. Memories of the love and support they had provided to Frankie were still fresh in my mind. I watched as they prayed by the casket. And when they were ready to leave, they embraced Teri and I and asked us to stop by and visit the City of Hope. Their love and heartfelt sentiments would remain in my heart forever.

On the third night, the casket was moved into a small chapel for the rosary recital. Once again, the chapel was filled to capacity. When it was over, Teri and I remained behind for a few quiet moments. We were alone, and while I held her hand, she listened as I explained what would take place the following morning.

IN A LITTLE VALLEY TOWN

The days segued from one to the other seamlessly, repeatedly leading me further away from the time Frankie was alive. Numb with grief, I wandered aimlessly from the past to the present but always back to the past. It was all I could do to keep from screaming. I wanted to turn back the hands of time, to the moments when we were together laughing, loving and dreaming of our future, to our days in Camp Lejeune—before he was ill—before California. I wanted to kiss him again, kiss him until he was breathless—kiss him until I was breathless.

With the wake and the rosary committed to memory, the burial was all that remained. On the morning of the funeral, I looked out the bedroom window to the pale gray sky. A slight drizzle was moistening the air, but it really didn't matter; the weather matched my mood. Actually I was happy the sun remained hidden. I hoped it would rain hard and heavy, enough to drown the deepening sorrow in my heart. I wanted to run from what lay ahead—I wanted to crawl into a fetal position and die.

A Requiem Mass had been scheduled for 10 a.m. at Our Lady of Lourdes, the same church where I'd spent countless hours praying and pleading with Jesus and all the blessed saints for a cure, begging God not to take him. Nothing mattered now; nothing made sense. I was merely going along for the ride, joining the friends and family who would come to pray for his soul.

I leaned over and kissed Teri, my sweet little angel who was still deep in a peaceful slumber. She would soon awaken, and I needed to keep my sorrow in check.

At 9:30, I took hold of Teri's hand and we walked out of the house to the limousine waiting by the curb. My parents and brother Tony followed close behind. In the distance, church bells from Our Lady of Lourdes were chiming a slow, mournful tone. My brother Joe was in the Navy stationed overseas and could not be with us. Wanting him to be represented, I tucked his condolence telegram in my purse. My sister lived out of town and was unable to stand with me.

Mary, Tommy, Chuck, Kelly, and Geri were waiting by the church when we arrived. Flanked by family and our dearest friends, we entered the church and walked past those who'd come to say goodbye. My eyes were drawn to casket centered in the middle of the aisle, and my heart sank to a new low.

The last time I'd heard the angelic sound of the Ave Maria was during a far happier occasion—our wedding day. But now, as the melody filled the air, I sat in frozen silence. I still had not cried; only dry tears filled my eyes. I glanced over to the statue of the Blessed Mother, the same statue where I'd tirelessly knelt before her in prayer. I remembered when I'd placed a rose at her feet during our wedding at Our Lady of Guadalupe and wondered why she too had abandoned us.

Dressed in white garments, Father Mackey recited the homily, and then briefly spoke of Frankie's illness, the years of suffering, and that he'd be rewarded in heaven. At the conclusion of the Mass, Father Mackey walked around the casket, blessed it with holy water, and commanded Frankie's soul to heaven. The thought of Frankie in paradise did not rest easily. Paradise was supposed to come later, after we'd grown old. When the ceremony was over, we followed the casket down the aisle and watched the pallbearers lift the casket into the hearse for the trip to San Diego.

Huddled close in the back seat of Kelly's car, Teri and I held hands and rode in silence, staring vacantly out of the window, at the dark, somber clouds following the caravan of cars for the three-hour drive to Fort Rosecrans National Cemetery.

When we arrived, guardsmen were standing at attention by the gravesite. Rows of matching chairs had been arranged neatly under a pristine white canopy. Teri and I and the family sat in the first row.

In this serene setting, we watched as the guardsmen lifted the flag-draped casket from the hearse onto a waiting stanchion. The ceremony was brief; a priest offered a short eulogy and a prayer and blessed the casket. He concluded the service by having everyone join him in a final benediction. As he spoke, the sky darkened and a soft rain began to fall.

Frankie was presented honors during a heart-stopping tribute. Holding Teri's hand tightly in mine, we listened somberly as the bugler began to sound *Taps*. While the haunting tone vibrated in the misty air, guardsmen positioned themselves and fired three rifle volleys directly over his gravesite. With the echo of the gun salute lingering in the air, the guardsmen lifted the flag draping the casket and folded it carefully. And when they were done, a lone guardsman began walking towards me. He placed the flag in my hands, and I heard his soft voice offer his condolences. I thanked him, and I noticed he was young, Frankie's age, and yet he was alive and Frankie was not.

Perhaps it was the breathtaking view of the ocean, or the tall majestic trees standing guard over perfectly aligned rows of headstones, or the wind gently whistling about and the soft rain on my face, but suddenly I felt Frankie's presence, and a calmness fell over me. Frankie was now resting in this peaceful place, in the company of fellow Marines, and for the first time since he'd become ill, I was at peace.

On our way back to the car, Mary took my hand and said, "You know, they say rain on a casket is lucky."

"Lucky?" I asked. "How so?"

"They say when rain touches a casket, a soul has winged its way to heaven."

THE FLAME

We loved for just a whisper of time,
Soulmates oh so brief,
Until your fate with anger came,
And filled our world with grief.
It stole the joy within our hearts,
And tears and prayers filled up each day.
And then a hand reached out to you,
On angel's wings you soared away.
Your image lives within my heart,
A tiny spark of light,
It flickers for the love you gave,
A memory I hold tight.
Although our days on earth were few,
I'll wait to spend eternity with you.

*Dearest Frankie, how happy the angels in heaven
must be to have you with them.*

JUST THE TWO OF US

As life in the house on Orchard Street began to inch back to normal, the fog in my mind lifted as well. My parents went back to work, Tommy left for home, Chuck returned to his duties with the Air Force, but Mary remained in California a while longer. I'd come to terms with my hurt feelings towards a mother and her anguished prayers for her suffering son. Frankie was gone now, and I'd let go of my annoyance towards her.

There was one challenging chore to tackle: packing up and releasing the apartment we'd lived in. The rent had been paid for the month, and the manager made a kind offer. He told me I would not need to move until the apartment was rented. I made a conscious effort to complete that task as soon as possible and decided it was best to tackle this chore alone.

During the next few days, I considered moving back into our small apartment. I wanted to be alone with Teri, but I quickly realized how difficult it might be to live where his breath and all the memories still lingered, especially that last night and Frankie's heart-wrenching prayers.

Casting aside any thoughts about moving into the apartment, packing became my priority. After dropping Teri off at school, I drove to the apartment. When I arrived, I parked the car, walked up the path to the front door, turned the key and entered what was once our home but was now a cold, empty space with no occupants. Everything connected to Frankie had changed, and it pained me to know I would never see him again.

Geri and Kelly had packed and marked boxes and stored them neatly along the walls and in closets. Thankfully my phonograph records and record player were still on the black slat bench against the living room wall. Frankie and I had shared many romantic moments listening to music. One of our favorite artists was Connie Francis. Just as we'd done so many times before he was ill, I placed the record on the turnstile and turned up the volume.

As the sound of her sweet voice filled the air, I walked into the bedroom, opened the closet where several boxes marked "Frankie" had been neatly stacked, and I began sorting through the items. I placed his Marine Corps hat and the triangular-wrapped flag given to me during the burial ceremony on the bed. It felt so strange to be touching his belongings, things he no longer needed. I felt detached—nothing was the same. As I sat on floor, my mind drifted back to Fort Rosecrans and the beautiful setting where he now rested. One thing I was sure of—I desperately missed him.

I began sorting his clothes, his belongings—things to save and things to donate. Personal odds and ends—his razor and toothbrush and comb made me tremble. When I opened his wallet and read Frankie's name on his driver's license and on the Marine Corps identification card, my heart sank like a brick tossed into a deep, bottomless abyss.

Touching Frankie's personal effects sent my mind soaring back in time, and I could see Frankie wearing his favorite shirt, his made-to-order slacks, his spit-shined shoes. At the bottom of a box was our wedding album. Instinct told me to leave the album unopened, yet I could not keep from reaching back to a happier time of my life, to the days and months before we ran off to get married, to the day my father found our marriage certificate in my wallet. Taking a deep breath, I opened the album and scanned over the recorded history of our second wedding day.

I took my time sorting through his things. When I was done, I placed the album, the folded flag, his wallet, his Marine Corps hat, and several personal items in the satchel he used for his trips to the hospital. Someday Teri and I would sort through his things together.

I placed his engagement and wedding rings in my jewelry box. Frankie had always worn his rings, except towards the end when they began to slip off his fingers due to his weight loss. I had planned on placing my wedding band in his folded hands, like Jackie had done for John, but somehow that didn't happen. By the time I remembered, it was too late, the casket had been closed. When I returned home, I placed the satchel with the saved memories in my closet and called Goodwill to pick up the remaining items. A few days later Karen and Gary picked up the furniture and the remaining items and stored them in my parents' garage.

Except for the legalities of social security and insurance, there was little left to do. After Mary left California, Teri and I settled in with my parents and adhered to their expectations. I owed them my respect, followed their Sicilian traditions, and wore black at all times. I became aware of many traditional expectations. One stood out and made me uneasy: I was to remain in their home during a period of mourning or for as long as I desired.

At times I found these expectations troubling, yet I did not challenge them. I needed to be with them as much as they expected me to remain in their home.

I turned my full attention to Teri. Frankie was such a part of her; I saw him in her eyes and in her smile. I began sharing what her daddy was like when she was a baby, before he became ill. Yet Teri only remembered sadness. And much like me, she began questioning the prayers she'd offered to Jesus.

"Mommy, why didn't Jesus make him better and let him live with us?"

My parents hovered over me, trying to make me comfortable. I had the run of the house. But soon their attempts to soothe my grief backfired. Nothing they said or did helped my sinking mood. I was sad. I was edgy. I was lonely. Sorrow had wrapped itself around my heart. Other than caring for Teri, my days were nothing more than empty moments in time.

It didn't take long to recognize that I was an adult child in my parents' home. When their friends visited, I sat at their table where the saga of Frankie's short life and tragic death was revisited nightly. When my friends visited, my parents entertained them in the same manner. What I needed was privacy, some quiet time. I needed a life of my own with Teri.

My friends noticed my life and my mood and advised me to move out. "Your parents love you, but it's time to move on. You and Teri need your own space. You're living under the black umbrella of endless mourning. You need to brighten your life, find a cute apartment, and for Pete's sake, stop wearing black. It's depressing. We want to see you in living color. You both deserve this much and more."

Moving out of my parents' home would hurt them deeply. The mere thought filled me with guilt. They'd done so much for the three of us. They'd set aside their own lives to help us. But now I was being strangled by their old Sicilian ways; wearing black was especially troublesome. My friends were right—I needed to move out. I needed alone time with Teri. I needed to sort out my life without distractions or my parents hovering over me.

By the beginning of the third month, having my own place became a realistic goal. With the help of friends, Teri and I moved into a cozy apartment. Once we were settled, I tossed out the black clothes and took a deep breath. Wrapped in the comfort of my own sanctuary, with my own couch and bed and a cute little bedroom for Teri, I felt refreshed.

On the afternoon of Teri's first school day, I anxiously waited for her to return home to see the surprised look on her face as she entered her bedroom. I'd decorated her canopy bed prettily with a green and white bedspread and matching curtains that resembled my bedroom in Brooklyn. I placed her favorite doll in the rocking chair by her bed, playfully scattered her toys around the room, and waited for the big moment. Needless to say, she was surprised and every bit as thrilled as I'd hoped she'd be.

For a while I kept busy and felt more relaxed. However, knowing that my parents were extremely hurt and angry kept gnawing at me. They refused to talk to me or visit the apartment. This was exactly how I expected them to react. In spite of their feelings, I knew being on my own was right for Teri and for me, and especially for my hurting heart.

Now that Teri and I were alone, I devoted endless hours to her. I loved watching her gobble up the cookies I baked or seeing her face light up when I prepared her favorite meals. After school we'd go to the park or to Farrell's Ice Cream Parlor. Sometimes I'd watch as she rode her bike or we'd sit on the couch and read books. And on weekends we visited friends.

While Teri was adjusting beautifully to our new life, I was not. Grief had embedded itself deep in my heart. When Teri was home, I was busy and happy; while she was in school, loneliness would inch its way into my heart. One long and lonely day led to another longer and lonelier day. There was no turning off the ache inside.

During the day, I'd lie on the floor close to the record player and endlessly listen to Connie Francis albums. As her voice filled the air, I would fall victim to melancholy, a mood that invitingly led to sentimental voyages to the past. Peering into the rearview mirror of my life, the past would come alive, the dreamy moments when we would snuggle on the couch or on the floor together. I missed everything about Frankie, especially the gregarious Frankie before cancer. I missed living in our tiny trailer, before California and the evil that crossed our threshold and stole him away.

Hidden below the surface, unseen by others, a subtle and insidious fever began blinding my senses. Memories fed my grief, and recalling his suffering and death kept me unfocused. I missed the euphoric happiness we'd once shared. His illness and death became a torment I could not set aside.

A few weeks after moving into our apartment, I received a letter from Dr. Sinclair inviting me to stop by his office at the City of Hope. He wanted to discuss the results of the autopsy. I was happy to see the doctor again and to touch the past just one more time. He continued to cross my mind—I respected him. He'd given us hope, taught us to gaze forward and not to sulk about the possibility of death. Although Frankie had not survived, Dr. Sinclair had my deepest admiration.

During Frankie's care and treatments at the City of Hope, I always wondered about the people and faces behind the names on the plaques hanging on trees and on the walls throughout the hospital campus. Approximately one month after Frankie passed away, I received a letter asking if I was interested in making a donation towards such a plaque. I quickly responded and sent a check. I wanted to see the plaque with Frankie's name hanging on a wall in the hospital library, and a visit to Dr. Sinclair provided the perfect opportunity.

Every nook and cranny of that hospital was still within my mind's reach—the reception area, the waiting rooms, the twists and turns of each corridor, the colorful pictures on the walls, and the children's ward. I knew the names and faces of the gardeners, the receptionists, the caregivers, and the wonderful doctors, and everyone knew me.

When I arrived, I drove past the large wall with words that had always sparked hope: THERE ARE NO INCURABLE DISEASES, ONLY DISEASES WHERE CURES HAVE NOT YET BEEN FOUND. The wall was a reminder that Frankie was now part of the

City of Hope legend. Someday, when a cure was discovered, I would be proud he had contributed to that goal.

As I walked down the curved path leading to the front of the building, I marveled at the lush gardens teeming with bright, colorful flowers, tall majestic trees, and shimmering greenery as far as the eye could see. Even the roses appeared more radiant, more than I remembered. As I approached the building, I hesitated for a moment to catch my breath and slowly entered the familiar lobby. My eyes scanned the room; nothing had changed. Some of the staff members recognized me, greeted me, and asked about Teri. Soon I was standing by the closed door of the doctor's office and I softly knocked.

"Come on in," said the warm voice still locked in my memory.

Although he welcomed me with a wide smile, I felt estranged from the office and the doctor I'd come to know so well. He appeared different. I sensed the change. And when he asked about Teri and how things were going—and not about Frankie—our conversation seemed out of sync, out of place. When he began discussing the drugs and treatments Frankie had received through the years, especially during the early months—those that held so much hope—the familiar attachment returned.

He reminded me how every treatment was a stepping stone towards a cure. "Someday, when a cure is announced to the world, you'll reflect back and realize how instrumental Frankie was towards reaching that goal."

"I know I will, Dr. Sinclair. But since he died, the cure I'd prayed for is the furthest thing from my mind. When I think back I only remember what he went through, especially the debilitating side effects from the drugs. He was so strong. He never complained, and it hurts to remember what he went through. I honestly believed he would survive. It was difficult watching him slip away inch by inch. At least you were doing something. I feel as though I brought little to the table."

"Yes, memories can be torturous. However, you have to make every effort to move forward, if not for yourself, for your daughter. Trust me; there will come a time when you will feel sure of yourself. You'll confront new and exciting challenges. Don't look back and cry; be proud you knew and loved someone so special!"

We chatted for a while, and later we walked to the library where a plaque with Frankie's name was now displayed along with many other deceased patients. As we walked past the rows of plaques, my feelings seemed skewed, off center. I stood silently in front of Frankie's plaque, read his name and the date of birth and death, feeling disconnected from the reality that he was now among all the heroes who'd bravely donated their bodies to the science behind the cures yet to come.

I WILL SURVIVE

The world around me was moving forward. All my friends had returned to their prior lives. My brother Joe had been discharged from the Navy, married his high school sweetheart Pat, and moved into an apartment directly across from mine. My sister was married and living in Orange County with her family, and my brother Tony, now in high school, loved music and played the guitar. My parents were doing well but were still angry and continued to keep their distance.

With the coming of summer, Teri was at home and my ominous mood was somewhat lightened. We went to drive-in movies, picnicked, and went to the beach every week. Louise invited us to go camping for a week with her family in Carpinteria State Beach. We continued to see our friends; Frankie remained close in their thoughts as well. I purposefully kept the void in my heart concealed.

With the arrival of fall, Teri returned to school, as did the sadness in my heart that created a path for the past to push into the present. In my private world, sorrow had leached into every living cell of my body. Nothing eased my grief. He was gone, and I had no purpose other than caring for Teri. Life was nothing more than a hazy fog of uncertainty.

"I feel so disconnected, unsettled unless I'm with Teri," I shared with Kelly and Geri during one of their visits. "I want to get out, go somewhere, but the only place I want to go is to the cemetery, to Fort Rosecrans. Sometimes I'm overcome with a need to take Teri and just keep going and going."

"I understand how you feel. I think you need to meet people and go places. Go back to work, part-time, like before," Kelly suggested. "You've gone from being super busy to doing nothing. What about your old job?

315

And Freeman's is looking for a cashier on Mondays. Just one day a week, during the day. That might be a good start."

Oddly enough, going to work made sense. It would occupy my days. Insurance had provided a healthy nest egg, and my monthly allotment allowed me to stay home and make up lost time with Teri. Working was merely a mental health program.

I stopped by to see my old boss and inquired about a job. He was delighted to see me and told me a position was available. However, it meant working at night, and I turned it down. Leaving Teri alone at night was not in the realm of possibilities. The job at Freeman's was a better solution.

I'd purposely kept away from Freeman's. There were too many memories of Frankie floating about in that store. Yet the job sounded intriguing. I talked it over with my sister-in-law Pat, and she offered to watch Teri for a few hours after school. Things had fallen into place, and I decided to move forward.

The following day, before the desire dwindled, I got dressed, took a deep breath, got in my car, turned on the radio and headed towards Holt Boulevard—the major road to many points of interest in Pomona—the street Frankie took on his way to work. Soon I was standing under the large FREEMAN'S SHOE STORE sign.

Mr. Freeman was standing behind the front counter and quickly came around the counter to greet me.

"Hey, look who's here!" he shouted. "I'm glad to see you. We were hoping you'd stop by. How ya doin' kiddo? How's Teri?"

It didn't take long for the guys to come bouncing up from every aisle. I had imagined it would be uncomfortable seeing them again. Surprisingly, seeing their familiar faces put me at ease. We chatted for a while, and when Mr. Freeman asked if I was interested in cashiering on Mondays, I answered yes.

The following Monday, I woke up excited about my first workday, and everyone went out of their way to welcome me. The happy and friendly mood was uplifting, I felt comfortable, as though Frankie was near. Although everyone asked about Teri, I noticed they were carefully avoiding any mention of Frankie. At first it seemed odd, but I soon understood that they were attempting to keep me above my grief. After a few more Monday workdays, I began looking forward to getting dressed, driving to work, and interacting with the world. It was a much-needed diversion, and I enjoyed mingling with old friends and customers as well.

A PETAL IN THE WIND

As time moved forward, my emotions continued to teeter erratically, and my friends attempted to nudge me forward. Most vigilant in this endeavor was Kelly. Now *I* had become his charge. He became more than a friend; he was now my advisor. When he'd remind me to lock my car and the front door of the apartment and to check the air in my tires, I found his thoughtfulness endearing. But when he began telling me I was vulnerable—that I was an easy target for unscrupulous people—and cautioned me to be on guard, I was perplexed.

"What are you talking about? A target?"

"Yes, a target," he said. "You have no idea how much of a target you are, especially at work. Someday someone will come sashaying up to the front counter and start flirting. Just be careful."

"I don't get it. Why and how am I a target?"

"Because you're young, and they might think you have money—a widow with money. Think about it!" he added.

"First you tell me to get out, go to work, talk to people, be around adults who speak English, and now you're telling me to watch my back! Which is it?"

"Of course it's good for you to be working. I just think you need to be careful. That's all I'm saying! Just come to me if someone hits on you."

Despite Kelly's warnings, working at Freeman's was fun. I felt safe. I felt Frankie's presence. The store was perpetually busy with people seeking bargains, and I enjoyed the interaction and inevitable conversations with customers.

Kelly wasn't the lone defender who took charge of my virtue and my life. Pete, another salesman at Freeman's, assumed this role as well. Pete

317

and his wife Sandi were among our group of good friends, and Frankie, Teri, and I had often been invited to their home on Sunday afternoons. I was not surprised when Pete invited me to lunch, but I was caught off-guard by his hidden agenda. After lunch, and sounding very much like Kelly, he told me to be cautious around men.

Yet there *was* a new salesman at Freeman's. We were introduced on my first day. He'd kept his distance, and I hardly had any interactions with him, except when he came to the front counter with a customer to complete a sale.

Kelly and Pete justified their warnings by telling me the new salesman was well aware of the now-legendary man named Frankie, about his illness and death, and that I was his widow.

"Mr. Freeman *does not* check backgrounds. For all we know, this guy may have been in jail in another state, and Mr. Freeman is not exactly thrilled with his behavior. Evidentially, he went ballistic the other day when Mr. Freeman questioned a sale," Don shared with me.

I didn't see myself as a vulnerable female. Kelly's and Pete's warnings only served to galvanize feelings of resentment towards them.

One Monday afternoon, as I made my way to the back of the store, I noticed that the new guy was standing by the time clock. As I approached, he stepped aside, waited for me to punch out, and then walked with me as I made my way towards the exit. I was polite but anxious to get home. Other than saying goodbye, we didn't speak. When I arrived to work on the following Monday, he was again standing by the time clock. I smiled politely and he asked about my weekend. I wasn't especially friendly, nor was I rude, but I did not want to encourage any non-work-related conversation. After a quick response, I quickly walked towards the front counter.

From that moment on, whenever the store wasn't busy, he would meander up front and engage me in small talk. Eventually he asked if I would like to have dinner with him. I turned him down. I told him I was not dating. I was still drowning in grief. Frankie's essence was all around me, and I had no desire to be with another man.

Kelly and Pete continued their mantra about his bad temper and hidden background, adding that no one had befriended him at Freeman's.

"No one likes him. Have you noticed that he's never included in our conversations, nor does anyone ask him to join us for lunch?"

My response to the temper comment was an honest observation: "If you've never loved someone or been loved, then you fight and argue to make a point. Maybe he's never been loved!"

I had noticed he did not fit the mold of his fellow employees— the older veterans, most with disabilities. The new guy was young and seemingly healthy. When he began to ask questions about things I knew he was already aware of, I was uncomfortable. Yet, it was difficult to ignore him or to be rude.

I decided to share my feelings with Geri. I told her I neither liked nor disliked the new guy. I also shared that Kelly's and Pete's hovering was beginning to annoy me.

"Honestly, you just don't get it!" she snapped. "They *hover* because they worry and care about you, and they flat out don't trust him!"

So Geri had joined the chorus as well. "I suggest you keep this guy at arm's length," she continued. "You have no idea what's out there. Trust me; Kelly and Pete know exactly what goes on in a man's mind."

After sharing the work conundrum with other friends, they interpreted Kelly's, Pete's, and Geri's comments as overly protective and intrusive.

"There's nothing wrong with going to dinner with this guy. You're young. It's good to get out and meet new people," they advised. "Just don't get chummy with him!"

Perhaps I was merely establishing my own boundaries with Kelly, Geri and Pete when I set aside their remarks and accepted a dinner invitation from the new guy. However, as the date night drew close, I had second thoughts. Being with "another man" was unsettling. I was still married emotionally, and seeing another man felt like betrayal. But it was all perception, and in an effort to push myself forward, we went to dinner one night after work.

At some point during the evening, I shared my feelings for Frankie with him. I told him my grief was still raw and it was too soon to begin dating. I also told him the guys at work worried about me. He said he understood but didn't see anything wrong with seeing me now and then. He agreed to keep our dates quiet and promised to respect my feelings about Frankie.

Amidst my trepidations and uncertainties, our first date had gone well. When he asked to take me out again, I accepted. Before long I was seeing him regularly. I met him away from the apartment. In time he began asking about Teri. He wanted to meet her. Although I was reluctant about taking that next step, he was persistent and very persuasive.

"Meeting Teri would be good for her, for all of us," he insisted. When he shared how much he missed his two daughters, I caved in and prepared Teri.

From the moment he met Teri, his attention turned to her. On that first night he gave her a pretty doll. From then on, he always arrived with a gift. Teri was now enjoying trips to the movies and to local ice cream parlors. He began cajoling his way into my life through an innocent child who'd recently lost her father and was just as vulnerable as her mother.

Teri accepted him immediately. She enjoyed his company, his attention, his antics and his gifts. And I could not deny how much I loved watching them together and fantasized that Frankie had opened this door for Teri and I to walk through. I was not about to test the waters and bring any other men home. Although I still felt guilty for entertaining another man in my life, I was enjoying an element of normalcy. When he promised to never hurt either of us, I believed him.

Except for some of my friends and my sister-in-law Pat, we kept our dinner dates quiet. But somehow Kelly found out and worlds collided.

"I knew it—I had a feeling you'd do this!" Kelly shouted. "You know absolutely nothing about him—no one does. No one knows where he's been, what he's been up to, if he's been in jail. He could be married for all you know. His family lives out of state. Can't you see the red flag waving in your face? You have a daughter, and you need to protect her. I think you should *not* see him again outside the store!"

My life was in a freefall. I decided it was best to quit working at Freeman's and to keep my distance from Kelly, Geri, and Pete. Their obsession with the new guy was maddening. They were acting like parents of a teen child, especially Kelly.

Kelly's obsession led him to make an unforgivable decision. Taking matters into his own hands, he spoke to my parents and told them I was seeing someone from work, someone he disapproved of tremendously.

Kelly's news flash launched a larger war between my parents and me. They were now convinced I'd moved out solely to seek out men. To my parents and to the entire Sicilian community, my behavior was disgraceful. When my mother called to tell me I'd dishonored Frankie, I wanted to die. Knowing she was speaking my father's heart as well, her angry words cut deep into my heart.

Things could not have gotten any worse. I began to wonder why my life continued to be a convolution of problems. Swallowed up in a war of words and hurt feelings, and distraught by my mother's false impression of my goals, my attention turned to the one person who seemingly presented an interest in making me happy—the new guy.

In my quest to find peace and tranquility, on Christmas Eve of that year, I accepted the engagement ring he'd placed inside a Christmas card. Later that night, when he asked me to marry him and promised to never hurt either of us, I accepted.

I was over my head, overwhelmed with uncertainties, especially my agreement to marry him. The now defunct relationship with my parents hung heavily in my heart as well. Still, his enthusiasm about marriage overpowered my qualms. He told me he'd make the wedding arrangements, including a Vegas honeymoon. He convinced me the qualms in my heart had all to do with the negative input from everyone, and especially those from my mother.

While he was busy with wedding preparations, I was headed in opposite direction, convinced it was not the best time to get married. Yet I found it impossible to tell him I wanted to call off all plans, at least for a while. His enthusiasm continued to override my insecurities, and I overlooked the red flags he began posting.

When I told him I preferred not to go to Las Vegas for a honeymoon, he balked—loudly.

"Are you kidding? Why would anyone not want to go to Vegas? It's a lotta fun. There is so much to do, especially the gambling and the shows," he insisted.

I suggested a quiet place, like Palm Springs. But he laughed and told me Palm Springs was dull and boring. I told him I did not enjoy gambling—he told me he did. The more I objected, the more convincing his argument became. He endorsed Vegas as the most desirable place for a honeymoon and eventually got his wish. Setting aside my feelings, I went along with his plans.

On New Year's Eve of that year, a strange twist of fate occurred and broadened the drama in my life. Kelly called with news that brought me to my knees. Geri had suffered a heart attack earlier that day and had passed away. He asked me to come over. The news sent me reeling. I was stunned. Geri had died, and we'd never made peace, never spoken since our confrontation.

"Kelly, my God!" I screamed. "What happened?"

"I'm not sure," Kelly answered. "She was busy in the kitchen when she collapsed. I heard a thud and found her on the floor. I checked her pulse, but there wasn't any. I called an ambulance, they worked on her, but she was gone. She never said she was feeling sick, not a word, not a hint. It all happened in a split second of time."

Kelly wasn't expecting me to bring anyone that evening, especially someone he was less than pleased with. But we had plans for dinner that night, and it seemed the natural thing for both of us to go to Kelly's house. After all, they were still working together at Freeman's.

When we arrived, the front door was wide open, and people had gathered in the tiny front room offering their condolences. When Kelly saw me, he greeted me and we hugged. But when he saw who had accompanied me, he asked about Teri and turned away. We left after a few minutes, and after that evening, Kelly and I had no further contact.

Geri's death plunged me into another emotional meltdown. I began to rethink the reasons that led up to the loss of friendship with dear friends. The added grief served to further my state of mental mayhem.

As plans to marry moved forward, I wanted to break away from him but could not. One Sunday morning—without warning—he stopped by and told me he'd like to drive us to Fort Rosecrans. Initially his heartwarming gesture lightened my heart. When we arrived at the cemetery, he parked close to the gravesite and instructed me to say goodbye to Frankie. His demand shocked me, and I imagined he was jealous. Not wanting to cause a scene in Teri's presence, I took hold of Teri's hand, and we knelt by Frankie's grave. I prayed, not to God but to Frankie.

Frankie, I'm so confused. What should I do? Frankie, help me, please . . .

A few days later, I kept Teri out of school and drove to Fort Rosecrans. When we arrived, we knelt down in front of Frankie's headstone. Looking out towards the peaceful bay, with only the sound of the wind whistling through the trees, I shared my heart with Frankie. I told him that I was troubled. I told him how much I missed him, and how he'd always live in my heart. I told him I was confused about my life, if I was headed in the right direction. I begged him to send a sign, if he could—something—anything. Yet, I saw nothing.

Strangled with doubts and pent up anxieties, I decided it would be best to cancel our wedding plans. As much as I wanted to taste love again, I was not convinced this was the right man that would bring me the happiness I craved. I also sensed that he'd get upset if I told him how I was feeling. In hindsight, I was more concerned about his feelings than my own, and could not step up to the plate and tell him how I felt.

On the night before the wedding, he stopped by and asked to use the phone to call his grandmother. He went into my bedroom and shut the door behind him. The simple gesture of closing the door and keeping his conversation private spoke volumes. I knew the time had come to tell him how I felt.

I'm not sure if it was the look on my face or the sound of my voice, or both, but after he returned to the living room, sensing the mood had changed, he asked if something was wrong. I found the strength and answered yes. I told him I was having second thoughts about getting married, that I wanted to postpone the wedding.

"It's just too soon," I said. "It's not even a year since Frankie died. I'm still hurting. It isn't fair to you or me. I need more time. I just can't do this right now."

My suggestion came as a complete surprise, and it shocked him to his core. He sprang up from the couch and began to rant loudly. He was trembling, and his eyes turned an angry red. He began marching back and forth, shouting, insisting that I was wrong. He told me marriage was the best thing for me, and I was making a big mistake.

Even my father's anger during my adolescent years and on the day he found the marriage certificate did not reach the level of frenzy I was witnessing. He was furious and I was frightened. However, after regaining his composure and apologizing for his temper, I—with little experience to guide me—added my own apology for making him angry and then agreed to move forward with our plans. He convinced me his anger was a one-time event and again reminded me that he would never hurt me.

My apology that evening marked the framework for our relationship—and his behavior set the tone for our life together.

CLOUDY WITH A CHANCE OF PAIN

Six weeks before the one-year anniversary of Frankie's passing, with the lingering uncertainties still in my heart as well as his disturbing behavior the night before the wedding, we married in a chapel in West Covina and drove to Las Vegas.

The Vegas honeymoon was less than a happy celebration of wedded bliss. While he gambled at a nearby casino, I sat alone at dinner as Kelly's, Geri's, and Pete's warnings quickly flashed across my mind.

Our marriage was never the euphoric frenzy of happiness I sought and longed for. In my determination to accept the decision I'd made, I set aside how little we had in common, his disregard for my fragile feelings, and somehow found the strength to sort through our problems and do my best to bring some semblance of stability to Teri's life and mine.

I learned to place blame from his continued tantrums on myself and cave in to all his demands. In this less than loving relationship, the only taste of love came from the children we bore.

However, there were happy moments in the marriage. The happiest, without a doubt, were the births of our children and grandchildren, the shining stars in my life. We remained together for many years and somehow managed to sort through our children's high school years, college graduations, marriages, my father's untimely death, and my mother's tormented life after his death, and yet we somehow managed to work side by side in our restaurant.

Through the years, recollections of the concerns I had before we married often returned to haunt me. I wondered why I had not been stronger, why I was so naïve, why I had shut my eyes and mind to the guidance of friends. But then again, hindsight is always 20/20. Had I ended the relationship, I would never have known the love from our three beautiful children.

I'd walked directly into the path of that tempest and survived. After thirty-three years of marriage, we divorced. And unlike the memories I have of Frankie, my regrets for having married again in time were surrendered to the past.

LOVE LETTERS TO MY CHILDREN

THERESA MARIE

NOVEMBER 7, 1958

Sweet Teri, you were my firstborn, born during the happiest time of my life. You and I share a unique bond: a love for someone special, someone whose short life left a deep void. Because of him, you are a precious gift! Through you, he lives. And because of you, I will never forget him.

Life led you on many paths, beginning with your father's tragic illness and passing. Adolescence was challenging, yet you persevered. Your most notable rewards were the births of your children Ryan and Kristyn, college graduation, a successful career in the field of your choice—health and fitness, your beginnings in prenatal care, including childbirth education for pregnant mothers. I know you'll agree that one of the happiest times of your adult life occurred after you met Brian, a Navy officer and a gentleman in the truest sense of the word. Your marriage continues to be blessed with love and understanding and respect for one another, which at times leaves me speechless.

As I reach back, my thoughts turn to Camp Lejeune, after the doctor announced I was pregnant. That moment launched a new chapter in our lives. Your dad and I were completely unaware of the amazing adventures that lie ahead.

And what a sweet little bundle you were! From your adorable little face with dark hair and eyes to your teeny, tiny toes, you stole our hearts and completed our happiness.

I remember the day we took you home from the hospital and the countless hours we spent staring at you while you slept. I fondly recall how your dad would race home after work and immediately reach for you. Watching both of you together was a joy.

The first year was incredible. From your first sweet coo to that incredible first step, each milestone was an amazing feat.

There was little room in our trailer. We mostly cuddled and played with you on our bed. Weather permitting, your dad and I would place a fluffy blanket outside under the large shade tree by the trailer. It was on that blanket where you began to scoot and crawl, where you sat up on your own and rolled over from your back to your tummy.

We didn't have much money, but your father often came home with something special that caught his eye—a toy or an outfit, always a precious choice. When you were about six months old, he came home with two adorable little dresses, one blue and one pink. I know I took a picture of you in your stroller wearing that pretty blue dress.

Your legs were strong, and he'd been coaching you to walk, determined you'd be running before our trip to California. He'd prop you up against the couch and you'd smile as though you understood what he wanted. Sometimes you'd plop to the floor and laugh. The day you took your first wobbly step into his arms, he was thrilled and deemed it worthy of a twirl around in his arms. By the time we reached California, you were practically dancing.

I remember your favorite stuffed animal, the soft pink bunny with floppy ears. The bunny had become your "binky" and "blankie" substitute and joined us for the trip to California—minus the one ear you'd chewed off.

The best part of the trip occurred the moment we pulled up to the curb in front of the house on Orchard Street. Grandma and Grandpa came running out of the house before the car's engine had been turned off. I'm sure their greeting could be heard for miles.

They were excited, ready to share their love with their first grandchild. And how thrilled my mother was when she introduced you to pastina. "*Theresa, mangia*" were probably the first Italian words you learned.

So many of the precious moments you shared with Grandma often come to mind, especially when she sang those precious old lullabies. I know you'll remember, "*E dae, dae, dae, stasera veni papa, porta menole e nucedre pa cordera la pitciridra, porta menole e castagna pa cordari la cu grani!*" Singing to her grandchild gave her great joy.

Your father considered you a genius and always made time to read to you. It didn't take long for you to associate words and pictures. In time you'd thumb through each page as though you were reading. We were so proud of your accomplishment. As were you!

You loved pretty dolls, and we'd watch you play house, feeding and cuddling your babies in your tiny rocking chair and putting them to bed at night in a tiny doll cradle. When you turned six, Kelly and Geri gave you a Barbie doll—your first grownup doll, one you enjoyed for many years.

I remember your kindergarten days in Monte Vista Elementary School directly across from Grandma's house. How adorable you looked as we walked hand in hand to school each morning. Uncle Tony would pick you up after school, and you'd both watch television until either Grandma or I came home. Television cartoon programs were very limited during this time. Do you remember "Deputy Dawg", "Huckleberry Hound", "The Flintstones", and "Rocky and Bullwinkle"?

Some of my fondest memories include Grandpa and how bright your eyes would get, how happy you looked sitting high on top of his shoulders! I remember your first tricycle. You were so petite, and your legs dangled far from the pedals. But Grandpa came to the rescue and attached large blocks of wood on the pedals. Your legs may have been short, but they were strong, and soon you were racing around Grandpa's backyard.

Remember Tommy, your first love? You were both five years old. Every afternoon Tommy would knock on our door and ask if you could play. Watching both of you walking hand in hand or riding bikes was endearing. Tommy was adorable, and his parents could not get enough of you as well. A bit young for "Teri and Tommy sitting in a tree," yet Tommy always managed to kiss your cheek every chance he got.

Do you recall the dairy farm close to our home? You and your cousin Shellie were only five years old at the time. Whenever you were both in the car and we drove by the farm, your sweet voices would echo loudly in the car: "Those are my cows! No they're not, they're mine!" The heated argument would escalate until the cows were no longer in sight. But you clearly had rights; the cows were in our neighborhood.

I remember when you joined the Girl Scouts and how cute you looked in your little skirt and sash. Then came accordion lessons with Mrs. French at the Milton Mann Studios. Before long you were playing on a beautiful instrument large enough to shield the pretty little girl sitting behind it. It was there where we met the Krader family—Annalese, Wendell, Kenny, and Susie—and we became close friends. Your music was a joy that remains with me to this day. Remember the beautiful duet you'd play with David, our neighbor's son? I remember how we'd proudly subject visitors to a musical jamboree. The music was wonderful and everyone enjoyed the concert.

And then came your mini-bike! Watching you scoot up and down Steeplechase Drive was a hoot. When you were older, you drove up and down that same street in your first car, a salmon-colored Mazda. Later on you bought a white car and buzzed around town stylishly.

Remember the party weekends with the Kraders or the Donatellis in Sunnymead? I still remember you and Janie, so young and so pretty. Memories of those fun-filled weekends on Steeplechase Drive often come to mind.

I remember the beautiful essay you wrote about the family. It was a high school assignment, an analysis of the family. Your essay was remarkable. I read it over many, many times. The teacher was pleased as well and graded you highly. Your clear perception and astute breakdown of each family member was insightful and spoke of your intellect. It helped me understand the dynamics of our family, why things played out as they did, the reasons we interacted and reacted as we did. It was beautifully written, and I knew then you had many talents behind your pretty face.

You were only a young teenager when you were shipped off to Uncle Lawrence to learn the pizza business. This was not a happy time, but we needed your help, and you came through—always a trooper. After one week, you came home as though you'd taken a college course in the "pizza biz."

It was at the pizza house where we met Truman (Todd) O'Doherty, and you developed a close friendship with his daughters Kitty and Erin, a friendship (I believe) that remains to this day.

One special moment occurred after a baseball game at your high school. Tommy Lasorda, Steve Garvey, Bill Buckner, and some of the Los Angeles Dodgers had taken part of an exhibition game and came to the restaurant for pizza after the game. What a surprise! You looked positively adorable in your blue-and-white uniform posing for pictures at the front counter with Don Sutton and Steve Yeager.

You worked hard during those days, and in spite of the turmoil at home and in that restaurant, you remained focused. Words can't express how proud I am of you, Teri. I have always been proud of you—so beautiful, so loving, so focused. Having you as my daughter fills me with tremendous pride.

I will never forget your college years and how much you cared for and loved Grandma. She would patiently wait for you to come home from school, and the three of us would watch *All My Children* and *General Hospital*. Watching you and Grandma together and the love you gave to her always put a smile in my heart.

I remember your first serious love, Jim, and your plans for an overnighter at the Rose Bowl in Pasadena. You were very young, and I wasn't sure the decision to let you go was wise. When you and Jim told us you wanted to get married, I was thrilled. I prayed Jim would bring great love and happiness into your life. Planning your wedding was so exciting, especially shopping for your wedding dress. Remember the lovely picture of you and Jim in the flower fields? I kept hoping your wedding day would be picture-perfect—minus wind, rain, clouds, and absolutely NO SMOG! I got my wish. And how beautiful you looked in that precious wedding dress with a sweet touch of blue—a princess bride!

Your birth made me a mother, and the birth of your first child, Ryan, made me a grandmother. When you called to share the news you were pregnant, I was completely unprepared for my new role as grandma. As the shock wore off and the months sped by, my excitement grew. And when you asked me to be in the delivery room with you, I was overwhelmed. After Ryan was born, I imagined that my delivery room antics had upset your doctor. Imagine my surprise when I received a card from the doctor thanking me for allowing him to partake in such a blessed family event. Witnessing the birth of each grandchild became a family tradition that continued with your sisters. How truly blessed I am. *Thank you, Teri.*

I remember your college graduation day and how proud I was of your accomplishment. You'd worked hard to get through school. Then on a wonderfully happy day, holding sweet baby Ryan in your arms, you walked up the aisle to receive your diploma. I knew your dad was watching and smiling from heaven and every bit as proud of you as I was on that day.

After graduation you introduced a new program to San Diego—coaching pregnant women from prenatal exercise through delivery and beyond—"Mom and Baby Fitness" classes. Doctors were impressed, and pregnant women flocked to sign up in droves. Venturing into this uncharted territory spoke of your entrepreneurial nature. In Utah you were not as confident about the potential for this program. But it made an impression on the doctors, and your program took flight. In Virginia, your resume led to the wonderful position you hold today: Corporate Fitness Director with Sport and Health. You have had an amazing career, and you continue to astound me!

Do you remember our trip to Hawaii? Ryan was only six weeks old. It was a memorable trip, as was our trip to Sicily years later. Having you and Brian with me to share those special moments in Italy made the trip special.

I know I'll never forget Utah and my first and *only* attempt to ski! It was a stormy day, and the major blizzard served to heighten the adventure. It was the day I invented a new style of skiing—my own!

The day you gave birth to Kristyn was truly unforgettable. I was not thrilled when I learned you were planning a home birth with the assistance of two midwives. You were living in Orinda, and when you called and announced you were in labor, your mother-in-law Barbara and I hopped on the next flight. By the time we arrived, your labor had stalled and our baby waited four more days before making her much-awaited appearance. But things did not progress well. After laboring many hours, the midwives were concerned, and we left for the hospital with your legs propped up on the dashboard of the midwife's car. You endured many more hours of a difficult labor before Kristyn was born. Good job, Teri, although after several hours with little progress you did finally call out for drugs—I heard you, young lady!

You inherited your delightful sense of humor from your uncles. No one will ever forget the cookbook (lesson) you, Ryan, and Jodi videotaped for Denise's bridal shower. It remains an all-time hit, a "stop it, my face hurts from laughing" video. And who could ever forget Jodi's wedding reception and the outfits you and Denise wore to greet guests? A funny prank few enjoyed as well as we did.

Remember the Christmas season when you opened a tiny gift box with keys to a Mercedes? I'll bet nothing has ever topped that Christmas surprise!

More recently you helped plan a surprise party for my 70th birthday. I did not want a party. Rising above my objections, the party was planned, and what a wonderful surprise it turned out to be—how masterfully you kept that secret. It turned out to be a truly memorable day. *Thank you, Teri and Kristyn!*

Teri, many nostalgic memories of your life often come to mind; the most endearing are of our time in North Carolina—moments that remain close to my heart. You brought so much joy into your father's short life. He loved you dearly—loved being a father to a precious child of his heart.

One of the saddest moments in my life occurred on the morning I had to tell you he'd passed away. You have never failed to amaze me, and you did that morning when you accepted the news with complete understanding. Your response spoke of your tremendous strength—much like your father!

Although Jodi was charged with the mission to design a family memory book, you had the tedious chore of collecting most of the information and pictures of past generations. I know the research time you invested was significant; however, it resulted in a beautiful book, a treasure that I scroll through often to remember our family. It means the world to me. *Thank you so much, Teri!*

Having been blessed with two children of your own, you know of the special bond between a mother and her child. The love you share is a priceless treasure. I thank God for the wonder that is you, for your sweetness, for the love you've given me through the years, and for all the wonderful memories. We are tied together by one heart, and you are never far from my thoughts. I treasure the sweet memories that visit me each and every day, and your love will live in me forever.

I love you, Teri!
Mom

GRANDCHILDREN

Ryan James Hansen and Kristyn Nicole Bothwell

DENISE MARIE

NOVEMBER 9, 1965

Sweet Denise, your birth was my second miracle, a gift that came at a time when my life was in complete disarray. Being pregnant was the glue that held me together emotionally, and I could hardly wait to hold you in my arms. And when you finally came into my world, so tiny and so small, I knew you'd blossom into a beautiful flower.

You were due late in November. There was no reason to expect or to foresee an early arrival. But you had other plans, and when that first sharp jolt announced you were ready to leave your comfy abode, I was surprised—and thrilled. Four hours later, when a nurse carrying a hungry little bundle placed you in my arms, my heart exploded. Holding you magically lifted the heavy weight in my heart. I wanted to keep you with me, and I cried each time the nurses carried you back to the nursery after feedings.

You were very petite, almost too fragile to unwrap and check every precious part. But I did—from your adorable, sweet face to your tiny little fingers and ten teeny toes. I marveled at the precious miracle that was mine, and I lovingly named you Denise.

I had not decided on your name, but it came to me the moment I looked into your precious little face. My doctor was a flamboyant French woman, Dr. Jacqueline Bordes. I loved her name and even considered naming you Jacqueline. However I chose the name Denise. Dr. Bordes was somewhat disappointed, yet pleased since *Denise* was a French name and better suited for a baby so petite.

Denise was also the name of an elementary school classmate at Our Lady of Guadalupe—someone I'd played with as a child, someone I'd thought about through the years. But now I had my own little Italian daughter with a pretty French name!

During the early months of your life, I was still working through issues with your father. But with you in my arms, my focus changed and my problems took their place in line. With you in my life, I was much calmer and happier. Caring for a newborn was a godsend.

During the quiet moments of those first months, I'd close the blinds, settle into our rocking chair, and while you nursed and slept, we'd rock away the day. Those precious moments of pure heaven are memories that will never be forgotten.

As the first year marched on, so many wonderful moments come to mind, the first time you looked directly at me and smiled, your first tooth, your first spoonful of solid food, your first words, and how peaceful you looked as you slept. Soon you were sitting up, crawling around and rolling over. And whenever I'd place a soft blanket on the living room rug and watch as you softly spoke to your stuffed animals, my heart would burst open.

Watching you play and sing sweet songs to your dolls remains within me today. You were so gentle and caring, as you are with your own children. After you learned to walk, you would stuff *all* your dolls and furry animals into a doll stroller and take them for a walk. You were so sweet and never left anyone behind.

You were tiny, but your legs were strong. One day I turned around, and when I looked back, you had pulled yourself up by the couch. I was flabbergasted. Each new development was a milestone, an endearment.

Although you were cuddly and sweet, you also enjoyed crying. And you did that well, as though you enjoyed wailing as much as smiling. At times you'd cry for absolutely no reason. As always, the moment I appeared in your field of vision, a pretty smile would blossom and squeeze away the tears from your eyes.

Back then Sundays meant a drive to Grandma's house, where we joined the camaraderie of aunts, uncles, and cousins in our happy and mostly Italian family. Those were such wonderful days, when Grandma was happy, and no one dared let her down by not showing up. The food was always a festive delight, and while the adults chatted and caught up, all the cousins played and bonded closely. However, for you, Sundays were intimidating. When anyone made eye contact or approached you, you'd wail. In time your crying blended in the ambiance of sounds from adults and the growing family of cousins. And in spite of your tears, everyone loved you. Especially Grandma.

During this time, someone was always pregnant. My mother was in grandbaby heaven. In spite of this, she never gave up on you. She'd often attempt to sneak a kiss, but never won. You'd cry, and she'd leave in frustration, but the hope that someday you'd accept her love remained in her heart.

I remember the day a door-to-door photographer knocked on our door offering to take pictures. The moment I opened the door, you began to cry. The photographer convinced me of his expertise in getting babies to smile. He told me he came with a bag of tricks and would accomplish that goal. After he tried his last trick and your crying had not stopped, he decided to take the pictures anyway. One month later I received a picture of a precious moment captured in time—one tiny teardrop as it began to cascade down your face, your bottom lip puckered ever so gently. Attached was a note that read: *No charge due to tears.* He'd taken many pictures that day, but that one stood out.

In spite of your tears, you were loveable. There was a sweet femininity about you. I loved that side of you. By the time you were eighteen months old, you knew exactly what you wanted to wear each day. When you didn't care for the outfit I'd chosen, you would march to your room and reappear with strange combinations of clothing. Your mishmash of clothes was a hoot!

There were times I'd find you playing dress-up in your room—a young fashion model holding a fashion show for her dolls, donning her favorite outfits one over the other. You certainly had a flair for looking adorable. It must have been fun to empty every drawer and not worry about repercussions.

I remember one very special moment when you were about two years old. As I prepared to wash our car, a bucket of soapy water with suds billowing in all directions attracted your attention. You seized the moment, and when I turned to wash the car, you placed your head in the suds and began washing your hair. It was a precious moment recorded by my camera.

Soon your strong legs helped you peddle around in a tiny tike bike for hours, yet it was the dolls that you loved best—many, many dolls. I loved watching you play house, feeding your babies, and doing things that came natural to a mother. When you became a mother, your early training came flooding back like an avalanche. Motherhood fell over you like warm sunshine on a cold day. I will always remember the look of joy on your face when you held your firstborn, Anthony, in your arms. What a remarkable mother you became.

When you were three years old, I decided to check out a nursery school. After weeks of searching, I chose a school I thought you'd enjoy. On the first day, we walked into a room filled with children your own age, but it was not to be. As I started to leave, you hung onto my leg as though it was the last time you'd ever see me again. With visions of my own first day at school still in my mind, we went home.

When it was time to enroll you in Kindergarten, I held my breath. After the nursery school fiasco, I worried you'd reach for me and create a wild scene. I knew I would not have the heart to leave you. However, things at home had changed; you now had a baby brother in your life, someone you adored. Much to my surprise, your first day in school was a breeze—no crying and no screaming. You'd grown up and adjusted to new people and places and things.

One special memory that often comes to mind occurred on the morning Grandpa passed away. You were seven years old and still shunning away from Grandma. Although she'd never given up on you, she eventually accepted your peculiar behavior. But it all changed on one sad morning. After Grandpa passed, we gathered at Uncle Joe's house. When Uncle Joe returned home with your grief-stricken grandmother, she was sobbing uncontrollably. She settled into a chair in the living room, and you sat on the floor close to her and latched onto her leg, consoling her, reassuring her that everything was going to be okay. And when she reached down to gently touch you, you stood up, kissed her, and gave her what she needed most—love—something she'd yearned for and needed most on that grief-filled morning.

I remember the matching bikes we bought for you and Tony. Yours was bright red, and his was royal blue. How adorable you looked riding your little red bike. You were older, and you learned how to ride without training wheels, something he aspired to do as well. But you sweetly mentored him until he was able to ride without the cumbersome training wheels.

I have many memories of our home on Steeplechase Drive, of you, your friends, especially the Stone girls next door. And ballet, those perfectly wonderful years when you danced. You LOVED to dance. With a perfect little ballet body, you never had to be told to practice. I attended each session, enjoyed every moment of the delicate and graceful steps. Remember *The Nutcracker?* That was a magical weekend, especially when I was asked to fill in for one of the dancers—my one and only moment under the bright lights. I'd never danced ballet, and I was worried I'd fall, but amazingly, I didn't!

We moved to San Diego the summer before your freshman year at Mt. Carmel High School. You weren't very thrilled about attending a new school in a new city. But once September rolled around, it didn't take long for you to adjust. You did well and had many friends. You joined the tennis team and became a star player. However, the real turning point in your life occurred when Campus Crusade entered your life. It was a welcomed change that guided your future choices.

I remember your first high school crush, and the drama this romance brought to our table, especially when he egged our house. And how could I ever forget Mark, your second and very serious boyfriend. When you and Mark split up, Mark and I both had broken hearts.

I know you've never forgotten your first car. Your dad decided to give you his truck and had your initials (or your name, I can't recall) imprinted on the door. I told him a truck would not go over well, but he went ahead anyway, and you were not very pleased to see your name on that red truck. I honestly understood how you felt. When your dad decided we needed another car, he traded my car for a camper. I was not thrilled. I felt like a truck driver. All that was missing was a large cigar and a mouth full of curse words flying off in all directions.

However, you were happily surprised when a fiery red Pontiac was waiting for you in the driveway one night. It was a beauty, perfect for your sense of style.

Do you remember the Fourth of July trip to Catalina when your friend Willy joined us as a stowaway? Taking him was not part of our plans. We had to make room for him, and your dad and I were not terribly happy. But after all was said and done, it turned out to be a fun Fourth of July!

I know you've never forgotten the short period of time when you worked in our pizza house in Rancho Peñasquitos. You were not thrilled about the job, but it had its moments, especially the day Hank Bauer from the San Diego Chargers rushed through the front door and asked the perky cashier behind the counter if she (you) knew his name. Although you didn't follow football or the Chargers, you were familiar with the name Dan Fouts, the Charger's star quarterback.

"Hmmmm, let's see, are you Dan Fouts?" you innocently asked. Hank nearly jumped over the counter. "No, not Dan, anyone but Dan!" he shouted. Your answer was dead-on funny, and his reaction was hilarious.

Remember when you and I worked at Scarcella's Pizza in Mira Mesa? You were in college at the time, and juggling school and work was difficult. You always looked classy, strived to look your Sunday best at all times, and restaurant work uniforms were not your fashion ticket. It was apparent that another type of work would best suit your style, a place where heels and pretty clothes were the preferred dress code. You were much happier when Dick Palmer, a local realtor, offered you a position in his office.

Earning a college degree was important. I never wanted you to be in the same position I was in. Your graduation day was a special day, and you can imagine how proud and overjoyed I was as you accepted your diploma from San Diego State.

Memories of your college days remain with me, but one stands stands out—the day I visited your dorm room. What a shock! Your mattress was on the floor, and I'm sure you never made your bed. I would never have imagined you could live that way. You were Miss Fastidious at home. But then again, I'd never been in a dorm room.

Although Jodi had the task of putting the memory book together, I know you had a part emotionally. It is a beautiful reminder of our family ancestry. The book means so much to me, Denise, thank you so much.

The births of your children were special moments in my life, and having been with you when they came into this world tops all other moments of endearment. You've been blessed; the joy of becoming a mom cannot be described or put into words.

I want you to know how fortunate I feel to have you as my daughter, and I hope you know how much you mean to me. It matters little where you are; children and mothers and never truly apart—they are only a heartbeat away. Denise, thank you for loving me, for being so sweet, and for all the wondrous memories that visit me each day, and know that I miss you so much.

I love you, Denise!

Mom

GRANDCHILDREN

Anthony John, Nicholas John, and Kourtney Nicole Palmer

ANTHONY WILLIAM

NOVEMBER 11, 1967

Tony you were my third love, and I loved you long before I held you in my arms. By the time you were born, my life had quieted down, and I'd had time to wonder about the tiny miracle growing inside me. I was sure a wonderful gift of love was about to enter my world.

When I learned I was pregnant and due on November 18th, I never gave November 11th much thought. As your sisters' birthdays on November 7th and the 9th approached, the number sequence became increasingly intriguing, and I wondered if the 11th would mark your birthday. *How unique*, I imagined. Not only would the number chain be extraordinary, November 11th was a much-revered day commemorating our veterans.

On the morning of the November 11th, I was scheduled for a checkup. Dr. Silas was aware of my previous November babies. It had often been a topic of conversation. After she examined me, I asked if my precious cargo would make its appearance that day. She answered with an emphatic *no* and told me there was no indication the journey was about to begin.

The mind is an amazingly powerful tool, and although I left her office disappointed, a slim glimmer of hope still remained. By dinnertime I had just about given up . . . until the first pain sat me upright. An hour later, contractions were steady and the doctor was notified. But she was not convinced, assumed it was probably false labor. After all, she'd examined me that morning. Although she had her doubts, this was my third pregnancy, and she suggested I meet her at the hospital.

"Okay, bring her in. I'll call her bluff," said the skeptical doctor who was just sitting down to her evening meal.

As they rolled me into the labor room, I remember looking at the clock on the wall. The window of time was narrow, but I knew what I wanted—a November 11th baby. There was time—six hours, still doable. Labor for me had never been a long and grueling span of time.

I still remember Dr. Silas' voice the moment you were born. She glanced at the clock and cried out, "Bingo, just what you ordered; a November 11th baby! And—it's a boy! Good job, Mommy."

It took a few moments for the event to register—I had a son born on November 11th. When she placed you in my arms, my world stood still. You were perfect, a healthy baby with all the correct parts, including a head full of thick black hair and big beautiful eyes that made my heart burst with love.

Without a doubt, you were a good baby. You hardly ever cried, except when you were hungry, wet, or just needed to cuddle. I was convinced you learned to cuddle inside the womb. You nursed well until the dreaded projectile vomiting made an appearance and you were placed on formula. It was then I noticed your healthy appetite. You would gulp down eight ounces of milk in what appeared to be one long, hard swallow.

Watching you develop was nothing less than a joy. Soon you were sitting up, crawling around, and exploring the world of boyhood adventures. I remember how you'd play for hours, completely engrossed in your toys, especially your Lincoln Logs. Sometimes you would crawl around with one log tucked in your mouth. I was never sure where your imagination had taken you or what you were imitating, but watching you made my heart smile.

The first year went by in a flash. I wanted to hold onto every precious moment, yet it seemed as though I took a breath and when I exhaled, twelve months had flown by.

I know you were too young to remember when we cuddled in the living room rocking chair and watched *Sesame Street*. Or when I read to you until you fell asleep in your bedroom. So many precious moments that we shared when you were young often return to remind me of those wonderful years.

You were never a mischievous child and far more sensitive than most. When you were four years old, I was pregnant with your sister Jodi. You loved my very round tummy. It was endearing to watch you watch me.

Sometimes you'd wrap your arms around my leg and squeeze tightly. Sometimes you'd pat my tummy and say, "Mommy, I love your tummy. I want you to stay like this forever." My heart still smiles whenever I'm reminded of those sweet words.

I'll never forget the days when you'd line up your fleet of Tonka trucks on the side of our home on Steeplechase Drive. I'd watch from a distance as you maneuvered your trucks into various positions. Your range of truck sound effects always added to the drama of your playtime.

You attracted attention, especially with the ladies. No matter where we went, be it the grocery store or the park, mothers would always stop to greet you. But it was the lasting impression you made on your kindergarten teacher that stands out in my mind. At the end of the school year, she came to our house, and with tear-filled eyes she told me how special you were, adding that she'd never forget her brown-eyed charmer.

I know you remember Gary, the tractor guy who lived up the hill on Steeplechase. You loved Gary and watched in captive concentration as he drove his tractor up and down the street on his way to work. Gary would often stop by and take you for a spin on his tractor. Sitting on his lap high above the ground was always a monumental highlight of any day. You were in truck heaven, and I was convinced that someday you'd grow up and become a truck driver.

Do you remember the Beatles song "Yellow Submarine"? You knew every word. Whenever that song came on the air, you'd go into action immediately, reach for anything that resembled a microphone, and sing and dance to the beat. I remember buying the album just so you could sing and dance any time you desired.

So many wonderful memories are etched in my mind. I remember your first two-wheeler and how you loved riding that tiny blue bike. And how cute you looked as you waved goodbye from the school bus window on your way to Kindergarten.

Do you remember the dinosaur books you collected and how fascinated you were with the pictures? Although you were young, you could easily pronounce and describe each gruesome creature.

I remember when you'd sit in your room for hours concocting imaginative games. Your imagination was remarkable, and the games were creative and riveting. I'd have to peel you out of your room at dinnertime.

Your devotion and love for animals began early. Your first love was for Sam (Samantha, a beautiful German Shepherd), then Shotzie, Rocky, Meatball, and our sister Siamese cats Misty and Dusty. Your love for animals was astonishing.

Do you remember when you'd sit in Samantha's makeshift doghouse—a large sheet of plywood propped up against the house? You looked so cute cuddled with your dog in that doghouse. Much like the other animals in our family, Sam loved you best.

You dearly loved another set of twin cats that came to live with us—Laverne and Shirley—and when you left home, you took Shirley with you. In your care she enjoyed a wonderful life. I remember the pain you felt when she died. The death of your beloved pet was a tremendous loss, and you grieved deeply.

I remember when you joined Little League. Baseball was your game, and you loved it! How adorable you looked in your uniform. You were a natural athlete, and I was proud of you. I attended every game, and when it was your turn at bat, I would shout cheers with the best of them, at times louder than Dixie Kingery. Remember her? I also recall when things didn't go well, how hard you were on yourself. Win or lose, the "after the game" pizza parties at Scarcella's were always fun. The pizza house brought everyone back to square one.

The Los Angeles Dodgers were your team of choice. I found this troubling. After all, we lived in San Diego. I expected your loyalty to be for our Padres. Yet the Dodgers held your heart captive. When I asked you why you loved an opposing team, you answered, "Because of you, Mom. You were born in Brooklyn; that's why I love the Dodgers!" Although I continued to cheer for the Padres, when the Dodgers were in town, my loyalty switched to the team with Brooklyn roots.

Our family was riddled with many picky eaters. I had to jump through fiery hoops to get everyone to eat. Much like your siblings, you had your favorites. Topping your list were *"piggies in the blanket"* and *"chicken enchiladas"*, meals you enjoyed with gusto. Leftover rice and cheese was your power breakfast. You also loved "made from scratch" macaroni and cheese. When you were older and learned to make that dish yourself, you boldly told me that you enjoyed your recipe better than mine! And last but not least, I have never forgotten Christmas and your favorite—*"forgotten angel cookies"*.

I remember when a pretty girl from school with a head-over-heels crush on you asked you to take her to prom. Her parents were good customers. When you agreed to take her, I was thrilled and gave you permission to take her to prom in style—in my Porsche.

I remember when your dad and I came home from Las Vegas and found his truck turned sideways in the driveway. I'm not sure if you were aware your parking was mightily askew. I don't remember how you excused your strange parking maneuver. Your dad was really angry. By the way, what was your reason for parking sideways?

Your cousin Johnny was your special pal. I remember the days when you, Joey and Johnny were a team. Although Johnny was in a wheelchair, he was never left out of the fun you and Joey enjoyed. We never worried when the three of you went out on your own.

Our first trip to Hawaii with Grandma, Uncle Joe, and your cousins was memorable, especially the afternoon when you, Joey and Johnny went downtown. Later that day, we received a frantic call about a sniper attack downtown. The entire area had been cordoned off and we panicked. But a stranger had given the three of you safe haven inside a large store and called to tell us you were safe. Nonetheless, our panic remained until we received a call telling us the sniper was under arrest and we could stop by and bring you home. What a memorable adventure!

During that same Hawaiian vacation, you, Johnny and Joey found a stash of money—approximately $800. The money was reported to the front desk of our hotel. After twenty-four hours and no reports of lost money, it became "finder's keepers." Later that day, we discovered the money actually belonged to Grandma. For safekeeping, she'd stashed the money in her bra, but somehow it had fallen out. Not wanting to take the money away from her grandsons, she refused to admit the loss until we discovered that she no longer had the cash she'd traveled with. We never figured out how the money slipped out of her bra.

You were not enamored with restaurant work, but it had its moments. Since the kitchen was in clear view of the dining area, many of the high school girls would stop by and flirt with you. You worked hard during this time, and it earned you your own set of wheels—a brand new Toyota truck.

Then one day you announced that you'd applied for a job at Price Club (later renamed Costco) and you'd been hired. It's been many years since that first day with Price Club, and you've remained a loyal employee. I'm proud of your dedication to this company.

Tony, you are a treasured part of my heart and my life. I'm proud to have you for a son. I'm so very proud of the person you've become, and I want you to know that you are loved more than you'll ever know, more than I could ever describe, and the love you have returned to me is priceless. Thank you for so many wonderful memories that often come to mind to brighten my days. Your heart and mine are forever locked, and no matter where you are, know I am thinking of you and missing you.

I love you, Tony!

Mom

JO-DINA MARIE

OCTOBER 20, 1971

My sweet Jodi, you were the last child to fill my life with joy. When the doctor announced I was pregnant with my fourth child, I was dizzy with excitement. Knowing this was probably my last pregnancy, I set a goal to enjoy each precious moment of my journey, and my reward would be another love in my life.

Once again I learned my due date was in November. Scorpio babies were my fate—one more child to add to the unique sequence of November birthdays. I wondered if you'd arrive on the fifth or on the other end of the chain. But you had other plans. On the afternoon of October 20, when I went into labor, I had mixed emotions—happy you would soon be in my arms, yet disappointed the November birthday theme was over.

The goal to enjoy this last pregnancy was snuffed out early on. I'd just completed my first trimester when my father passed away. With his untimely passing, my focus changed. I missed him and began grieving deeply. The realization that you would never meet your grandpa and he'd never meet you became an unsettling sorrow. At times it was more than I could bear, and it became a daily battle to keep priorities in perspective.

We were living in Fountain Valley when he passed away. In my second trimester, we moved to Sunnymead. Grandma was living with us. Consoling Grandma and keeping my own grief at bay was exhausting. The remainder of my pregnancy is somewhat vague, until the day I went into labor and my world changed.

Back then general practitioners delivered babies. We were new to the area, and I selected Dr. Hillyard, a well respected family doctor. He was young and had his own agenda for pregnancy. He was adamantly opposed to drugs and highly in favor of the Bradley Method for natural childbirth. Dr. Hillyard's confidence persuaded me to following his advice. I read the *Natural Childbirth the Bradley Way* book, practiced the program and schedule recommended in the book, and I had nothing but the highest of hopes the method would pay off.

And when it was time to practice what I'd learned, I was fully prepared. Labor was less painful and less stressful, and it led to an incredibly beautiful moment—that last memorable push. I still remember those last moments, as well as the doctor's voice announcing the news. "It's a girl, and she's a beauty!" he said as he laid you down across my chest.

"This one's a real cutie pie," he added. "I want one too," he said, turning to his wife who'd assisted in the delivery. One year later he got his wish; his wife gave birth to their second child, a precious little girl, and he told me you were his inspiration.

I wanted to name you Genna Marie; however, with my father's death still weighing heavily on my mind, I wanted to honor him but please my mother as well. I decided on Jo-Dina—parts of their names in combination—and I immediately nicknamed you Jodi.

You were a cutie pie, a precious little bundle with bright blue eyes that gradually turned green. You nursed well and hardly ever cried. Being the last baby, I desperately wanted to hang onto every precious moment. I honestly didn't want to share you, but I did, mostly with Grandma. The distraction of a precious baby was just what she needed, and having a new love in her life was healing.

Watching you grow was a joy. You enjoyed cuddling and always flashed a smile when someone crossed your path. You loved everyone, and everyone fussed over you. Your brother Tony was especially attentive. He loved playing with you and would ask about you the moment he came home from school. Your doting sisters always wanted to hold you, and I felt as though I had to take a place in line. In spite of the attention you received, you remained unspoiled, and the expression "you can't spoil a child with love" now made sense.

The first months went by in a flash, and I enjoyed every moment, especially the early morning nursing sessions. It was the only time I had you all to myself.

You loved your dolls, the colorful trinkets in your playpen, and our walks up and down Steeplechase Drive. Hands down, you were a profoundly happy baby.

By this time, I was an old hand at mothering. I knew the stages of child development and what to expect next. Still, each new event was a fresh miracle I welcomed warmly.

By no means were you a picky eater; however, much like your siblings, you had your favorites. When I introduced you to Le Sueur canned peas, you were immediately addicted. Watching you eat peas was a kick—two tiny fingers picking up one pea at a time was hilarious. You would have eaten peas for breakfast, lunch, and dinner! It was no surprise that "peas" was one of the first words you learned.

When you were three years, old you developed the perplexing habit of hair twirling. I worried you'd soon have bald spots. Breaking the habit became a difficult endeavor. Thankfully hair twirling fell by the wayside. When your daughter Haley was born and began twirling her hair, I suspected it was an inherited peculiarity.

You were a happy child with eyes that sparkled whether you were quietly playing in a playpen, chasing our cats around the house, or playing with our dog Shotzie. When we opened a restaurant, our time at home was limited. You were good-natured and quickly adjusted to our new routine. Every morning I'd tear you away from your toys and take you to work. Lorenzo's restaurant became your home away from home. I felt fortunate to be able to work and still have you by my side. Soon our regular customers began asking for you.

Do you remember Conrad? He was our first pizza cook, and you took an immediately liking to him. You also loved music and memorized the words of a popular song "You're No Good" sung by Linda Ronstadt. Each time Conrad walked through the door you greeted him by singing this tune. He loved your serenades. At times, even when he was too busy to give you his full attention, you'd pull on his pant leg until he stopped to listen to your song.

"Conrad listen, *you're no good . . ."*

You looked adorable, and watching Conrad's reaction was hilarious. He'd smile and pick you up and thank you. Thankfully, he never took offense with the words.

When we moved to San Diego, you easily adjusted to a new environment. It seemed as though your first semester in a new school had just begun when Halloween rolled around. I had no artistic skills, but I thought Pocahontas would be a cute costume. Making use of a flour sack from work, sandals, and a hair band with a pretty bird feather I found in the backyard, I marked up your face and *voilá*, you became Pocahontas—much prettier than the original Indian chief's daughter. You looked adorable, and I should not have been surprised when your costume won for uniqueness.

Remember soccer? It didn't take long to realize you weren't the least bit interested in participating in that sport. I'd watch you standing midfield and talking to other players as though you were chatting with friends between classes. But you gave it a whirl, and no one could deny how cute you looked in your uniform.

You had many friends, including your cousin Angie and her friends. Remember our boat? You were too young to be left home alone, and I would invite your friends to come with us for the weekend. I was never sure if you had fun on a boat that never left the slip.

Do you remember our home on Sawtooth Way and your legendary bike ride down the hill, directly towards the open door of our garage, and into the water heater? The sound from your contact with the heater penetrated the garage wall into the living room. After seeing the condition of your mangled bike, you were rushed you to the emergency room. Thankfully, you were fine—not so for your bike!

You never worked at the family restaurant, except for your time at Lorenzo's Pizza serenading Conrad. While in high school, you applied for a job at Au Cuton and you were hired. In time you became the manager. Having a sixteen-year-old manager made little sense. Soon your closet was overflowing with the baggy cotton sweats sold at this store. Your comfort clothes never suited my taste, but you looked adorable and beautiful in your style of choice.

Although you never worked at Scarcella's Pizza, your first boyfriend Chris did. He was our weekend delivery guy. You and Chris were two peas in a pod. Do you remember when he failed to show up for work on a Friday night? When your dad called and asked if you knew where Chris was, you nonchalantly told him he was waiting for you by the hot tub at our condo. Your father was furious. In a fit of rage, he landed a hard right into the oak bookcase and broke his hand. Luckily you and Chris were not his target.

I am sure you remember your first car. The scenario resembled Denise's truck debacle. Your dad decided the pizza delivery car would perfectly fit the bill, the price was certainly right. But you began complaining, and in time he took you to buy a car, one you preferred driving.

I will never forget your last day at home. You were the baby, the last one to leave home, and I was *not* looking forward to that day. I began fighting back tears long before you left. Yet I knew the reality—someday you'd move away. As the time drew close, an avalanche of emotions fell over me. I dreaded that day; the moment when you'd close the door to our home and embark on your own life. When that day arrived, I packed a basket of goodies and placed it on the counter. I decided it was best not to be home during those last final moments. But things didn't go as planned. When I returned home that evening, you had not finished moving. On the counter was a note telling me you'd be back the next day to pick up the remaining boxes.

For the second time, I planned not to be home during your final exit. Unfortunately you came home early the following morning, and I was still home. You looked so pretty and happy and excited about your new life, and I tried to be strong. I hoped I would not cry and spoil your happy mood.

I could see how anxious you were to be on your way but as those last moments approached, I was desperately fighting back tears, and my good intentions nearly unraveled during the last final moments.

Forcing a smile, I kissed you, we hugged, and I followed you as you made your way to the front door. Suddenly you turned and looking directly into my eyes you said, "Mom, thanks for the basket of goodies. That was sweet of you." In that same breath and in a sweet and unforgettable tone you asked: "Mom, you won't forget me, will you?" I shook my head and said, "Jodi, no, of course not. I promise. How could I possibly forget you?"

A moment later the door closed, and I froze in place, feeling empty and lonely. I ran to my bedroom, sobbing uncontrollably, and cried the entire day, into the evening. And when I woke up the next morning, I could not stop the tears from running down my face. My emotions were so raw, I felt so alone, and I cried through most that day as well.

The memory or our moments by the front door still brings me to tears. I had been warned about the day your last child leaves home. And it was every bit as emotional as I'd been told.

Sharing an apartment with friends, you worked hard and attended college at Cal State University San Marcos. And when graduation day arrived, wonderful plans awaited you, including a great future with your new boyfriend and future husband Mark, and I was proud of you.

I call it fate, others call it kismet—when you meet someone special, someone who enters your life and changes your world forever. You met your certain someone after a phone call to the police regarding a neighbor's problem. Mark, a handsome San Diego Police officer who immediately captured your interest, answered the call. I learned that you'd called to thank him for his help, and after playing phone tag for a few days, Mark left a message with his home phone number, a signal he was just as intrigued with you as you were with him. After several telephone conversations, you joined him for lunch, and two strangers who met as destiny deemed began pivoting towards a meaningful relationship.

Later, you shared an account of an exciting adventure, a police ride-along where you were introduced to Mark's work in the world of law enforcement. It turned out to be an exciting jaunt through the streets of La Jolla and past the home of Dr. and Mrs.Theodor Seuss Geisel, aka Dr. Seuss.

Part of your graduation was a European vacation, a trip you'd been looking forward to since you met friends from Spain at school. They'd invited you to visit them after graduation, and you were excited. However, you'd recently met Mark and you were in love. By graduation day, the relationship had become serious. I was surprised when the trip to Europe remained on your agenda. You explained that you did not want to disappoint your friends, and you proceeded with your plans.

The first leg of the trip was England. I wondered how well your European vacation would play out. I was not surprised when you called from England to tell me you were flying home—immediately—and your plans to visit friends in Spain had been cancelled. You told me you were frightened to be in Europe alone, but I knew full well that you were returning because of Mark.

Mark soon became an important part of your life. He bought a house on Chocolate Summit, a home that holds many wonderful memories—those of his parents, the parties, the menagerie of dogs, cats, snakes, and desert urchins as well. Of course it was Haley's and Taylor's first home.

When you and Mark announced your plans for marriage, I was thrilled. I learned the ceremony would take place aboard a ship sailing to the Caribbean. Knowing I would not witness the ceremony was somewhat disappointing. Even so I was happy for both of you. We picked out your wedding dress, and I was positive you'd look beautiful. Yet I can't deny I was somewhat disappointed that I'd only see you wearing that dress in pictures.

Before you left for your wedding, a surprise party was planned at "Joey and Maria's" hilarious faux wedding production. It took some coaxing with the theater company to include you and Mark in the evening's performance. When they agreed, I was thrilled. The show now had a special meaning; one that included a surprise for you and Mark and became more than just a funny dinner show.

To help celebrate your nuptials, when you and Mark returned from the Caribbean, a party was planned on Chocolate Summit. It was a wonderful celebration shared with long-time friends, family, music, and an array of tasty foods.

Before long you were pregnant and precious little Haley came into our lives. Soon after, your second joy was born, Taylor. And following our family tradition, I was delighted to be a part of their births. Those endearing moments are locked into memory forever.

And let's not forget the surprise birthday party for my 70th birthday. I did *not* want a party, but you and your siblings had other plans. The surprise worked out as you'd hoped, and I had a fabulously happy birthday. I truly appreciated all the work it took to make it a special day. *Thank you, Jodi!*

I know I could never find the perfect words to express my deep feelings about the beautiful memory book, a priceless reminder of our ancestry. Designing the book was time-consuming, but the reward was just; the book is beautiful, a treasure, and I love gazing through the pages and remembering back. *Thank you Jodi. Thank you so much*!

You have been blessed with two precious little girls, and you know the compassion and depths of a mother's love for her children. It is timeless, as mine is for you. Thank you for the many wonderful memories you have brought into my life. I am proud of you, proud you are my daughter. No matter where you are, you are never far from my thoughts, and I hope you know how much you are loved.

I love you, Jodi!

Mom

GRANDCHILDREN

Haley Nicole and Taylor Lou Willhelm

POST SCRIPT

Dearest children and grandchildren, a few friendly reminders . . .

Please remember to always lock your doors before going to bed, value friendships, fall in love, be loyal, keep promises, never go to bed angry, daydream, sing and dance and laugh with reckless abandon, pick your battles, finish what you start, treat people the way you'd want to be treated, take your vitamins, eat healthy, work out, don't smoke, take ownership of your responsibilities as well as your actions, make lists, and believe in God. Last but not least, love one another and say you're sorry—God knows you can't always be right!

EVEN THE MOST BEAUTIFUL CLOCK
IN TIME WILL STOP TICKING

When parents leave your world, an eerie feeling of having become an orphan enters your heart. The loss settles deep. You feel alone with no ties to the past, and no one to turn to for comfort. Their passing brandishes a heartache no one can heal, and the though of never seeing them again is an agonizing reality much too difficult to accept. Parents are your heart—mine certainly were.

Daddy . . .

My father was the consummate daddy. He worked hard, loved his family and music passionately, and was much too young when death stole him away like a thief in the night.

He wasn't easy to deal with during my teen years, nor when he learned he was a diabetic. My father was a difficult patient, refused to accept the dynamics of this illness and the diet regimen that needed to be diligently followed. My father loved pasta with his evening meal. Like most Italians of that generation, life without an overflowing platter of pasta during *pranzo* was unacceptable.

My mother did her best to guide his diet but often yielded to his demands. All attempts to educate him on the perils of not following the diet fell on deaf ears. It was no surprise when his sugar count continued an upward trend, and daily injections of insulin became a part of his routine.

Long before he fell ill, my parents had a dream—a goal—a return trip to Sicily after retirement. When the time to retire drew close, preparations began to take shape, including the hope of remaining on that island for one year, maybe longer.

Four months before retiring, while driving home from work he experienced severe chest pains and was later rushed to the hospital. Tests revealed he'd suffered a heart attack. He miraculously recovered, but a second attack occurred a few days later. As we gathered by his hospital bedside, waiting and hoping he'd recover, the long vigil, with no improvement was telling.

During this time, I was in the first trimester of my pregnancy with Jodi. After hours and days at the hospital, I'd gone home to rest at my brother Joe's house. The sound of a telephone ringing in the early morning hours can be ominous, and the moment I heard my bother Joe's voice, my thoughts raced to my father.

For as long as I live I will never forget the somber tone of his words when he spoke . . .

"He's gone, Daddy's gone, he passed away," were the only words Joe uttered. My heart sank, and my mother's world went into a tailspin of grief.

He left us on March 20, 1971. My father, still young and vibrant, was only sixty-four years old. Death was not justified after a lifetime of backbreaking work and endless sacrifices, and his passing plunged each of us into a world of grief.

With retirement around the corner, and the much-planned trip to Sicily pending, his passing was the furthest thing to enter our minds. Their bags were packed and ready for travel, yet his journey was not to his beloved island of Sicily.

Our hearts were heavy with pain and sadly the family was never the same without him close by. Left with a lifetime of memories, my mother felt abandoned, the rhythm of her life had been shattered, and she never found peace. His passing launched an inconsolable anguish that remained within her until she took her final breath.

Mommy . . .

My parents shared a silent but strong bond, their marriage a harmony, depending entirely on one another, and when the music died, she struggled to find her way in a world without him. She never learned to drive and her English language skills were still lacking, even after all her years in this country. She was far more independent in Brooklyn where mass transportation was available on every corner, and everyone spoke the familiar language of her youth. In California, my parents functioned as one. After his death, she depended on her children, who by then were busy with their own children. Nothing, absolutely nothing, could fill the void left by my father.

Having lost the one person she loved and depended on, it was obvious my mother could not live alone. Their home was sold, and she lived with her children for extended periods of time. Assimilating into the American lifestyle enjoyed by her children was difficult for her to accept. In reality, her life was a ship headed into a storm. She wanted the impossible—a home that valued Sicilian traditions and my father by her side.

In our desperation to bring an element of happiness into her life, when Villa Scalabrini—an Italian retirement home in Burbank came to our attention, my siblings and I were delighted. At the Villa, the Italian language was mostly spoken, and the colorful taste of old customs were part of the everyday environment. It appeared to be an ideal setting for her lifestyle. When she agreed to make the Villa her home, we sighed in relief.

For a while she appeared to have adjusted, but in reality, she never acclimated to her new world. It was soon obvious the Villa was not where she desired to live. Adding to the pain-filled certainty of life without my father, arthritic hip and joint pain, and cognitive memory loss added further misery.

However, sorrow runs deep. My father's passing continued to torment her, and twenty years of relentless mourning eventually took a toll on her general and emotional health. In time, the grief-induced dementia began to drown her memory, and arthritis locked her knees until she was no longer able to walk. As her thought processes diminished, she was no longer aware of her surroundings or the faces of those who loved her. Unable to care for herself, she was placed in a full-care nursing facility close to home.

In some small way, we were thankful she would never be aware of her environment. My mother spent the last years in her life in bed, mindless of her surroundings. She lived in the world of the past, where only memories of my father existed.

I found it ironic how she no longer recognized her children but never forgot my father. During my visits, I would often hold up his picture, the one she kept by her bedside and ask her to identify the handsome man in the photo. She never wavered in her response.

"That's my husband, Joe," she'd answer while patting her heart.

"Where is he?" I'd ask teasingly.

"Oh, he's home cooking. He's waiting for me. Can you take me home?"

In her ninety-fourth year of life, my mother died peacefully in her sleep. With Teri and Lisa, two of her grandchildren at her bedside, her last moments were described as peacefully serene. My mother was finally where she always wanted to be—with my father in paradise.

At the time of her death, she'd been a widow for thirty agonizingly lonely years. Unlike my father's death, we were prepared. For my siblings and me, the years of sadness and grief she carried in her heart will never be forgotten.

My parents lived simple lives, where love of family was the quintessential essence for life. They loved, forgave, and deserved much more than they ever received. They left behind a legacy of devotion for family to be carried on to the generations that follow.

As a teardrop runs down my face it touches my soul
knowing you are no longer in my world.

Young Tony, Dad, and Mom in Venice, Italy

WHEN GOD CALLS CHILDREN HOME

The death of a child leaves a unique and unparalleled ache. Two such losses occurred in my sister's family. Each passing reminded us of the haunting reality of death and of the inescapability of God's timetable.

Five-month-old Michael Dean passed away from sudden crib death. Lacy Lynn passed away at the age of forty-five after a lengthy illness.

If I should go tomorrow, it would never be goodbye,
For I have left my heart with you, so don't you ever cry.
The love that's deep within me, shall reach you from the stars,
You'll feel it from the heavens, and it will heal the scars.

Ron Tranmer

JOHN (JOHNNY) ANTHONY SCARCELLA

APRIL 18, 1968-JUNE 15, 2010

Johnny

On April 18, 1968, a champion was born into the Scarcella family—John Anthony Scarcella, Pat and Joe's third child. Born with an unforgettable smile, he earned the title of "champ" by his incredible journey through life. His extraordinary courage, coupled with an unwaveringly positive attitude, was the hallmark of Johnny's strength of character.

During the early years of his life, Johnny followed a normal pattern of development, but it was short-lived. At the tender age of six, he began to stumble and walk with a gait, and it became painfully obvious his development was not progressing normally. Medical tests soon revealed Johnny had Duchenne Muscular Dystrophy, a debilitating genetic disease. From that day forward, the normalcy of life that Johnny and his family were enjoying came to an abrupt halt.

In the early years, Johnny was too young to understand his illness and the dire prognosis. However, Pat and Joe were painfully aware of what lie ahead. Shedding rivers of tears and sleepless nights became a way of life. The reality of this disease was clear; the illness would generate immense challenges. Shattered with the news their young son was gravely ill, they worried where this incapacitating illness would take him and how long he would remain in their loving arms. However, God had charged Pat and Joe with this heart-wrenching cross knowing they were best suited to meet each obstacle.

Their goal was a firm commitment, a resolve to provide everything humanly possible for his comfort. Throughout the course of their journey, no stone was left unturned, and they always kept the hope that Johnny would live long enough for that much-needed cure to make him whole again.

During the early years, Johnny played normally, romping with his brother Joey, his sisters Lisa and Angela, as well as his cousins and friends, and in time, his nieces and nephews. Joey—eighteen months older—was closest to the challenge. In time he became Johnny's arms and legs. And with his help, Johnny was able to attend school and participate in functions long before special education and handicap aids were available in schools or at social functions.

In his teen years, Pat and Joe purchased a handicap van. With the help of his family and friends and the new van, Johnny was able to participate in special events and activities and attend movies and ballgames. The van meant freedom for Johnny and brought an element of normalcy to his life. Although he was confined to his wheelchair, for many years he welcomed customers at Scarcella's Pizza, their family-owned restaurant. Later, with the patient help of his nurses, he would play poker on Friday nights.

Johnny's passion for sports included a profound appreciation for the San Diego Chargers, the Padres, and the Los Angeles Lakers. Later, when he was no longer able to speak, he developed a unique way to communicate and provided perceptive and astute analysis of the games. He traveled with his longtime friend and caregiver Carl Brown and entered the World Cup Power Chair tournament sponsored by the San Diego Power Chair Soccer Team and became the proud recipient of many Special Olympic medals.

Despite the many obstacles Johnny encountered each day, no one would ever know what lay in his heart. He never complained, and visitors were always met with a warm and welcoming smile. Johnny was strong-willed and had an unwavering determination to face each day with an appreciation for life, such as it was, and to never let go of the hope that he'd someday be cured.

During the later years, life for Johnny was confined to his bedroom on Torcida Way, connected to a myriad of medical equipment. Life-saving machines eventually provided breathing, nutrition, and other necessary functions to sustain his existence. He spent most of his waking hours in a state-of-the-art bed or in his high-tech wheelchair. With the help of caregivers, he enjoyed sports on a big screen television set and a computer with his own Facebook account.

Johnny's room was more than sleeping quarters; it was a sports Disneyland that housed scores of memorabilia on shelves and walls, including autographs and paraphernalia of famous athletes. Building on the sporting ambiance of his room, a close friend painted a colorful ballpark mural on the walls of this room with many symbols and images of our San Diego stadium.

If there were a Lifetime Parenting Award, a "Purple Heart for Parents," I'd nominate Pat and Joe. Casting aside their own needs and comforts, Pat and Joe challenged the mindless bureaucratic red tape, never wavering from the goal to meet all of Johnny's changing and demanding needs.

On April of 2009, Johnny celebrated a milestone birthday. Sporting his famous smile, and with the help from family and friends and his nurses, Johnny was able to participate in the celebration of his big day in the backyard of their home.

Johnny was an inspiration. His remarkable journey remains etched in our minds and hearts. For those of us whose lives are controlled by deadlines, money, clocks, traffic lights, careers, and other such energy-draining commitments, none of these obligations compare to Johnny's life. When one is fortunate enough to enjoy good health, one is truly blessed. Johnny would have willingly traded places to enjoy one hour of our so-called hectic lives.

Johnny was indeed a champion, a hero to those who were privileged to know him. He left much more than a legacy in his wake. Those who watched his journey came to understand the fortitude of his persona, his ability to push forward in spite of the complications and impediments of his illness. Had it not been for Johnny, we would never comprehend that the strength one needs in life is often found within oneself. We would never have learned to embrace an appreciation for life—no matter what obstacles come your way—had it not been for Johnny.

During his life, Johnny enjoyed the companionship of three faithful pets: Tiny the Basset Hound, who was with him during the early years, followed by Rocky the Cocker Spaniel, and later his service dog Lilly, who sadly passed away shortly after Johnny's death.

On June 15, 2010, Johnny left his pain behind and claimed his due reward in heaven. On June 19, 2010, a commemoration and celebration of his life was held privately at the family home.

It is the heart of a hero that lightens a dark world.

ISOLA BELLA

Castellammare del Golfo

Throughout her life, my mother had often invited me to travel with her to visit Castellammare. She wanted to share the beauty of her childhood home. She wanted me to see where she was raised and where she had often told me I was made.

As far back as I can remember, my perception of Sicily was that of an island where technology had not yet touched its borders and where young people left their childhood homes and traveled to large cities to work and embrace a better life. With the passage of time, I learned that Italy had greatly modernized, and my views began to change.

My brother Tony had often traveled to Italy and Sicily. He became my inspiration, a stimulus that eventually led me to gaze differently upon the land of our ancestry. His enthusiasm convinced me that the time to embark on this long overdue journey had arrived. As the planning commenced, much like my mother, I wanted all my children to see Sicily, but only Teri and her husband Brian were able to accompany me on this journey.

There was an element of sadness in my heart—I wanted my parents to stand by my side to see the excitement in my eyes as I set foot on their beloved island. I wanted to hold their hands as we walked their walk. I wanted them with me as I gazed on the houses they once called home, the marina where my father swam and fished, and the farm where my mother was raised. And although this desire was not to be, I knew they would accompany me in spirit.

In June 2005, I boarded a plane in San Diego—destination Atlanta to Rome to Sicily. Tony had traveled earlier that week, and I met Teri and Brian in Atlanta for the longest leg of the trip. We were too wired to sleep and remained awake for most of the flight. We reached Fiumicino Airport in Rome weary and anxious for the short trip south to Palermo. Soon my eyes would gaze upon the bay my father had eloquently described as "more beautiful than any other sea in the world." As the plane soared over Sicily, I could hardly believe my eyes. The sea in Castellammare was every bit as mesmerizing as he'd often described.

It was mid afternoon when we arrived in the Punta Raisi Airport in Palermo, Sicily. My cousin Vito met us at the airport and drove us to our destination, the home of his parents and my first cousin Joe Genna and his wife Anna.

Along the way, Vito noted various roads and landmarks, those familiar to my parents and to me through their words and descriptions since I was a child. And although my feet were firmly planted on *terra firma*, I felt as though I was soaring high above the clouds.

As far back as I can remember, whenever I thought about Sicily, it was the castle that came to mind. My father's descriptions of the bastion created a fascinating charm. On the first night, the lights from the castle flickered under the dark sky. Yet nothing seemed real, not until the following morning when I awoke and gazed through the tiny porthole in my bedroom. The castle at the end of peninsula was sparkling under a brilliant sun, and the sight exploded in my mind. Later that morning we visited the towering monument, now a museum, and I touched its beautiful stone walls and marveled at the ancient artifacts used by fishermen of a bygone era. It was then the reality of being in Sicily touched my heart.

During our visit, we met the relatives I'd known all my life by name only, strolled along the promenade by the bay, and walked the narrow cobblestone streets. Sadly, a gas station had replaced the house and farm my mother once called home. The house my father once lived in, though still intact, had been renovated. As we walked along the quaint streets and paths they'd once strolled, I sensed their presence; I sensed their eyes seeing through mine.

Our two weeks in Sicily was nothing short of remarkable. We strolled along the promenade where weathered fishermen still went to sea at night, returning each morning with fish to feed their families or to sell to restaurants. We met relatives, visited breathtaking beaches, ate scrumptious meals at quaint restaurants, shopped in the nearby towns of Scopello and Palermo, and visited the salt ponds in Trapani and the winery in the seaport town of Marsala.

We also toured two of Sicily's prized jewels: first the medieval city of Erici—located 2,400 feet above sea level—where we strolled along the cobblestone streets and winding touristy paths; next San Vito lo Capo, a town located in a valley, nestled between spectacular mountains on the northwest tip of the island. San Vito is considered a "secret" resort spot popular for tourists and Europeans.

Along the coastline—a breath away from a shimmering sea—the old dirt path had been replaced by a beautiful stone promenade, home to extraordinary fresh seafood restaurants, bars, and shops where curious tourists leisurely stroll while eating creamy gelatos and tasty pastries. During late afternoons we enjoyed espresso in contemporary coffeehouses while gazing at the tranquility of the sparkling emerald bay.

The centuries-old paths where donkeys once lugged colorful Sicilian carts had been replaced with the Autostrada, a super highway that snakes through valleys, towns, and tunnels and allows one to drive without speed limits.

Spilling down to the sea are the majestic Madonie Mountains, with tall peaks that reach to touch puffy white clouds—a natural habitat for hawks and eagles. Beautiful floras add a blanket of stunning color as far as the eye can see, and many cliffs and paths offer breathtaking views of the village below. Perfectly manicured rows of olive, grape and walnut orchards line the rolling hills, and in the springtime the intoxicating fragrances from the groves fill the air and touch one's soul. In the shadow of these majestic mountains, colorful homes dot the narrow streets of Castellammare.

The Madonie Mountains

Overlooking the panoramic bay is the Hotel Al Madarig. Bearing an Arabic name, it is located on a wide piazza where visitors stroll, children run and play, and vendors display their wares. On this romantic seascape is the Hotel Cala Marina where guests can enjoy a cozy, romantic setting with a delightful blend of modern amenities. Teri and Brian chose the ambiance of this hotel to rest each night.

My visit in Sicily was nothing short of extraordinary. Although the crystal clear seas, white sandy beaches, rocky coasts, cliffs, and grottoes remain untouched, Castellammare was no longer the sleepy fishing village of my father's tales. Yet the ambiance of the past blends beautifully with the present, allowing the genuine taste of a bygone era to remain untouched.

The citizens of Castellammare remain unscathed from a past plagued with immoral wars, crippling famine, and the corruption of the Mafia. Each new generation replicates the strong family values and traditions of their ancestors, and they embrace their colorful history with a new modern flair. Castellammare is a town endowed with an enticing charm for those who journey to her shores.

With a smile in my heart, I vowed to someday return to Castellammare—to the island my parents once called home.

Open my heart and you will see,
Graved inside of it, Italy.

Robert Browning

JANUARY 13, 2008

It seemed as though a moment ago I was a child sitting next to my father enjoying *pranzo* at our dining room table in Brooklyn, and when I blinked my seventieth birthday was breathing down my neck. Although one may be grateful to have lived a long life, the sobering realism that most of your life is now behind you can be distressing.

I dreaded my big birthday. But others did not and made plans. And when I received an online invitation that read: "Shhhhh . . . Surprise Party for Nicole", I realized a party was being planned and my e-mail address had inadvertently been placed on the guest list. The thought was sweet, yet I did not want a fuss and asked Jodi to please cancel any plans.

A few days before my birthday, Jodi suggested we meet at Café Zucchero for coffee. As I sat waiting for her in their outdoor patio, I was startled to see her walking towards me with Teri and Kristyn following close behind. I was not expecting Teri and Kristyn and assumed they had traveled west for my birthday—the cancelled plan for a surprise party was now a distant memory.

On the day before my birthday, we woke up to a beautiful January morning and Teri, Kristyn, and I spent the morning leisurely shopping at a nearby mall. I was looking forward to lunch at Point Loma Seafood with Jodi and her family. Suddenly Teri announced that plans had changed and we were going to meet at Café Zucchero instead. I had been looking forward to a delicious fish sandwich. Although I was slightly disappointed, sharing a meal with family was all that really mattered.

When we arrived at Café Zucchero, Teri and Kristyn led the way towards the back patio, a charming spot any time of day. Suddenly, I caught site of several friends sitting at a long table. My dear friend Manny Cepeda was at his keyboard singing "Besame Mucho", and I quickly realized that the surprise party had in fact *not* been cancelled.

In hindsight, there had been clues—Teri and Kristyn's surprise visit—the sudden change of plans for lunch—yet I did not suspect. *Yes I was surprised—completely and totally surprised!*

The tables were beautifully decorated with lovely blue flowers, thanks to my dear friend Dorothy. She'd contributed in part to the scheming and loved every fun-filled moment of the planning.

Two especially touching moments occurred when Gaetano sang "Non Ti Scordar Di Me" and Rebecca sang "Besame Mucho" in English to her sweetheart Gaetano.

Surrounded by friends, family, and music, the day was much more than a wonderful surprise. It was a day that pacified my anxieties and eased the transition into the seventh decade of my life!

FOOTNOTES

At this writing, my siblings are all well and thriving in Southern California.

Rose: After years as a devoted stay-at-home mom, Rose and her husband Larry owned and operated successful Italian restaurants. After retirement, Rose pursued a career with the California Department of Corrections and Rehabilitation. Larry, a former baker and restaurateur, worked for a service company before retirement, but now enjoys baking for special occasions. There were six children in the household: Michelle, Lacy (deceased), Michael (deceased), Joey, Chris, and Johanna. Rose and Larry live in Temecula, California.

Joe: As a young man, Joe joined the Navy and was stationed aboard the USS Midway. During his tour of duty, Joe married his high school sweetheart Pat. Later, Joe and Pat became successful restaurateurs. After retirement, Pat pursued a career as a realtor. Joe now relaxes at home in Rancho California. With a view of the spectacular rolling hills of Temecula Valley as the backdrop, Joe enjoys gardening and the tranquil ambiance of his secluded patio. Pat and Joe have four children: Lisa, Joey, Johnny (deceased), and Angela. Pat and Joe live in Temecula, California.

Tony: After enlisting in the Army and serving a tour of duty in Vietnam, Tony pursued a music career and earned a masters degree in music at the University of Santa Barbara. Music is the heart of Tony's life. He is a music teacher at a local high school, an opera aficionado, and a cellist with the Inland Valley Symphony. He has two children, Camille and Stephanie, and travels extensively during the summer. On May 28, 2011, Tony married Darlene Williams. On that special day, we welcomed Darlene's daughter Lauren into the family. Tony and Darlene live in Temecula, California.

Inspired by my brother Tony's desire to obtain dual citizenship with Italy, it didn't take much prodding for eighteen family members to climb on board.

In 2010, my siblings and I, three of my children, Teri, Denise and Jodi, my grandchildren Ryan, Kristyn, Anthony, Nicholas, Kourtney, Haley and Taylor, my son-in-law Mark, my sister-in-law Pat, my nephew Christian, and my niece Stephanie were awarded dual citizenships, an inspirational endeavor to honor my parents and the land of our ancestry—Italy.

LEGENDS

Paternal Grandfather (deceased): Giuseppe Scarcella, August 14, 1878—died in 1933. At the time of his passing, he was fifty-five years of age.

Paternal Grandmother (deceased): Nicolina Mione, September 17, 1887—died 1942, also fifty-five years old.

Paternal siblings: Giuseppe, Marianna, Carlo #1, Nicola, Leonarda, Camillo, Filippo, Vito, Giuseppina, and Carlo #2.

Carlo # 1 (deceased): Carlo was born in 1911 with a weak heart, lived his childhood years as an invalid, and passed away at the tender age of 17. His death was caused by the trauma from a dog bite that further damaged his already weakened heart.

Filippo (deceased): After an injury to his leg when he was barely two years old, the wound became severely infected, and amputation was anticipated. However, the doctors decided to scrape the infection out of his leg down to the bare bone, with hopes that scraping would spare his leg from amputation. Each day his mother patiently took him to the sea and soaked his leg in the warm seawater. In time the skin began to adhere to the bone, the infection cleared, and to everyone's amazement it never returned. My mother often spoke about the healing benefits of salt water. She also spoke of my grandmother's dedication and the doctor's foresight that prevented a tragedy from occurring. The deep scraping caused a disfigurement of the leg that remained for the rest of his long life; a small price to pay considering the alternative. He died at 84 years of age.

My grandfather died during a time when most people were buried in crypts or burial chambers. With little money, the family could not afford a proper burial. With no other alternative, he was wrapped in sheets and placed, unprotected, directly into the earth on cemetery grounds. When my grandmother passed away, Filippo went to the cemetery, and in the darkness of night, with the help of a caretaker, they dug up his father's remains. His mother's coffin was still in the chapel awaiting burial. In the morning, before anyone arrived, Filippo and the caretaker placed his father's remains into my grandmother's coffin. Only the family and the caretaker were aware of what transpired and where he had been placed to rest with his lifelong partner, the mother of his children.

Vito Scarcella is the only surviving sibling and is enjoying his golden years in Castellammare del Golfo, Sicily.

Maternal Grandfather (deceased): Antonio Genna, birthdate unknown.

Maternal Grandmother (deceased): Rosaria DiBenneditto, birthdate unknown.

Maternal siblings: Giuseppe, Antonina, Leonarda, Barbarina, Calogero, Leonardo, Giovanina, and Mario.

At the time of my writing, there are no surviving Genna siblings.

CAMP LEJEUNE WATER
CONTAMINATION INVESTIGATION

For many years, viruses and the human immune system were considered to be a possible link to cancer, the most likely cause of Frankie's illness. I was also aware of cancer clusters, notably the one in Bergen County, New Jersey, where we had lived for over a year. I was convinced any of these scenarios might have played a part in Frankie's cancer, yet there was never any documented proof.

In 2005, I became aware of another very logical possibility to the cause—a water contamination that occurred while Frankie and I lived on base. It occurred from 1957 to 1987. During that time, USMC service members and their families living on base and in the surrounding areas bathed and ingested tap water contaminated with harmful chemicals. The toxin concentrations were more than 240—3400 times higher than permitted by safety standards. An undetermined number of former base residents later developed cancer—as well as other ailments—which many blame on the contaminated drinking water.

Victims claimed that USMC leaders concealed knowledge of the problem and did not act properly in trying to resolve it or notify former base residents their health might be at risk. In 2009 and 2010, the United States federal government initiated investigations into the allegations of contaminated water and failures by US Marine officials to act on the issue. To this date, no further information has been made available.

ABOUT THE AUTHOR

 Nicole Scarcella is retired and makes her home in San Diego, California. She enjoys the simple things in life: relaxing on her balcony with a good book, listening to music, dancing, or taking long walks by the bay. Near and dear to her heart is her family and the camaraderie of friends, including those in San Diego's Little Italy and the gang at Café Zucchero.

Book cover design & photograph edits | Sheilani Romero
Cover picture | Bob Francella